It Rained at Harvest Time

It Rained at Harvest Time
Memoirs of the Forever Prairie

Reta Evens Simons

EDITED BY S. LEIGH MATTHEWS

REASK PRESS

Copyright registration number TXu000523346
All rights reserved.

ISBN 978-0-9992672-7-1

First Edition: 2017

It Rained at Harvest Time by Reta Evens Simons

Edited by S. Leigh Matthews
Keneth A. Simons

Book and cover design by Dona Simons

Andri S. Muth has preserved and maintained original manuscripts,
typed and electronic copies as well as included photographs.

Kathleen D. Simons typed the first copy of the manuscript from the
original longhand.

Reask Press
for more information visit: www.donasimons.com/reask

Forewords

Back in April of 2017, my life was on the verge of chaos. Positive chaos, to be sure, but chaos nevertheless. I had just sold my home and was about to move myself, my two daughters and my two cats into a townhouse, a move that, for a variety of reasons, demanded a great deal of physical and emotional exhaustion. At that same time, a really exciting thing happened to me: I received an email from Dona Simons asking for my opinion about a memoir that her mother Reta Evens Simons wrote about growing up on a farm in Western Canada in the first decades of the 20th century. This simple request had the ultimate effect of grounding me, of bringing me home.

Dona mentioned that she had come across my book about Canadian women's prairie memoirs, the study that had started as my PhD dissertation. As often happens in an academic career, my research and writing interests had migrated away from that area of specialization and, although I had been teaching a course on Canadian Prairie Literature in recent years, I had not read or dealt with a prairie memoir in a very long time. I was very pleased just to be asked to read portions of Reta's memoir and provide some aid to Dona in the process of having it published. But then Dona asked me if I would be willing to help edit the manuscript and, all of a sudden, I realized how vital such a project would be in my life at this particular time.

On a professional level, working with Dona on *It Rained at Harvest Time* brought me back to a passion I've always had for literature about the Canadian prairies during the period of settlement. As I read through Reta's text, I understood once again why the memoir genre in particular has always interested me. Her memoir is a very fine example of the form, and she is incredibly adept at bridging the detailed recreation of a time and a place with the exploration of her real-life characters' experiences, motivations and conflicts. Memoir is a balancing act between the sometimes contradictory demands of historical and auto/biographical narratives, but Reta's literary effort is a successful embodiment of Francis Russell Hart's assertion that memoir is "the personalizing of history; the historicizing of the personal." It is with great pride that I helped to bring Reta's voice to publication and I look forward to sharing her story with my students.

On a personal level, working with Dona on her mother's text was exactly the kind of concrete project that I needed in order to offset the flux of my own life. It settled me to spend time each day reading and editing this astute and humorous text. Reta's relaxed writing style and her engaging narrative flow between the lived experience of the past and the present moments of recreating that past were a pleasure to read. Together Dona and I navigated our way through an online working relationship, and I enjoyed the incredible privilege of being warmly embraced into another family's story.

With gratitude to both women for sharing their creative spirits,

S. Leigh Matthews, July 2017.
editor

Once I began designing this book, I could only wonder what took me so long. Many things have changed to make publication possible since my mother completed the manuscript in 1968. When, at last, I decided to proceed, I started by doing research online. Through the wonders of the web, I pinpointed the single individual who appeared to have the most knowledge and expertise regarding the circumstances surrounding my mother's early life on the Canadian prairie. S. Leigh Matthews literally wrote *the* book on the subject, *Looking Back: Canadian Women's Prairie Memoirs and Intersections of Culture, History, and Identity*. Since she is a university professor, I was able to get in touch with her by email, to ask for advice. Incredibly, not only did she reply, she agreed to edit this book. I can't imagine anyone more capable of doing it justice. It has been both a pleasure and an education to work with her. I truly appreciate all she has done.

Thanks to my father, Keneth Simons, the manuscript was preserved, updated and copyrighted after my mother's death.

It Rained at Harvest Time gives me a perspective on my mother's early life that I never truly appreciated as a child. Just as she writes about her own mother, I can also say that "she had much more than we realized until too late."

Reading these pages makes me feel like she's sitting at the kitchen table telling her wonderfully true stories. And now anyone who reads further can experience these stories for themselves.

Dona Simons, 2017
book and cover designer

This book was written by Reta around 1965. She wrote the entire document longhand with illustrations. She made three separate copies. It was typed into the computer in 1986 and edited by myself in 1990. I attempted to leave her style unchanged, while making minor changes in grammar and punctuation.

Keneth A. Simons, 1992
author's husband

Preface

The house is quiet. Life has settled down, some. I often read that it is good to try something new.

My life has never settled down, except for very short periods, which has made it interesting. Given a choice, I'd rather have it so settled that I'd be free to choose an interest. As it is I snatch at things of the spirit only in odd moments. Having time to reflect helps me so much to grow.

All the arts are a challenge and pleasure to dabble in, regardless of a person's capabilities. Doesn't every young person dream of being a beautiful dancer or of pouring out his feelings in song? Most young people have a restless feeling, without ever realizing just what specific form to express it in.

Perhaps I'm out of date. The young today seem to do a large amount of expressing themselves. Some are wholly devoted to it in a very noisy way. This didn't happen in our day. Thoughts took the form of daydreaming and were tucked away for the future when we'd be "on our own."

When I became 18, and felt very grown up, I decided to write a book. How to go about it never daunted me. Its title was to be "It Rained at Harvest Time" and naturally it was to be the story of my life.

Many years later, I can say I've read much and a favorite choice is stories of real people, how they lived and what they thought. Almost anyone's life is a good story.

I'd like very much to know how my poor mother grew up. Yes,

poor Mother. She was an orphan. We all loved her as children, but felt sorry for her at the same time. Sad to say, we rarely respected her. I'm oh so sorry now. She had much more than we realized until too late. But isn't this most often the case?

It took reading about someone who as a very little person loved to lie on the grass and watch the cloud pictures overhead, to remember how often I have enjoyed the same thing, but never thought to put it in words. You see, I grew up out west on a big, bare Canadian farm, not so big as western farms can be today, but because it rained one harvest day, my whole life was changed. At 18 this was a very romantic thought.

Now, a generation later, my only excuse for writing this is my children's interest in "things way back in Mother's time," or the "olden days" as we used to say.

Reta Evens Simons, 1968

Sketch from Reta's Art Notes book, made in eighth grade

The stillness is vast and noise helps fill the emptiness.
    —Attributed by Reta Evens Simons to O.E. Rölvaag
         (author of *Giants in the Earth*).

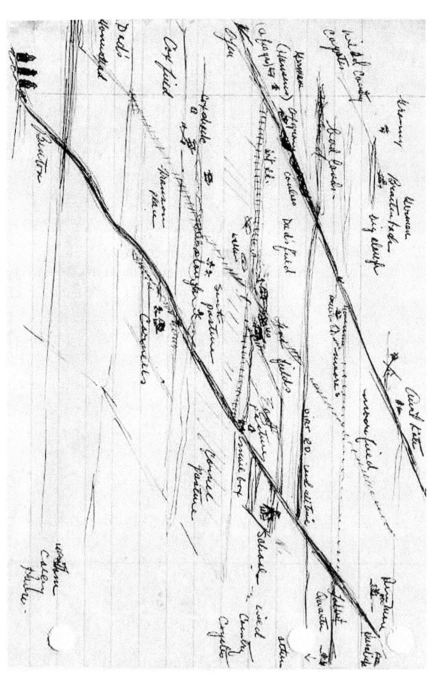

Scan of area map around the farm as drawn by Reta on lined paper

Contents

 Chapter 1

THE FIRST DAY OF SCHOOL

Once upon a time, when I was six years old, there came a day when I was taken by the hand and walked across a grassy pasture, a long ways away, to a building called a school. I'd not seen it before and had never heard of it.

I don't remember getting cleaned up or my hair fixed in readiness. The hateful procedure of a hair-do meant a stiff brushing and then a combing, ending with a part on the side. With hair that was heavy and straight - wiry straight - how could there be at least one big "tat"? But there always was. Last came a ribbon bow, if I was lucky, or more usually, a string of binder twine. This was used for tying sheaves of wheat and looked like small cheap rope with many loose ends, stiff enough to be prickery. With the bow tied on tightly - too tight chances were - I always left home feeling very clean and tidy.

We arrived at the school door and knocked. An enormous woman took my hand and the parent disappeared. I can't and don't remember which parent and I never saw them leave.

On the timeless prairie, nothing different ever seemed to happen in our everyday lives, except punishments. Dad's were strict and most often unexpected. I wondered if I'd done something very wrong to have brought about these strange events. What might it lead up to? But this woman had a kind voice. My mother was very small but this woman was so big and tall it was impossible to see the top of her!

She held tightly to my hand (what a thoughtful person she must have been) and we walked through a cloakroom and on through an open doorway into a big room. There were rows of desks with children in some of them, all strange and all looking at us. My goodness!

We walked all the way over to the far side of the room and there, at exactly the right height, was a row of small pictures tacked on the brown wooden wall. In one sat a frightened-looking little girl in a blue dress, while hanging beside her was an extra-big black spider. Another picture showed a boy and girl with the boy fallen down and water running out of a pail.

"Do you know the story of these pictures?" Whatever was she talking about? Thus, I was introduced to learning.

Next, and it seemed to have happened suddenly, I was sitting on the funniest little bench, fastened on to a whole row of them. The sides were of curly black iron and my seat could be moved up and down. Sitting on it, my arms rested on a small sloped table in front of me and there was a space underneath. The woman had gone, but there she was at the front of the room by a big flat table. She'd pulled open a drawer from under it and came back with a clean white piece of paper. We never saw such a thing at home. Also in her hand was a yellow pencil all new and long. At home was only a stubby pencil or two which Dad was forever trying to sharpen with his jack knife, which took such a long time. They were his too, not ours to use. The teacher pushed me over to the far side of the seat, squeezed down beside me and wrote a great big "A" on the paper. It almost filled the whole page.

"Now I want you to take the pencil and go exactly over this until you think you can do one like it." She stood up and left.

Over and over it I went until my fingers got too tired. Looking up I saw the children again. They'd been forgotten. They were all looking back. On the far side of the room were a couple of big ones, in big desks. Toward my side they got smaller. In front were two boys just my size. They were so quiet, all was so strange, it was frightening. I wished I could go home but I didn't even know where home was. It was a mighty long day but at last we were told to stand up by our desks and sing "Now the Day is Over." Never have I liked that song.

Everyone left except the teacher and one big boy. He promptly got out a tin can and a wide brush broom from a small closet at the back of the room. He sprinkled handfuls of green smelly stuff from the tin, up and down the aisles. Then he started sweeping it up, on my side first, while I sat there in my desk. Along the opposite wall was a long bench. Stiffly, I got up and moved to it to be out of the way. There I sat. I didn't know what to do and in no time could not move anymore. Eventually the boy came sweeping down the aisle past my bench and stopped. "That big puddle wasn't there before," he said.

Memory fails, I don't know how I got home. The first day of school was so startling an experience, I remember nothing before it.

SCHOOL

Soon it was understood that school was a place you went almost every day and you must not be late. We'd grown up on our own time, which had nothing much to do with clocks. Morning time was chore time, springtime was planting time, and so it went. Now my mother saw to it we had an alarm clock that worked.

Something to eat was put in a nice new empty syrup pail. They had handles but the jam pails didn't. After a goodbye hug, it was off to school.

I'd learned to walk alone across the pasture, over its hill that hid home, and to find the school, which could be seen across a dirt road. In springtime there was a big pond of water on this side of the hill, called a slough (pronounced *slew* by everyone), which had to be walked around. Very near school, on the other side of the hill, was an almost round rock, about five feet high, standing all alone. Often an effort was made to climb it but there were no footholds. Then I went on under the barbed wire fence and across the important dust road that went all the way to the town of Benton, where the mail came from. Best of all was the stile to be climbed, which went over the high schoolyard fence. Wide steps went up to a platform from which one could look around to see if anyone else was coming before going down on the other side. A short dirt path led up to the school door.

I put my lunch bucket under the girls' cloakroom bench and then went outside to play. Teacher came out on the front step with a heavy wooden-handled bell and rang it loudly. This meant time to line up, two abreast, on the front path and march (mark time, one, two) inside to stand by our desks until she said "Be seated." This happened also after each recess.

First thing in the morning, while standing by our respective desks, we sang a song. The favorite was "Good Morning, Merry Sunshine." Rarely was there no sunshine. Not only was it a pleasant time but also there were actions to be done while singing. After this, and perhaps having coaxed for a second song, we were given the order "Be seated."

One teacher taught all grades from one through eight but at that time some grades were missing. With the possibility of only one person in a class, they pushed the odd child ahead or behind into an already existing one. While one class did arithmetic, another studied geography, and a third group might be standing at the front of the room reading aloud, first one and then the next. At the end of the very long day, we stood to sing again. Being so far north in Alberta, it gets dark early in the fall. Maybe that was why "Now the Day is Over" seemed so dismal.

Each day I raced home to tell my sisters what the teacher had told us that day. Sister Irene was avid to learn and especially interested. It turned out there were two boys in my class, one called Jim, the other Richard Moore, and they too were reported on.

One of the first things I remember about school concerned the big boy, Tom Colby, who swept the schoolroom that first day. He was in about 8th grade, anyway far ahead of mere beginners. He was the first person I saw put his hand up, actually his whole arm, to ask teacher a question. He wished to sharpen his pencil. When permission was granted, he walked over to the wall and, with the pencil in his left hand, reached way out with his right one to turn the handle, using only his wrist. This looked strange, though I was not acquainted with pencil sharpeners. It so happened he was the only one who did it that way. As soon as this was discovered, I waited to get home and ask Mom why he had such a funny stiff arm.

It came about from his breaking his arm at the elbow when young. In that land no one went to the doctor (if one could be found) unless there was something serious! So his arm had healed straight and could be moved only at the shoulder and the wrist. It was a first lesson in factual evidence that people could have something wrong with them and still not be hampered by it. For days I was fascinated watching him do all sorts of things in his own way.

School became routine and the only awful part was when someone was punished. They got the strap, right in front of everyone else! For the first long while I could not discover the reasons why and was all the more alarmed at seeing the strap used. Each time it came down, it might as well have been on me. Made me miserable.

Somewhere toward the end of first grade, I did the only thing in school that came close to my thinking I'd get the strap. We'd just learned to write numbers from one to ten. I'd finished work and was looking for something to do until recess time. Under the top of the desk was a beautiful box of crayons, used rarely for coloring pictures. Looking them over carefully, I chose the purple because it had been used so little. With it, I wrote the numbers across the back of my seat. I had no idea I was doing anything wrong, or at least I didn't stop to think. We'd had no wall scribbling problem at home; there was nothing to scribble with! Then it was recess time and we all ran out to play. No sooner had we gotten out when teacher opened the window and called me back inside. I couldn't imagine why and went in with that scared-to-death feeling. Being called in in this fashion had always meant trouble for the unlucky person. The other children had stopped their play and were standing quietly, curious. I could see the strap in the offing.

The teacher, a different one than I'd started with, was standing at the front of the room. Without a word we walked down to my desk. She had a white faced (I'm sure) and trembly, wondering child accompanying her. Stopping in front of the desk, she seemed patient when asking, "Why did you do it?" My mouth was dry; I had nothing to say. She must have been understanding because she ended up saying nicely, "Never do it again. Get a cloth from the cupboard and rub it off." With rubbing and rubbing, finally all signs were gone from the varnished finish and no one needed to see my disgrace.

It was fortunate that the school windows outside were high enough above ground level and the ledge too narrow for anyone to climb and peek. Someone always tried, however. This was the one time I was called to terms in all of school. I took care to do only what was asked. Perhaps Dad's sure punishments at home added to this attitude of it not being worth taking any chances.

JESSIE CAULKINS

One event happened around the beginning of school that really left a lasting impression. In our sparsely-settled country families came, settled here and there, only to move on again before long. As youngsters we saw abandoned buildings - some bought up again by newcomers. Such a family, the Caulkins, lived to the south of us for a short while. Their house was one of the only ones we could see from our place. They had a daughter, Jessie, about my age.

One summer's day, Dad was going to go to town, five miles away, with the team and wagon. He liked these neighbors and took me along to be dropped off with them while he went on to town. He'd stop and pick me up on the way back. Somewhere, I'd seen Jessie before and because we'd had such a good time her mother had suggested Dad do this. There were not such things as telephones to make arrangements beforehand.

After quite a bumpy ride over the dirt roads, hanging on to the sides of the wagon to stay on my feet and unable to talk with Dad because of all the noise, we stopped on the road in front of their house. Dad dropped me off and, with a "giddyup," was off in a trail of dust. I ran into the yard and knocked on the door. No answer. Then quick to the barnyard. No one was home, so I went back to the road to look for Dad. He was quite a ways off, climbing the first hill to Benton. Once he went over the top he'd be lost to sight. In bare feet, as usual, I tore after him, calling as loud as I could yell. He disappeared and I *tried* to run faster. Soon came the tears. Right away I discovered nothing could be seen through tears. It was a distinctly unhappy setup.

I ran and ran, sometimes seeing Dad come into view on a hill only to have him disappear again into the valley beyond. This was just enough encouragement, while the hills lasted, to keep from feeling all the way lost. For the first long way a great deal of energy was spent in hollering, but eventually I gave this up, since it didn't do any good. By this time my feet were hurting from all the ruts and pebbles.

Not watching where they landed was a large part of the trouble. I was dusty, exhausted and thirsty, besides being in a panic. Whenever the horses slowed to a walk, I felt sure I could catch up if I didn't burst before then. A most discouraging sight was seeing Dad flick the reins to start the horses running again. At the beginning it didn't seem impossible to catch up, but the further we went the more desperate I became. I had no legs anymore; all feeling was gone from them. At times nothing was in sight, nothing but space with grass and sky. There was only the sound of my own running.

My heart was beating into the sides of my head. Veins stood way out on my feet. It was the first time I was ever aware of my physical self. Maybe I'd die! But I wasn't going to stop.

If only Dad would look back at the right time. Finally he did just that and what a wonderful flooding feeling of relief, the feeling of being rescued. He stopped the horses and waited for me to catch up and I gratefully climbed into the wagon and sat down on its floor. We weren't far from town but the idea of getting there, usually such a treat, was flat. I didn't even feel like myself! Dad was very matter of fact. I'd expected him to be happy he'd found me but all he said was, "Why didn't you go back home?" while giving me barely enough time to climb aboard.

I couldn't tell him home had looked so far away at the time, and he so near. Left feeling stupid, I thought I'd never learn to figure things out. Probably Dad didn't mean to, but he always made us feel dumb. When around him, his remarks were made after things that had happened went wrong. He said nothing if they were right. His favorite was "Why don't you keep your wits about you?" As a result, I grew up feeling I had no wits. He didn't take time to explain or warn. The back of his hand across the mouth meant "no more talking like that." And so it went. But he was a good man and we very much respected him.

There's a P.S. to this story. Not long after the attempted visit to the Caulkins, they moved away. In our mail a package arrived for me. What should it turn out to be but a red-backed book, *The Story of Mother Goose*. I coaxed awhile for somebody to read it but nobody did. After several years I learned to read myself and discovered "Jack and the Beanstalk," "Jack the Giant Killer," and best of all, "Rumpelstiltskin"!

GROWING UP

I learned that the Cornells, with three redheaded boys, lived in the only other house we could see in all that flat expanse around home. This was to the south where the Caulkins had lived. A boy named Richard lived on a farm adjoining ours to the north and another named Jim to the northeast. East behind the schoolyard fence, as far as could be seen, was *nothing*, and beyond that was more of the same. And so, knowledge of a little broader spot than just the yard at home grew as to people and places.

All the farms were large and spread over slightly rolling hills. There were no trees. Our school was known as Wavy Plains and a very apt name it was.

Four sections of land, totaling 640 acres, made a square mile. Most fields were broken up into a minimum of 160 acres (a quarter section). Farmers talked of their fields as the Homestead quarter, the Talbot quarter (originally owned by Talbot) or the west field, etc.

The roads were absolutely straight, running one mile apart going north and south with two miles between those going east and west. I can remember still, seeing the four holes that had been dug by the surveyors to mark our corners. That's how new the country was.

Dad owned 2000 acres, which was one of the biggest farms in our school district. This meant that most children traveled quite a distance to school. If there were only one or two, they rode horseback, but, as the family grew, they drove a horse and buggy. In winter it was a "cutter," the sort of sleigh seen on Christmas cards. They were light in weight and could be pulled by one horse. They were attractive and comfortable but cold to ride in. We never owned one.

About three families lived near enough to the school to walk. We were one of these and always wished for a horse to ride or drive. Our horses were all the heavy work sort, geldings that Dad called "plugs" because "they plugged along at a steady pace." The children who did drive were not too happy about it. Horses had to be harnessed, hitched to a buggy and food for them brought along. Upon arrival they were unhitched, unharnessed and fed before the bell rang. There were inevitably family quarrels as to whose turn it was to care for the horse. The oldest child always took the responsibility of driving.

GETTING INTO THE SWING OF THINGS

The school and its yard became familiar parts of life, almost the whole of it. The school was white clapboard with green trim. So was the small barn with its two-way pitched roof. The barn housed the "facilities," girls on one end, boys on the other. Around the yard ran a high wire fence made up of oblongs perhaps 1x1½ feet in size, the only fence anywhere that was not barbed wire. I remember it because when Richard's family, the Moores, were quarreling with the new German family, the Braitenbachs, also their neighbors, the Moores threatened dire reprisals. The B's then said they'd get their awesome mother after them, whereupon the Moores laughed and said they'd climb through the fence. Mrs. Braitenbach was much too big and fat to follow! Over this fence went the stile where we played, marching up and down.

Inside the school room, up front, was teacher's desk, a big table with a bell on it. She later added a small bell, to pop her hand on, for dismissals and for bringing the room to order. All eight grades were taught in the one room, though there weren't that many at first. Behind teacher was the long blackboard forever needing its chalk brushes dusted out. Pupils were never allowed to write on it. In front of her were rows of desks fastened to slots, but not the floor, so's they could be pushed up close together for certain occasions. They ranged from little ones, next to the south wall, on up to the biggest on the north. Against the north wall was that bench, memorable from the first day, with a big bucket of drinking water and its long-handled dipper standing in it. This was carefully brought each morning by someone with a horse and buggy. There was no well at school.

Next to the bench, in the corner, was a big round furnace, or at least the shield of zinc that stood out from it was big and round. This protected those in the desks, right next to it, from getting too hot. Teacher arrived early each morning to get the fire started. A small shed, close to the back of the school building, stored heavy black chunks of soft coal. The boys were asked to pound this up into smaller pieces and to carry coal scuttles full into the school. Hard coal was not even known.

There was a library on the back wall of the schoolroom, a very small closet where brooms and everything were kept. There was a fat dictionary, rarely touched, and one shelf of books titled *What Every Child Should Know*. Teacher never asked us to read them and none of us did. Let well enough alone. We had too many "shoulds" at home.

Next to the library, on the same wall, stood a small, brown, ornate organ with two beautiful slanting pedals. The red cut-velvet carpeting on them was the prettiest thing in the brown wooden room. Its long row of stops was fun to play with when teacher wasn't aware. It was never played properly in all my eight years of school. We hoped each new teacher would be able to play it when we sang, but all some could do was to find the first note. The children, however, gave it regular workouts as long as teacher could endure the noise.

The other spots of interest and color were two small pictures hung high on the side wall. These were of King George V and Queen Mary. He wore a wide blue ribbon and medals across his chest and had a very black beard. The queen's hair was all fixed pretty, under a sparkling crown.

In cold weather, if we weren't playing Fox and Geese in the snow, or even Four Sticks, the barn was often fun. There were rafters for the boys to climb, while the girls watched, and right inside the door was a swing, always fought over or never used at all. Sometimes two would swing at once, standing up together and taking turns pumping. After trying it once when invited by someone bigger and having them gleefully pump so hard we nearly hit the ceiling, that was that. I was a coward in many ways.

The bigger we got, the more fun to play games. The one or two older pupils had left and my grade was growing up with no gap in classes behind us. We lived for recess. There were two short ones, morning and afternoon for fifteen minutes each, and a whole hour for lunch. Dry old sandwiches were only nibbled on and so little time was taken for eating. Teachers tried to persuade us to finish up lunch.

We were lucky to have jam or butter, and occasionally both. Once in a while, when Mom ran out of her baked bread, we'd have to go home to find something to eat - miserable days - and such a rush to get back in time. There was rarely anything good at the best of times and other times almost nothing at all. There would always be flour on hand and, when worse came to worse, baking powder biscuits could be made. A cold one for lunch, after it sat in a lunch bucket for hours being banged up, isn't so good. To find them on a candlelit table, in a fancy restaurant today, still holds no thrill. I rather detest them.

The teacher wanted us to play in the great outdoors winter or summer. Perhaps the poor creature craved peace from her noisy charges. She made an exception when it rained. No one owned a piece of rain gear, but with an average rain fall of about 10 inches a year, this was no problem.

GAMES

Four Sticks was our favorite, played most often both winter and summer. Any number of kids could play. Two or three were "It." All the rest ran from one base to the next in either direction. If a player was caught between bases by a person who was It, he was put inside the "Pen" formed by the four sticks in the middle. The prisoner's feet had to stay in the Pen, but his arms could be stuck out as far as he could. If someone running between bases could swerve in and touch a prisoner's hand he was then free to run to a safe base. If he was caught on

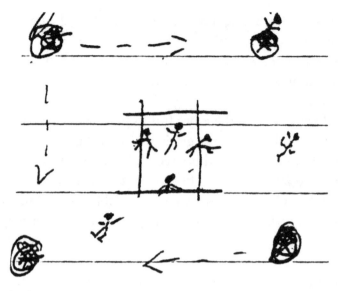

the way he became It, and his catcher became free. When the Its were quick, and the rest daring, the Pen could get pretty full. This game never ended of itself; the school bell stopped it. Everyone played and the bigger ones gave the younger kids a pretend chase occasionally, but with all ages playing there were plenty of challenges as to who could keep the jail fullest and who could get away, being caught least often.

"Anti Over Pigtail." This game required a ball and a large building. The school barn with its two-way roof was just right. Two kids picked their sides until all were chosen. One team stood on one side of the barn, the other team on the opposite side. The team with the ball threw it up over the roof, at the same time yelling, "Anti I Over." If the ball didn't make it over the roof and came bouncing back down we'd yell, "Pigtail."

The idea of the game was not to let the ball go over the barn. When it came down Pigtail, anyone who caught it could run around the barn to touch as many of the other side's players as possible, before they got away. When touched, a player became a member of the team that had the ball. If he reached the area at the end of the building before being touched, the player was safe. When one side was so far ahead that there were too few players on the other side, the ball was purposely thrown over the barn so they could have the fun of chasing.

OUR DESKS

All desks had a groove across the top, supposedly to keep a pen and pencil, but there was only room for the pen. The teacher disliked having pencils forever rolling out of desks and wished pencil boxes could be afforded by each and all. No one could, but an effort was made to tuck them in behind a book and remember they were there.

on desks screwed to floor

All work handed in to teacher must be done by pen. The only ones in use then had straight tapered wooden handles and pen nibs. In the top of the desk, at the right-hand corner, was an inkwell where the ink dried up too fast. The only thing to do was pour it back into the bottle at the end of the day. We often didn't, and this added to the cleaning problem. With no paper towels or Kleenex, and a scarcity of cloth, it was messy going. Even during the day, in such a dry atmosphere, much ink evaporated and we'd then guess how much water was needed. The guess was rarely correct.

The inkwell was a small recessed glass bowl with a metal lid, flush with the top of the desk. It snapped open and shut. Many times over teacher would say, "Stop playing with your inkwells and get to work." In the lower grades she kept the ink for their wells, but older ones had to have their own and take care of it themselves, a chancy chore. Fussing with ink and pens took up much time in school. Pouring it into the small wells was difficult and it was easily spilt in the process, thus terrible to clean up. It didn't come out in the wash either. Ink was the most borrowed item in school.

Pens were a worse problem. Nibs were so hard to come by with the scarcity of money. If dipped in too far it meant ink all over fingers and eventually papers. The nibs got bent and paper got into them and the well. Inky fingers were a chronic part of school, yet no paper was to be handed in untidy.

The worst spell came at writing period. Each day, time was set aside for long, boring exercises when it appeared everyone did their worst writing. We had to do whole rows of them. Unless done with a light touch, they were just the thing to make a mess of. Teacher walked up and down the aisles watching how we went about it. She carried a metal-edged ruler, not that the edge made much difference, but who could be sure? As she came by, we'd try to get away with fixing paper, dipping for ink, anything. She had the idea papers should be well up on the desk and that only arm movement and not "Uncle Wiggly" should be used (Uncle Wiggly was using only the thumb and forefingers). This practice was to ensure that a light touch would develop uniformity into perfect penmanship. If she caught us using no arm movement and the pen not a finger's width in front of the big knuckles, but only "Uncle Wiggly" at work, we'd be rapped over those knuckles.

Everyone loathed writing period.

THE SCHOOL TERM

The school term was handled in a unique way, due to the cold winters. It started when the weather was warm enough and stopped when it became too cold. No one could go out in some of the blizzards and 20-40 below temperatures for long. It was enough to keep warm inside.

Along about February, the grown-ups (I suppose on the school board) would begin unpleasant talk of when it might be possible this year to start school and where to find a teacher. It was always under way by March.

Now at the same time great bustling spread through the area as to what clothes for starting school in could be bought or gotten into shape by mending. At our house this problem was the big issue after Christmas. By now my next younger sister was going to school and the one after that had started, so the fat Timothy Eaton's catalog, about the only book in the house, was taken down again. There was a difference though. At this time of year some things were always bought, whereas Christmases came when all we did was to feast our eyes and wish. At Christmastime, we chose playthings to hope for that were possible and then ones to wish for. Our imaginations soared over these.

Before school started, the catalog was looked through over and over again, with the same intentness. Mom focused on best buys, we girls on pretty dresses. Such beautiful dresses were pictured, yet Mom, without fail, looked for navy serge. She had a feeling about the fitness of things. Navy serge was proper for school, besides being a practical fabric for wear and color too. Ugh! These winter dresses were never washed, just worn out. They'd shrink too much if washed. Many clothes were worn underneath: long-sleeved, fleece-lined shirts and long-legged underwear which were so warm and soft when new but never the same after the first washing. Over this went at least one very sturdy all-covering petticoat.

The Eaton's order would finally be sent with rarely more than one thing per person. It had to go all the way east to Winnipeg, Manitoba. Then began the inevitable worry as to whether the clothes would arrive on time. Our family was long on worry and last minute in doing. Lucky for us if everything fit and such a calamity when it didn't and had to be returned. We then missed the first bit of school and it took a long while to get over that being-behind or missed-something feeling. The new teacher came when school opened in spring and stayed until it closed in November or the first bit of December. Rarely did one come back for a second year. This made for a grand hodgepodge because we'd be in the middle of a grade! Regardless of when school opened or closed, exams were given in June. We'd go home on a Friday having finished one grade and come back on the following Monday to begin the new one. The next teacher to happen along in the spring wouldn't know what the one before had covered in many subjects. This meant a double dose in some instances and gaps in others. There weren't the well-planned books of today, so we could say, "Yes, we'd learned that," to some things.

In one clearly remembered instance, it saved the day and I had a second chance. 'Twas in the middle of 5th or 6th grade, we took up fractions. They were impossible. The teacher came around to my desk several times in an effort to explain but there was no understanding them. Thank goodness winter came with school closing. Next spring the new teacher explained them away so easily.

THE WALK TO SCHOOL

By now the walk to school, with company, was rather fun, if we weren't *always* in such a hurry. Our family was apt to be very unorganized and as a result often late for everything. But we certainly rushed around trying to be on time. With Mom so small and not too strong physically, it was hard, and at this time she was very busy having brothers and sisters. I felt burdened down with things we should do but never did. The parents' lack of organization was due to their not knowing how to do any better.

Right after the snow melted, the first tiny, gray, soft, furry nubbins of the crocuses were eagerly sought on the hillsides. Then one day their swelling lavender buds became wide open flowers with snowy white interiors. Later we found bright yellow buffalo beans, looking like small sweet peas, all in a cluster on their stems. Another favorite were tiny white daisies, with a bluish tinge, no more than three inches tall with petals as soft and fine as a painter's brush. Dainty bluebells grew in the ravine on slender green stems. They were so perfect looking. It was surprising how many flowers grew in that dry earth and all so fragrant. The wild pink rose, Mom's favorite, had tough stems and many thorns were braved to pick for her. It was among the most fragrant. Mom's name was Rose.

The slough (pronounced *slew)* we skirted could be investigated for polliwogs. Such tiny black ones they were. Then they grew up to be only tiny frogs, but a very bright green. We could not understand what happened to them when July came and the slough dried up into big black cakes of dirt, with cracks, which later turned to dust. How did they survive to be there next year?

With luck, in the springtime there might be a duck nest with lovely blue eggs. Sometimes they were taken home to eat. Meadow Larks and all the other birds built their nests on the ground because there were no trees or bushes. In some spots a tough little bush called buckbrush grew, no taller than a foot. This was a wonderful place to hide a nest! The cows didn't go near it for food and it was impossible to walk among it in bare feet. Most nests were cleverly hidden among the short grass and clumps of hoofprints. Meadow Larks were our favorite birds because they sang, "I love dear Canada, Canada, Canada."

The big round rock stood where we climbed under the barbed wire fence, just before leaving the pasture. That fence was a real hazard to school dresses! We often helped each other up and had a look around and a turn at feeling big and tall.

When there was school, and hopes for even a few minutes to play before the bell rang, we kids did not idle in the school yard. Every precious moment was spent playing games. A quick one, with only a few there and others added as they arrived, was Red Light. Another was Statues. There was no opportunity for informal play such as children have in towns and streets, so the one chance to be with other children was never wasted.

When the time came that four were going to school from our house, there wasn't as much chance for idling on the way. There were still more young ones at home and it was all too much for Mom without help. There was much more of the last-minute rush and it took longer to get so many off to school on time. The teacher scolded and I felt blamed. She said I was big enough to get them there on time. I certainly did try. She didn't seem to know that younger sisters never do what you want them to do!

Then it was that the only fun times were the stolen moments on the way home to see things to be seen, though it was not nearly so enthusiastically done as it had been in the early mornings. It was more a time to catch up on my thoughts. Also to take that much longer before having to get busy with some unpleasant job.

All jobs are unpleasant at that age!

CHORES

There was so much work at home now, I was only too glad to be at school and not because of the learning. Also, I wasn't at all bookish-minded.

Conditions had certainly changed. All the things I'd begged to try, now were expected to be done as regular chores. The list had grown. It started in the first grade when I'd pleaded with Dad to let me try milking our gentle white cow, Molly. The pail was awfully big to hold between my knees and Molly herself was very big, as I discovered after sitting on the stool. What if she stepped on me while I was so far underneath her? It was bad enough being clouted unexpectedly on the head with that long heavy tail. The first time or two the bucket went flying on this account because I'd jumped so with fright and there'd been scolding words from Dad. But I was keen to fill the pail as he did, and have it all foamy like that.

When starting in to milk, it must be done steadily, and after a while it becomes rhythmical. This ensures a steady giving down of milk, otherwise the cow dries up faster. Dad never took a minute out to rest, once he began, and was strict about others doing the same. So, after Dad had given me a chance or two at Molly, I was ready to try something else. He didn't see it that way. The time had come for me to do it through busy times like spring and harvest. When I became somewhat older it was an always job and there were at least three cows to be milked. A new one would be freshed, adding a fourth, and dad would take it over until the calf was weaned and one of the other cows dried up.

My wrists and fingers didn't get so tired by then but some of the creatures posed problems. The young cows were often skittish when I got seated next to them and wouldn't stay put. Cows were never tied up. Dad didn't believe in it. Maybe it had something to do with keeping them contented so's they'd give more milk. Anyway, he seemed to prefer their reactions unfettered. If a cow didn't like you, she'd run away. If tied, she'd kick. The worst times were when some of those same young ones had tried to climb through fences and torn themselves. They still had to be milked.

There was one time we had a peppy black and white spotted beastie that got an especially bad tear on a teat. Upon sight of her, I begged off. Dad insisted, "If you keep away from behind her you'll not get kicked and once you get started she'll settle down." Cows can also kick forward and with your head against their flank (the only way I ever saw anyone milk) you can get a good whack also. It's a bit of a nutcracker feeling because of being in a wedge. After quietly getting near enough for a pat and a bit of "so-o Bossy," I sat down. It didn't last long. With one gentle touch, she was off. I tried again and again, on the good teats, to relieve the pressure. These were on the back and we finally got under way, with much hesitating on both sides! After more talking, I slid my hand over to the front where the sore one was and she started off with a foot in the bucket. It was ruined, milk all over me and Dad mad. He finished the milking that time.

One thing that was fun when milking was squirting the cats. When anyone started milking, they collected to sit and mew for a share. We'd seen Dad squirt them a few times; he did it to get rid of them. For us it was a game. Could we aim squarely for their mouths? They never gave up and would stick it out even though soaking wet and dripping with milk. Sisters kept watch to be sure Dad didn't catch us. He thought it was a waste of milk and naturally interfered with the milking procedures.

When mosquitoes were bad it helped to make a little smudge fire. With the barnyard being soft with powdered dust, it was safe but carefully guarded. The cows didn't much like it and sometimes moved on. Then the fire was tramped out and a new one started. These were so small and hard to keep going, it kept my little followers happily busy.

The worst chore, which I was anxious to try but heartily sorry about later, was washing dishes. You know how kids like to play in water? Mom was delighted to discover someone was old enough to give a hand! I could play all I liked!

On the farms, people lived in their big kitchens. Actually, the houses were small but the kitchens were the largest room. All sights, talk and smells were centered there. A person scurried upstairs to jump into bed, having undressed in the warm kitchen. Home had only one other small room downstairs, sparsely furnished, rarely used, called the sitting room.

Our house was pretty untidy, especially the kitchen, and we were ashamed. Mom fussed about it so we knew it should be different, but there wasn't much chance of it. She had too many hurdles all at once and no conveniences. Now I know that even a coat closet would have been a help! Under the west kitchen window was a long wooden table, pretty good-sized, always piled up with dishes needing to be washed. Mom complained there was no place to work and cast a look around. Dishes were kept there at all times. Why was it they took up so much room when dirty and hardly any when clean? Most meal times we scrambled around to get enough plates and cups for eating.

Under that table sat a big, round, gray granite dishpan, used for many things besides dishes. Butter was worked in it, wash carried outside to be hung on the line, and it was the only thing big enough for raising bread dough. Bread, being a staple diet, was baked on the average every third day. All this helped to interfere with the dish washing use of the dishpan. A front corner of the table was cleared for the dishpan, and the square roasting pan, if clean, was used for draining some of the dishes. Mostly dishes were just drained on the table and we tried to mop up as necessary.

With a dipper, Mom scooped warm water out of the reservoir on the end of the stove. Some very hot water was added from the big tea kettle, forever steaming on top of the stove. Soap was useless in the hard well water. Dad tried to keep the reservoir filled with rainwater for such chores as washing dishes, as well as faces and hands. The reservoir did keep the water warm but it didn't hold much water.

I tried a wooden apple box crate to stand on so's the dishpan could be reached, but it wasn't high enough. I soon found dish washing was no fun at all. The food was dried on and even one plate took too long. A knife was the only thing owned as a pot cleaner. Mom took a very long time scraping pots and pans even after they were soaked. Soon the water was cold and greasy and, worst of all, rivers of water ran down to my elbows, and my front was all wet, to say nothing of the floor. Mom made encouraging remarks, wishing a bit more done. After that it was all too often, "Get busy and do those dishes," but I don't ever remember doing them all. If she was right there in the kitchen, more were done than when she wasn't. Poor Mom, we gave her a bad time in many ways. Usually enough were done to get by, plus the frying pan, which was used for every meal. We'd then disappear as fast as possible, leaving the pan of water for Mom to empty. It became pretty full from adding hot water from time to time, so was cumbersome and heavy. It was hard to balance, and on the way to the door, where it was thrown out, could so easily spill over us and the floor. It did often enough for poor Mom. Then there was that awful grease ring left with no good way of removing it.

THE KITCHEN

I don't know where those cozy, picturesque farm kitchens were that people wrote about. There were none out West. They must have belonged to second generation farmers in the affluent East! Ours was stark, bare and colorless, when it came to the pretty things, with nothing that could possibly become an antique! The only decoration was a calendar given each year by a merchant in our town.

All work was mirrored here in a glance: Dad's greasy overalls, worn to work on the implements; barn coats, children's coats; milk pails and the big cream separator; the large wooden flour bin next to the always hungry stove; school books and the desk bulging with bills; and oil lamps. A fat bucket of drinking water sat in the lame old sink and perhaps another steamed on the stove ready for washing. In winter clothes would be hung on a line overhead to dry. There were dishes to be washed and bread rising. In most respects a grim room, full of reminders of the everlasting chores. Steamy wash day smells were most unappetizing. The floor was constantly washed, yet never clean.

This same room heard all the news: Dad coming to say, "Yes, the hail finished the crops," and also happy news in the morning, such as, "In the barn is a new baby calf" (in my entire life, I never saw a thing born on the farm, Dad saw to that). There wasn't such a thing as a comfortable chair, nowhere in the whole house. Children used benches at the table.

The kitchen was the only warm room in the house, due to the big black cook stove. The heat diminished as it traveled toward the walls, which didn't hold it in. Insulation *wasn't* in those years. The time the room was most inviting was after coming in from the cold, which stayed near zero and below. Then the red glow around the stove lids in the poorly lit room were good to see. To sit on a chair with half-frozen stockinged feet on the oven door, and leave the wind to howl and whistle outside, was a cozy feeling. Even though our house was amazingly small for all the folk it contained, Dad said it still was too big to heat.

On one wall hung a sink, with a drain pipe running outside. This froze solid every winter. This meant opening the door, when you least wanted the cold, to throw out dishwater and shaving water. In the sink stood the bucket of drinking water and next to it a small granite basin for washing face and hands. Toothpaste cost too much money. Wash-cloths were rare so faces were lowered over the basin and sloshed with handfuls of water. On the wall hung a towel from a nail, everybody's towel. On the narrow ledge of the sink sat a brush and comb, again for everybody. Above hung a small mirror. On another nail, beside this, was Dad's long black razor strop with a nubbin on the end. This was held while he stropped his long-bladed razor, to sharpen it for shaving. 'Twas used as often for lickings and the nubbin was nasty.

Sitting on the floor, next to the sink, was a large wooden box known as the flour bin or the bread box. Sometimes bread was kept in it. It was homemade with leather hinges. Inside, it was divided into two parts: one side held 100 pounds of white flour and the other home-chopped wheat for porridge. It was piled with coats but we sat on it too when lacing up shoes or putting on boots.

On the wall were a few hooks, but never enough. After the stove and a door to the sitting room, came the tall oak desk in the corner, the most treasured piece in the house and the only thing that could be termed a piece of furniture. It was amber-colored. On top of it was an odd magazine and dad's porcupine quill and birch-bark collar-box, rather old and dusty but very precious. Behind the glass doors were the Writings of Swedenborg, Dad's religion. He read them, believed them and argued with his neighbors when they'd listen. No one else went near the desk. It was Dad's. When he sat down at it, we were quieter. He had a letter to write or was trying to figure out bills. These seemed to be important occasions.

The big table took up the whole south end of the kitchen. One small window let in the sunshine and a view of outdoors. On the table sat the lamp, sugar bowl and perhaps a pitcher of milk and loaf of bread. Bread was always handy for a slice when we were hungry. We might come downstairs in the morning to find the milk frozen solid in the pitcher and inches of ice on the water bucket. Then we'd know it was very cold outside. By the kitchen door stood the tall black cream separator with its dull metal bowl, ever so broad, on top. Everything about it spelled work.

But the kitchen was home. We lived in it and there was no lack of togetherness while we did, eight children and their two parents making up a family.

Dad was first one up in the mornings to tend the kitchen fire. We awoke to his shaking and poking the clinkers through the grates. Mom woke Dad on extra cold nights to put more coal on the fire so's we'd not freeze in our beds. Ordinarily, with dampers closed down, it lasted, with banking, through the night. Next we'd hear a rumbling in the dirt cellar as Dad loaded a coal scuttle. Often we children had to pound these big chunks with a sledge hammer until they were a manageable size.

After the grate was shaken down with a detachable handle known as a shaker and the fire all set, ashes had to be shoveled out. This had to be done carefully to keep the smothering dust to a minimum. All this was my alarm clock.

Dad put the tea kettle on, filled with water. Too often he complained later that no one had cleaned it out. The very hard water formed thick layers of lime on the bottom of the kettle. A hammer was the only means of removing it. So upside down went the kettle and we pounded the bottom to break it up and at the same time tried not to ruin the kettle. Even so, the bottom got pretty bumpy after a while.

My first job when I got up was to start the long-cooking wheat porridge for breakfast, leave it simmering on the back of the stove and then to go milking. When I got back to the house, the milk had to be separated. If there wasn't enough time, I didn't. It was a nasty, hard job.

Mom would be fixing and feeding babies.

 Chapter 2

THE BADGER

One summer's day, Dad came home with a baby badger and let us have it. The animal was pretty heavy but we carried him around and soon he followed us everywhere. He slept in the house, under our beds, on the beds, or anywhere he pleased.

He was built low and looked rather clumsy but could ripple along when he ran. We had never seen a creature who could dig so fast. Badgers live in deep burrows in the ground and we often climbed down them, feet first, up to our armpits. We'd seen our dog, Purp, dig after the wild ones. They could dig out fresh sod faster than he could keep up on the soft dirt left behind. Face to face in a fight a dog wouldn't stand a chance as badgers are so strong and quick.

While out playing with us, we watched Badger dig numerous holes around the house, which the parents didn't like. He ate only raw meat and looked very vicious while about it. He could take good-sized bites. However, he never bit us and Purp gave him a wide berth. As he grew older, he played rough and we didn't quite trust him (Mom hadn't from the beginning). We were dubious as to whether he was following us or chasing us. He growled when crossed but there were times we preferred him out of the way at play. He had to be shut in the house.

One day, halfway to school, we discovered him rushing to catch up with us. Taking him back would mean being late. After standing still till he caught up, we tried jumping at him, scaring him away. He stood still and watched. He was picked up and put down facing home and we ran on. He turned around as fast. We tried running a piece toward home so's he'd get the idea. Nothing worked so we gave up and went on to school, hoping he'd leave on his own. But no. When we tried slipping in the door, he was in the cloak room with us. The other children were already seated and quietly working. We quickly pushed him under a handy wooden box of slates and hoped for the best.

Soon the teacher asked if anyone knew what all the strange noises were about. After going hot and cold, I put up my hand to be excused. What to do? Badger was happy to see a familiar, friendly face and stopped his noise. My next idea was to get him outside. I carefully raised one side of the box. My hand reached for him. Out he rushed. He had never been penned before. On around the corner and into the school he ran. The teacher went into a panic, shrieked, climbed up on her chair and then onto her desk, wringing her hands. That's where she was when I came in. I'd heard her shriek before reaching the room; maybe he'd bitten her. My sakes, what a state of affairs! There was pandemonium among the kids. Of course there was trouble all around. Badger had to be caught and taken home.

Mom decided something had to be done about him. He wasn't trustworthy and he was an awful nuisance to her with his insistence on being with us kids every waking hour. Dad's idea was the quickest solution but we set up such a howl, he relented. We couldn't think of our beloved pet being killed. There must be some way we could still see him once in a while.

Any number of kids had wanted the unusual pet so he was given to one of the older neighbor boys, whom he promptly bit. That was the end of him. For a time we sorely missed him.

DUST STORMS

You haven't lived unless you've been through a dust storm. We kids enjoyed them because we thought they were fun-scary, not scary-scary, and they came unexpectedly.

It could be a nice summer's day with birds singing and sun shining. We might be playing Jump on Your Shadow, when suddenly the forever blowing wind would stop. The quiet could almost be heard. No bird sounds, everything was still. We'd stop, look up, and sure enough, way to the south and east was an enormous wall of soft sand color. First thought was to get to the house and yell, "Hey Mom, a dust storm's coming," and see her bustle to shut the windows. Even so, we could write our names afterwards on the sills.

Then back outside to watch and stay as long as we dared. The whole world was a funny yellow now and that wall of color was darker and nearer. It had become big rolling clouds piling higher and higher up the sky. Anticipating who knows what, we raced around for the sheer pleasure of the unexpected. First, little puffs and pieces of wind, then rough gusts, caught at our hair and clothes. Lids, or whole tin cans, in the yard were blown up in the air, maybe way, way up, and dropped again. The birds glided and wheeled in circles. We laughed, watching the last chickens scurrying for shelter while being pushed by the wind, noisily objecting with their feathers all fluffed out in anger and their tails blown almost backward. Tumbling weeds came from nowhere and sped across the yard and fields to pile up against the fences. Horses would come galloping home or race in the pasture and whinny. Even the cows made an attempt at running.

This was the fun time and it lasted a very short while - a matter of minutes. We waited for the big boiling storm to catch right up to us. By this time we'd be fairly close to the kitchen door. Suddenly the wind hit, full of choking dust. Sometimes it wasn't so very dusty, then it was sport to lean on the wind before obeying Mom, who was braced against the open door and calling, "Come inside, what's the matter with you, do you want to be blown away?" It never did get that bad, but she'd told us that if ever we were caught away from the house, we should lie down on the ground. We might try that too before coming in.

Only a year or two after I left, devastating dust storms struck that country. The Dust Bowl time had come to stay for several years, wiping out animals and farms. Dad's survived because he had a bit of life insurance to borrow on, but it was a long way back restoring the farm for usage.

A NEW ERA

One day a strange man drove up to our house in a car and said he wanted to talk with the parents. Mom sent one of us to bring Dad from the field, which meant it must be important. When Dad came, they sat down at the big kitchen table and talked a long while. We gathered something *momentous* was taking place; some different new thing was to be installed but we couldn't comprehend it.

Within days, men arrived who dug small deep round holes in which they put great tall poles, all along our dirt road, clear to the mailbox on the highway. Giants, marching in a straight line, precisely spaced. Very near the top of each was a pretty little green glass dome and a foot lower down was another one on the other side. From the house, two endless wires were next put up, running from pole to pole, much straighter and tighter than Dad's fences, which we had thought were very good. Then we waited, still marveling at these big things on the landscape and wondering what they were for.

Next time the man came, he brought a good-sized crate and asked Mom where she wanted "it" put. She pointed to a spot by the south kitchen window. Out of the crate came a polished brown wooden box with all sorts of things on it. The man fastened this to the wall with screws while a silent audience watched. On the left side was a heavy black bell shape, dangling from a brown cloth wire, which he hung on a hook and called a receiver. At the top, on the front, were two round black hollow half balls he told us were bells. Below these was a long black spout. This was right in the middle of the box and the end of it moved up and down. On the right-hand side was a little crank. He pointed out a small flat button on the left below the receiver. By cranking the handle while pushing the button, "Central" could be reached, always. If we forgot what he told us, and it seemed to happen a lot, she could give any information needed.

The box just put on the wall was called a telephone. We listened as Mom was told how to ring longs and shorts. Each near neighbor had a combination of these, besides having a number in the book. Our ring was a long and a short. Aunt Kate's was three shorts. The man asked Mom to try it out. With his help, she talked with Aunt Kate, who didn't know what to say either on her new phone. We could even hear her voice while standing near. She almost shouted. Shouting over the new telephones was common, although Central tried hard to talk people out of it.

We finally got the neighbors' combinations of rings written down on a paper with long and short lines after their names. Most everyone was afraid to use this new contraption and among themselves only admitted to having it for emergencies. It took time to become accustomed to its use, and longer to enjoy it. A few never did. Our number in the book was 411 but, like everyone else, the book was forgotten. If we couldn't ring the person in town, Central was asked for them by name. She became a busy information center for almost anything. She heard all telephone conversations and on many occasions saved much time, especially in emergencies. She seemed to know more than anyone else. People felt freer talking to her than to their neighbors. We children thought it strange the woman had two names, "Information" sometimes and Central at other times, for no clear reason.

When people began to use the telephone more often, we'd hopefully listen, in case the ring was for us. News began to travel fast and going to town lost some of its spice. There came to be accusations of people listening in or impatient ones butting in. At times several got on the line to talk with each other. This was apt to be the women. Mom wished she'd be included. When Central didn't answer after repeated ringings, you knew something was up somewhere. Receivers quietly clicked off their hooks and were cautiously held to ears to find out what was going on. Mom was much too timid to do much of this. Central might have to put a stop to it by mildly scolding. She played many a role besides doing her duty, cheering, comforting, calming and encouraging others. We wondered what we would have done without her. There had to be a few who held only a grudging respect for her because they thought she knew too much.

At this same time Uncle Nelson got a wireless, the first in the neighborhood. When he got it working, he called several people to listen all at once. Music! Dad put the phone receiver in an empty wash basin so the whole family could hear and we stood around it to listen. The music was full of crackles but a wonder even then. So there were two totally new events close together: the telephone and then the radio!

Life was never the same after that.

EVA

That same year the telephone was a blessing to us; a doctor could be reached in emergencies, and we had one.

For some reason there had been few childhood diseases in our family, and we weren't accustomed to calling a doctor (I didn't catch most of those diseases until later with my own children). There was little a doctor could do for them then, anyway. Nevertheless, sooner or later he was informed, when he was available. He traveled far, covering a wide area.

Outside of a round of mumps that swept through the school and then the grown-ups, I don't remember any epidemics. It was funny to see fat-cheeked grown-ups!

When a disease did hit a family, someone on the school board came to the house and nailed a big cardboard sign on the front door. The name of the sickness was printed in large black letters for any passerby to see.

These signs came in different colors, one for each disease. Our terrible one was pink for diphtheria. These signs meant the family was shut up in quarantine for perhaps two weeks. It gave us the feeling they must have had in the Dark Ages when the plague struck.

After the time was up, and one could go about again, the house was disinfected, an enormous chore. All beds and bedding were washed in Lysol, as were floors and woodwork. The place was sprayed and sulfur candles burned. The house was closed for hours and there was nothing to do but take a ride. When mumps came they gave up on quarantining and that's how we got out to see other grown-ups about town.

Why is winter time, sick time? This is when Mom worried that the kids, who were not yet fully recovered, might catch something worse from being out in the cold too soon.

Tragedy struck our house that November.

Blonde, quiet, six-year-old Eva, Mom's third child, was being dried after a Saturday night bath in the kitchen. She said, "I'm going to die." That was all she said and we looked at her in surprise. Why should she say such a thing? we all wondered. "Oh, go on, of course you're not," said Mom, after a moment's hesitation. The next morning she didn't feel good; her throat hurt and she stayed in bed.

Exactly one week of horror set in.

Maybe because of what she said, there was an anxious, uncomfortable feeling about her being sick from the start. Within a day or two, her neck was all swollen up and two bright burning spots of color on her cheeks made her very pretty at first. Her throat inside looked very bad indeed. I still remember the sight. She didn't want to eat anything but seemed anxious for a drink of cold water. Most surprising to us sisters was the fact that she stopped talking to us. Of course we were right there to see it all, as with everything else. That is the way it is when people live simple lives.

The new telephone was used to call the doctor and he came to our house for the first time ever. He said it was diphtheria and there was nothing he could do. He didn't come again. So Eva was brought downstairs to the unused sitting room where she would be near all of us in the kitchen. She was put on the flat couch with its legs unfolded to make it wider, and the door was left open.

Because she was burning up with fever, she'd get up and head for the outside door. Then she would collapse on the floor where the cold drafts from underneath chilled her. Mom tried to keep a close watch, but soon gave up. We were all home from school, shut in with the pink card nailed to the door, so had to help. From then on, all day long we were given turns as a lookout. We sat on a chair in the kitchen doorway and called Mom every time she started up. She was desperate enough that she was too strong for us to keep in bed.

After that first day or two, she moved very slowly but determinedly, and not talking made it a desperate thing. We wondered if she could hear. By now her throat was completely swollen shut and she tried *so* hard to take a drink of water. Her hands reached eagerly for the cup, but it ran down outside her mouth.

She tossed constantly on the bed and we worked hard to keep her covered. The worst part was seeing the big spots of bright-red blood left wherever she lay. Under great difficulties, Mom washed and washed the bed clothes. She and Dad took turns sitting with her through the nights. From being pink and rosy, Eva became terribly thin and it made us ache to see her. The family became so quiet. The parents looked sad and anxious and we heard Mom crying.

The last night, at supper time, Eva sat up against her pillow and stayed still on her bed. After being delirious the last days, she now seemed to recognize us. Her eyes were extra bright and shiny. From being blue, they now looked very dark but pretty. We sisters thought she looked much better and were glad. Right away Dad got out a soft little white book and read about "Children in Heaven." I can remember wondering why he did that when she looked so much better. When Dad finished, she got up off the bed, which she hadn't done in the last day, and again was headed for the outside door. This time she put her arms out and said, "I'm coming to play." After not talking for days, we were startled. Mom rushed to catch her in her arms and carried her back to bed, crying herself.

Early next morning, with just a pink sign of dawn and the lamp still burning low on a chair by Eva's bed, Dad was resting upstairs. I heard my mother call frantically for him. I rushed downstairs in time to see Eva stiffen out in Mom's arms and then go limp. Dad was close behind me. Turning right around, I rushed back upstairs to wake the others. We ran into Mom and Dad's room, crawled into their bed and sang all the songs we remembered as loud as we could.

I knew she had died. In only three days she would have been six years old. Though we had no birthday celebrations, we were sorry she'd miss the day. This was Friday morning, less than a week since the Saturday night bath, but it had seemed a very long time ago.

Then followed a long hard time for the parents with more trouble.

GRANNY

The next afternoon, a knock was heard on the door. In came a strange old lady with white hair and a "funny" eye. She said she'd come to help. Our house had been so miserable, I was glad something different was happening and she was certainly different. For one thing, she was old. There weren't many older people out there and she was the first we'd seen.

Dad said she was known as Granny McDonald. She kept house, miles away to the northwest in a little shack, for her no-good adopted son. He worked on the railroad when he worked. We suspected then that she wasn't really a granny after all.

She was most energetic and bustled about at once. Most interesting to see were the strange things she did. First of all, the silverware was collected and put in a pile under the tablecloth. Next, the small kitchen mirror was turned around to face the wall and she said we must be quiet. We were already spellbound.

We could tell that Dad, who was always so full of theories, didn't know how to handle this and was hard-pressed when faced with our whispered questions as to why she did all this. Soon she went into the room where Eva was and shut the door. She was going to "lay out the dead" and do something that sounded like "putting money on her eyelids."

Mom was upstairs lying down.

Before long, out came Granny waving her arms up and down in front of her and wailing. I wondered what had happened to her. However, we got used to it because from then on she'd periodically stop what she was working at and do this same thing. We didn't like it, but even so she was a big help to my mother, who was overcome with grief and tiredness.

The next thing to happen at our usually undisturbed house, took place soon after Granny's arrival. This time there was a knock on the outside sitting room door, the door that Eva went to, and not the kitchen door, which everyone used. When Mom went to answer it, we followed. She opened the door to see some men standing there with a long white plush box. She burst into fresh tears and Granny started wailing. We children stood in awe and misery.

After the men had put the box down inside the door and left, curiosity got the best of us. We had to see and touch. There on the lid was a tiny silver plaque I could read which said "Our Darling." We thought it was quite something for Dad and Mom to have thought of having that, even though it didn't sound like them. It had really just come that way.

Another man came to the door. He brought a round circle of pink and white flowers Mom called a wreath. She didn't look very happy about it. We'd not seen or smelled flowers like that before. They were so perfect, but we kids decided we didn't like them. I'm still not too fond of carnations due to the association.

Mrs. Pooke, a sewing lady, came and showed us a pretty white voile dress and bonnet she'd made. Around the edge of the bonnet were little pink rosettes made of ribbon. After Granny had put it on Eva, she insisted we go in to see her. I didn't want to. She was lying on the neatly-made couch and looked asleep in her pretty bonnet with a blanket over her. Granny picked up the blanket and told us to touch her. I refused, so she took a firm hold of my wrist. It was horrifying. She was stone cold. I could never remember anything else about Eva after that, except that it was a few days before her 6th birthday.

The day after that, neighbor men came and helped Dad put Eva's casket in the wagon and take it to the graveyard. When he came back we asked where it was: "Off a little dirt road, not too far from Oyen," which was nine miles away. He said there were very few people buried there as yet. There wasn't much snow on the ground, but it was very cold.

We children did not see her grave until spring, when we went out with Mom to put some wildflowers there for Eva.

Dad stayed in the wagon.

GRANNY LEAVING

When Eva died early in November, there was a light snow on the ground and afterwards several more inches fell. Almost a week later, we had bitter cold weather. On a clear dark night, as Mom was going to bed, she asked Dad what had happened to Granny. She had gone outside with the barn lantern and no one had heard her come back. They waited awhile upstairs and still no Granny. Perhaps she was still at the "little house."

Dad went downstairs and called out the kitchen door. No answer. He dressed, pulling on his heavy rubber boots over three pairs of stockings, and put on his cap and coat. He found no sign of her, called some more and took a look in the barn. All was the same. No horses were missing. After searching around the buildings, he spied some tracks out back toward the field where there was a lane. He followed them as best he could and found they went in circles. He figured she must have gone for a walk as she had several times before. He went back inside to bed. He was still very tired and upset over Eva and was trying to help Mom over the same hump. To add to their problems, she sometime later had a miscarriage.

The following morning dawned bright and crisp and Dad was up early. He found no sign of Granny about and upon investigating saw she hadn't slept in her bed. I was up and saw how upset he was about this, but he decided to leave Mom sleeping. He hitched the team of horses to the large box sled and set out to see if he could follow Granny's tracks from the night before. He had a hard time. They went back and forth, under fences and across fields. He ended up going straight northeast to her house to find out what had happened.

She had decided to leave our house just like she arrived, out of the blue. A neighbor, who lived across the road from her, said he heard a howling sound coming from the great big frozen slough in front of his house. It wasn't daylight yet. Thinking it was a stranded animal, he went to investigate. There on the frozen ice lay Granny, so he carried her inside. By the time the sun came up, she'd been taken to the hospital.

She was very frostbitten and in bad shape with both her feet frozen. A long time was spent in the hospital and people talked about us. Some people said her toes dropped off eventually, but I don't know. Often we kids couldn't get a straight answer to our questions.

Some children were still sick at our house and Mom was terribly anxious about them getting worse.

It seemed Dad and Mom had had enough trouble without Granny's catastrophe!

INOCULATIONS

After that first awful week, one after another of us got sick. We had the big pink card still nailed to our door with "Diphtheria" in those horrid large black letters. The doctor decided to come and inoculate the rest of us.

When he arrived at the door with his black bag, we ran and hid upstairs in the best places we could find. Of course the youngest crawled under a bed and I helped the next when she climbed into a big new empty drawer Dad had built into a wall of the north bedroom. She didn't much like it when I shut the drawer, but she did say she wanted to hide! I quickly slid behind some clothes in the closet in the parents' room.

When Mom called, no one made a sound, so she had to find each one and drag her out. Dad helped. I was the last one they found. Having heard the screams of the others, I couldn't imagine what the doctor was doing, but it must be awful.

When I was "licked" down the stairs, there stood the doctor by the kitchen table. A blanket lay across the end of it. I expected him to look at my scratchy throat. He was a dark, swarthy man with heavy glasses and, of course, all dressed up, very unlike the neighbor men, who looked friendlier. In his sternest voice, he told me to get up on the table and unbutton my bloomers. How mortifying! And on the table! I stood stock-still and clutched a handful of clothing, one on each side, right over the spot where the buttons were, underneath.

After a grand hassle, with arms, legs and other parts stinging from Dad's attempt at discipline, they had me face down on the table and the back of my dress pulled up. It was *such* an improper feeling. I managed to pull it down again and then Dad pinned my hands and arms over my head.

I was *so* ashamed! We were a most modest family. I felt that Dad and Mom had turned traitors. Besides, I had on a pair of big black and white checked bloomers that embarrassed me in themselves. They were awkward to hide. I don't know where they had come from but they were hateful (usually bloomers were made from plain white sugar sacks). It was bad enough for someone in the family to see them, but this public display!!! The doctor got them unbuttoned and started pulling them down. This was too immodest to be thought of and I managed to get free a couple of times to pull them up again. Even rolling over helped for a while.

Finally I felt a sharp, stinging stab on the hip and knew why the others had screamed. In a minute everyone let go so I knew the worst was over. I sat up to see the doctor with a hypodermic as huge as Dad's big darning needle.

He said that was all.

I'd figured he would work on our throats; that's where it hurt. When Eva was sick he had swabbed them with some vile stuff and for no reason. They hadn't hurt then.

It was not a good winter!

By spring brother Leslie was very sick. He was the baby, a cute two-year-old with now only three older sisters. One afternoon Mom said, "Run quick to the field and get Dad." I did, and ran all the way back, not waiting for Dad and a ride, but on into the barn to hide in the hay loft. Nothing could be seen or heard up there.

Not so Irene.

The doctor had come ten miles and gone again before I showed up. Irene had run into the room to see it all and then had come to find me. She told me how interesting Leslie was: "They put a clothespin in his mouth, his eyes behaved funny," and she described all the details of the doctor's visit. She made me very happy I wasn't there.

We lived in fear for a while but Leslie got better and life was good again.

THE COX GRAVE

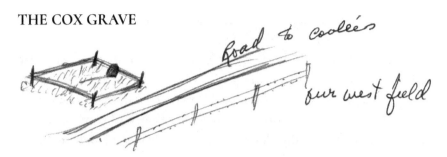

We talked among ourselves about people dying. Of course Dad and Mom would die first because they were oldest and then on down. It made me sorry to be the oldest of the children. We knew people were put in the ground because there was a grave across the road from our west field. It was a landmark and everyone knew Granny Cox was buried there. We figured she must have been very old because she'd died before our time of remembering. None of us had ever seen her.

After Eva died, we asked the parents many questions, and some of our ideas changed. Since Eva had died out of turn, we first asked about that. Then, what happened to her if she went to heaven and was also put into the ground? This had called to mind the Cox grave, which was the only one we'd seen. Instead of a very mysterious feeling about Granny Cox, she became a person and we wanted to know something real about her. So Dad told us what he knew.

She had come out West with at least four grown sons and was one of the first settlers in that part of the country. Whether they'd lived in sod houses to begin with he didn't know. They had plowed the land with oxen because these beasts could live off the then abundant grass. The abandoned farm buildings, not more than a quarter of a mile away from us to the west, were built by her sons.

They must have had money because her grave was very impressive. Besides, they must have thought highly of her to go to so much trouble where nothing was available. There was a little fenced-in yard. Remains of white paint could still be seen on the 4x4s. In a dry country, things last a long while. Her name was engraved on a big gray granite headstone, polished smooth. The sun sparkled on it.

Whenever we got the chance, we'd run over and look at it while Dad dumped rocks in the nearby coulees. He'd always give orders to stay outside the rail. It was shaky with age, which added to that ghosty feeling whenever we climbed over or under it. We just *had* to try walking over it a few times to see if it would cave in.

To the south, in the pasture next to ours, was a shack still standing that she'd lived in originally. The first family we'd known that lived on that farm were the German Hansens, and this pasture was part of the old Cox land. Later still, after the Hansens left and the place was abandoned, we'd climb under the fence and look around. Deserted places held a fascination and were a bit scary. The door was locked and windows boarded up.

back

One year an eagle built her nest on top of the roof, right next to the rusty chimney pipe. Now we had an excuse to go regularly to watch the nest. A ladder of sticks was still nailed to the outside end wall, put there maybe to wire up the pipe against the wind and then for cleaning out the soot. We climbed this ladder, with a missing rung or two, for a peek at the nest, never any higher than roof level. The mother bird might be nowhere in sight but the minute we got up there, she'd come swooping down out of the sky with talons spread. Then we'd quickly duck below the roof, climb down and give up for that time.

Soon three very fuzzy snow-white eaglets were hatched on the pile of debris. They looked decked all over with cotton wool and we wanted to pet them. They were good-sized birds for babies. From the start, they sat on their first joints looking awkward but alert. They seemed to be kneeling with their legs in the wrong direction. There never was a chance to pick them up or pet them. We managed to dart out a hand to touch the soft down and that was all. They'd be upside down in a flash to cut with their sharp claws when still very young. No doubt we'd have become tired of them if we'd had the chance to handle them, but they stayed fierce-looking with their bright, beady eyes and curved yellow beaks.

The mother eagle foraged further and further afield for food. We got bolder and climbed higher and they backed off. By now we were armed with a good-sized stick, which they grabbed but would never hang onto long enough! Sometimes we had several minutes before mother eagle returned to swoop at us. We watched her bring gophers and mice and eventually teach them to fly.

Coming regularly to watch the birds grow, we got braver about investigating the shack and the time came when we went inside. There was only an old iron stove, a small wooden table and a barrel of rags, nothing very interesting, except the stove. It became fun to light a fire in it. To do this we collected old dried cow chips in the pasture. When Dad saw smoke coming from the chimney one day, we were banned from the place.

After I left home, my younger brothers and sisters took over and one day burned the shack down. I'm told they lit a fire and, because of all the tell-tale smoke, decided to put it out. Cow chips must be very dry to burn well. After poking at it many times, they got tired of waiting and dumped it over on the floor. After righting the stove, they tramped it out and left.

It smoldered into flames and burned the building down.

TONSILS

After Eva died, the parents became aware of doctors and sickness. Mom kept a closer watch on what we wore outside, though we didn't need much encouragement with such cold outdoors. Dad muttered about not mollycoddling, but listened more than usual. It wasn't long after the recovery of the household from diphtheria that I complained that I had a feeling that I needed to swallow what was in the back of my throat, but it wouldn't swallow!

My parents dressed up for town and we landed, along with the doctor, at the small hospital. What a nasty place! It made me dizzy! What was that smell? It constantly reeked of chloroform. Instead of the doctor we'd known, who had left, a new young surgeon had come to town. His name was Macphail, and he was a very tall, bustling fellow. He used a flat stick on my tongue and said, "Those tonsils have to come out." They were much too big.

Into a room I was ushered, no bigger than a closet, and undressed. Next came one of those awful white, scratchy gowns. It opened down the back! How could anyone clutch it shut? Surely they weren't going to work back there again?? I leaned back against the wall. Maybe it was put on that way so's they could get you out of it in a hurry.

While left there in that back room working on the problems of the gown and teeth chattering, the parents went on home. I was fearfully afraid of this smelly place. A woman in white came and asked if I was cold. Of course I was cold, half-frozen was more like it. She led me into a long room with several beds. Many of them contained people, Granny MacDonald being one of them. Oh dear, I'd forgotten about her. What would take place next?

Very soon the woman in white came back pushing a long, shiny table on wheels and helped me onto it. We rolled into a back room with odd stuff in it. She wrapped a white cloth around my head. I asked what that was for: "To keep the blood out of your hair," she answered. From then on, I fought 'em tooth and nail until firmly tied down, hand, foot and middle, to the table. Now I was sure I saw the doctor with a butcher knife! And that's the truth. He put a white cone over my face, or at least tried to, while I jerked my head from side to side. Soon bright circles began to float all around and then only my head was left floating with them.

I woke up in bed having to swallow. It hurt something awful. I felt sick as sick besides. Needing to swallow again and again became all-consuming, I was bleeding to death! Even the nurse mentioned it and I couldn't tell if she was teasing or not. When I recovered enough to look around a bit, there was Granny with her awful-looking feet sticking out of the covers. She seemed very happy and said dinner was coming. It was fish and baked potatoes. Nurse said, "Eat." Just try *that* on a sore throat of the first order!

It was embarrassing seeing Granny there because I knew people blamed us for her missing feet. When I could bear to take a quick look, I saw that some parts of her feet were still there. There seemed to be bits of bones protruding and I wondered if flesh would grow back around them. As a diversion, she told me all about going home and then proceeded to show me more of her feet.

Someone in another bed, in a not very nice voice, asked how many kids there were in our family. This wasn't pleasant either because I'd heard them talk about no-goods having so many children. A large family was a sign of weakness, not something to be proud of. Instead of popping out with the answer, I was nonplussed and couldn't think. There was nothing to do but name them off on my fingers, which made it seem like twice as many.

I sure was glad when Dad came to take me home.

After this, Dad decided (I guess with the doctor's help) that the whole family should have their tonsils out, and they took mine out again at the same time. They had "grown back in," the doctor said. This time I felt he'd taken out the back of my throat.

The town had quite a few operations. Any number of appendixes were removed and most every one of those patients died. Surgeon Macphail stayed in Oyen only two years and moved on to the next city; some people said he was booted on and chased out of town. Everyone agreed he was sure "practicing" his profession!

One other time comes to mind in relation to health and its ways on the prairie.

Sister Mabel complained of a tooth hurting. Everyone waited till they hurt and then looked up a dentist to pull them out. Mom was too busy at home so I went along instead, my first time in the dentist's office. There was no telephone call; you just went and waited. People didn't think or know how to make arrangements on the phone; some still don't. If there wasn't time for everyone, they went home to doctor it as best they could and came back another day.

Even today a dentist comes to Oyen perhaps once in six months and stays a day or two. Too bad if there are folks left over for next time.

The dentist sat Mabel in his fancy chair and she pointed to the bottom and back of her jaw in her open mouth. He pulled the tooth and we went home. Mabel kept right on fussing and when Mom looked in her mouth, there sat the bad tooth. The one next to it was missing. They were second teeth so Mom went after Dad and he admitted, "Well no, he didn't watch what the man was doing."

The truth was that the real dentist couldn't get there that day so his brother had substituted! The brother sold farm implements, as I remember.

MORE ABOUT OUR NEIGHBORS

Half the time school life was peaceable, but the other half was filled with feuding and whole families teamed up. It was somewhat reminiscent of the Hatfields and the McCoys, in that the same two families were always pitted against one another. Not once did I know what started the fighting. Before the fight was over, everyone had joined one side or the other. Time passed and there were many more children in school, many of them younger brothers and sisters of those I'd started with, but the pattern didn't change. Never at any time were there more than four or five girls, even when the school grew to its peak of twenty-six pupils.

Loyalty was an unspoken law, taken for granted among members of a family. I suppose it came about as a means of survival in such a loose-knit society. Certainly it gave the younger members of the family a feeling of protection. On at least one occasion a parents' meeting was held to call a halt to a particularly bad squabble. Only men attended meetings. All we heard afterwards was that the fathers had had fist fights over the differences. No further meetings were held! From then on the teacher handled the rough spells as best she could, anxious, but unable to do much. Those were tense times; the boys fought rough and mean. Some of us who were more timid stayed inside as much as possible, but we fought when we had to, mostly in self-protection.

We lived west of school and the only farm west of us was the old Cox place where that German Hansen family had come to live. They walked to and from school with us and had the worst and roughest boys. Being old country German, they still spoke in their own language. Some men were called by both first and last names and father Pete Hansen was one. He had a mustache, was small, quiet with people, and mean. Maw Hansen was enormous, capable and dour.

We heard they tied their bad boys up with a logging chain fastened to a wagon wheel. There they spent the night as punishment with only the howling of coyotes for company. At least this is what the boys told us and we believed them. Beyond them for miles was poor land of small gullies, buckbrush and stones with no farms, and the coyotes did come from that direction. It gave them better cover than most places.

The oldest in the family was a daughter, Myra, a sturdy, unimaginative girl. Next was a boy, Walter, the meanest thing alive, and usually white-faced, which added to our fear of him. He gave everyone trouble. Youngest were the very much unwanted twins and we heard Maw Hansen say she'd "like to drown 'em," right after they were born. She had earlier wished twins on our 42-year-old prissy Aunt Kate, who was having her first child. Mom said that Maw Hansen's having twins served her right.

The two oldest Hansens were about our age and we tried to avoid them. On the way home from school, Walter amused himself with pastimes such as aiming fast-skimming rocks at our bare feet. Once there was a violent hailstorm with very large stones. It was an ordeal hobbling home over the icy coldness in bare feet and he pelted us with hailstones all the way besides. We arrived at home bawling.

Our house still shows the marks of that storm. Farmers went to town after it was over to swap tales of their adventures during it. They talked about playing a game of pool with the icy balls. That's how big they were.

The barn in the schoolyard had girls' facilities built at one end, boys' at the other. The strictest rule in school was that the girls' area was strictly off limits to the boys and vice versa. The few girls that were at school were a little afraid of using the "room," preferring the great outdoors where possible. Teacher frowned upon this but knew we did it only as a last resort.

Once during a feud, Walter was after me and I made a dash into the room and slammed the door, but his long arm was already inside so I leaned heavily on the door. In a flash, I took off my heavy canvas shoe with a thick rubber heel and sole and his head got a good pounding. It was most satisfying but I was afraid to venture out afterwards. When the bell rang he didn't loiter, so I dashed safely up to the schoolroom. It was a turning point; now I was someone to reckon with and he didn't feel so free to be dastardly.

The teacher had a thick, heavy length of threshing machine belting made of rubber and canvas. This she used as the strap. Walter got it often. Once he bit a teacher so hard on her arm she carried away permanent scars. He threw scissors too. When anyone was due the strap they were called to the front of the room to stand by the teacher's desk. She then asked them to raise their hands with palms up. One funny time Walter was called up and marched forward with his hands in his pockets. When he took them out he had on his heavy leather mittens. He'd been so bad, teacher fixed him. She licked him anywhere she could land the strap.

This was a family who stayed only a few years in our neighborhood and then moved on, no doubt to find some neighbors of their own nationality. The Cox place where they lived became an abandoned farm again and the buildings later disappeared. Dad eventually got their pasture, which adjoined our south one.

For years World War I could never be mentioned without my remembering this family. When thinking about them, we felt anyone could easily see why we'd want to fight the Germans! Apart from this, the Hansens were like everyone else out there when it came to making do with little money. The saying "necessity is the mother of invention" was often quoted by elders and I first applied it to them. When winter arrived, the Hansen children showed up at school in surplus army boots and khaki wool soldier jackets, much too big for them. However, with those stand-up collars and rows of beautiful brass buttons, they were the envy of many. The Hansen girl Myra wore the same boots and coat as the boys. Once I got up enough courage to ask, please could I try hers on, thinking I'd like one too. Not only were the sleeves too floppy and uncomfortable feeling, but also the collar was impossibly scratchy around the neck. The wool might look soft but was actually coarse, thick and harsh. Boy, was I glad not to have to wear it every day! I felt sorry for Myra and was glad this particular mother of invention was not tried at our house.

North of us, on the other side of the highway, lived the Moores. The oldest in their family, Florence, who was oldest in school too, was a tall, pretty brunette who helped her father on the farm and was aggressive by nature. She was a real stir paddle during feuds. Next came Richard, my classmate, who was nice-looking but plump, on the awkward side and inclined to be sassy. He was considered cowardly and his tongue often cornered him during the big fights. The kids all called him boob and when mad at him, ninnyhammer boob, which was for us a terrible epithet! He helped his mother in the house, come to think of it. This was the usual pattern: the eldest helped outside and the second one inside, regardless of whether he was a boy or a girl.

One time I sat down to explore the school organ. It took concentrating. The pretty pedals had to be pumped so hard to keep the keys sounding, while all the stops were tried one after another for their different tones. Richard came along to tease, pulling hair and darting a finger out here and there on the keys. After repeatedly telling him to stop it, he stuck out his tongue right beside my face. I let go with a good right-arm swing backward to get him out of the way. Chasing him had done no good so maybe the element of surprise would. "Look what cha' did to me," he bawled with his hands to his face. Blood was running profusely through his fingers. Not having intended such an outcome, I was afraid of punishment but teacher never said a word. I was a little pleased then to have stopped his teasing for once. He was so much bigger than I.

There's a P.S. to the Richard story.

He grew into a rather sensitive person and considered himself my boyfriend, which I didn't know for a long time. He liked to draw and sew. Once he made me such a pretty little doll dress, even tho' I had no doll. The color was considered out of taste then. The top was of bright orange cotton with a pale blue scalloped band around the bottom. Drawstrings on neck and sleeves were of heavy dark red wool. He even brought a drawing one day, of a dress for plump sister Mabel to make her look prettier.

Richard was a completely misunderstood person out there among the farm boys. After I left, he wrote romantic letters for years about "a little gray home in the West," etc., then "scrimped and saved" to come to my wedding. We had a fun visit and he was goggle-eyed over all he saw down East. Afterwards, he joined the Merchant Marines. His ship sank in a storm off the rocky coast of British Columbia on a Christmas Eve.

Richard's next younger brother, Walter, was a wiry, pesky kid, always in the thick of things. Their father was known as A.R. He was a hard and shrewd man, quiet, except on such occasions as a meeting of the school board. Their mother must have been Irish; her name was Coleen. She was kindly and pleasant with straight black hair bobbed to the ears. No other woman had short hair then. Her eyes were very blue. She looked like a typical farm wife with work-worn red hands and weathered skin. She always wore an apron and kept a most tidy house.

The Moores hailed from Illinois and were forever saying how much better everything was in the States. The standard rebuttal was, "Why don't you go back?" This one thing played a big part in my being naturalized as soon as possible after I came to the States. If I was to live in a country, I felt I should join it and be a whole-hearted citizen.

The Cornells lived south of us, on the east side of the graded highway. Ungraded ones with only two ruts were called roads. Reg, the father, was also a school board member and couldn't get along for five minutes with A.R. Dad said that was where the feuding stemmed from. Reg's three boys were wiry and redheaded with lots of freckles. Arthur, the oldest, was a grade behind me. He came to school looking so tidy. By nature, he was methodical and studious. One day when in seventh grade, he came to school wearing a beautiful, new, navy blue sweater with a bright green band across the chest. My, he looked nice and he was always polite to the girls.

He was my first crush. After growing up, he joined the Pentecostals when a group came through to evangelize, and he became a preacher. He mailed me literature from time to time about being saved. One piece, titled, "How I Found God in a Chicken Coop," caused much merriment among my school chums. It was a testimonial of a fellow who was about to steal someone's chickens, stopped, and, standing still in the straw, thought better of it and so was converted. Arthur became very righteous, thin and earnest, and narrow-minded too. Every pleasure was a thing of wickedness. Much to my surprise, he gave a skating party for me when I returned to visit. We skated as couples to mouth organ music. His people enjoyed pair skating, but dancing was taboo.

The next brother, Bert, had the redhead's temperament and was a good match for his classmate Walter Moore. They fought to beat the band. My sisters and I were always on the side of the Cornell boys because they were consistently our protectors, and Arthur was particularly chivalrous.

On one occasion, I truly felt I saved Bert's life from Walter Moore. A very high snowbank drifted up on the north side of school, often too high to see over from inside. Going out one recess during a feuding spell, I saw Walter sitting on top of the snowbank with Bert's head under him, face down. Bert's struggles looked hopeless. Asking Walter what he was doing, he said, "sitting here till he dies," and he looked as if he meant it. To interfere in a person to person affair wasn't smart, but because the Cornell boys were our buddies, it was worth a chance! These two boys were both wiry and quick and capable of outrunning any of us. To save time walking around the bank, I backed up and made a quick run up the steep face of the drift and gave Walter a swinging clout and was gone again as fast. I was enough bigger that this sent him sprawling, and I was safe inside before he'd recovered. After a day or two of watching out, he forgot his threats of retaliation. By that time a bigger and better war was on and we were walked part-way home by the Cornell boys as a safety measure.

The Othens lived north of us, in a house east of the highway. They are mentioned only because their eldest, Jim, was my other classmate. This family never got directly involved in anything at play. Jim was colorless, skinny and without much get-up-and-go. He rarely played without being coaxed, but liked to read. He was a nice boy though. Whenever we three were reading aloud, as each class did, Richard and I stumbled over some of the words. Whenever we hesitated in the least, Jim would pop out with it before teacher had a chance of noticing there was a break in the reading. She was often making minor preparations of one sort or another and not paying full attention. We made fun of Jim's ability instead of admiring him, but he took it blushingly, without a word.

His younger sister, Alice, was of note because she was a mere wisp and wheezed so badly. She was a person apart. Cheerful and patient, all the kids treated her as someone special and she never complained. She was the only one who didn't get mumps when it swept the school. She grew up to be very religious, which didn't surprise anyone. She often carried little Bible pictures around in her hands and liked to sing hymns in her quiet way, even when alone. No one made fun of it either. She died young of T.B.

The next younger brother, Bob, was fat all over and quite innocuous. I felt he was the one who should have been called by Richard's name, Boob.

Mother Othen was stocky, loud and had many large hairy moles on her face. When we read about the Wife of Bath in *The Canterbury Tales*, we all thought of her right away.

THE MAILBOX

The tin can, which was an odd shaped cream can as I remember, was long and thin compared to the usual bulgy, fat ones. It was nailed to our gatepost and we barely managed to reach the bottom, standing on tiptoe. If a letter was flat on the bottom we climbed the fence to get it. This was our mailbox, but it was a sometimes affair as far as mail was concerned. Mostly, it was a designated place on the map of the farm. Over a small hill, out of sight of our house, it seemed to enlarge the boundary of home.

A barbed wire fence ran alongside the pasture, dividing it from the highway to Benton. Our own two-rut road joined the main one at the mailbox. Here was a wide gate also made of barbed wire and fence posts, and it lasted for many years. It was nothing more than a break in the fence wide enough for large implements to pass through. A smooth wire loop was thrown over an adjoining post to keep it closed. It was quite a chore to open and drag this lot of wire and posts out of the way when Dad came through with the horses in his usual hurry. Dragging it back to close was much harder because it so easily tangled.

Dad would yell impatient directions from the wagon. If we managed past this stage, it took all our strength to stand the posts upright and an extra spurt of energy to keep it so until the wire loop could be slipped over that adjoining post. Another sister's help might make it possible but most often, in the end, Dad had to get down himself and do it, which left him cross. When we climbed back into the wagon with him, hurrying also or he might leave us behind, we were very

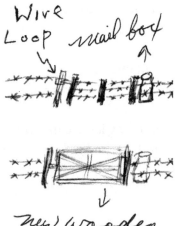

Wire
Loop mail box

new wooden

quiet for a spell or he might have quite a bit to say.

Eventually, when more money was available, he replaced this arrangement with a nice wooden gate with a latch on it. One push and it swung open. All we had to do was run to hold it open. Given a chance we'd jump on for the ride while it swung out. Dad forbade this and was on the watch; he thought it pulled the hinges loose.

The mailbox brings to mind any number of happenings of one sort or another. Certainly it was put there for mail once upon a time, a hopeful idea that didn't last long.

One could always manage to get to it from the house if any going was possible because our road was on the highest ground. Once outside the gate, Dad started some of his treacherous trips to town down a steep hill. It could be either with a heavy load of wheat any time of year or in the Model T Ford on the still-slippery surface after a rain or in late spring. The slough at the bottom could so readily overrun the road and then its culvert was a mere bump in the sea of mud.

Ordinarily we climbed under our pasture fence directly in front of the school and walked home that way. But when the Moores and Cornells feuded we were automatically in the fray. If we didn't choose a side we'd be in trouble anyway from both sides for nonsupport. We always chose the Cornell boys because they were trustworthy. It was a lucky thing they were the only family headed south after school, so we walked with them a piece down the highway to our mailbox before heading safely home. On such days, we brought home the mail, if there was any.

One spring day after a first big thaw, a feud was on. We'd hoped to make it directly home but the Braitenbachs, who were the Moores' supporters, were after us, so we walked down the road with the Cornell boys to our gate. In front of the mailbox the ditches on the side of the highway were cut much deeper than they were in front of the school due to the hill. Trying to get across the ditch, I sank to my middle in the wet snow, with water running underneath. That year's navy wool serge dress was ruined! It was the prettiest I'd ever had, and school had just gotten underway. The skirt was pleated all around and at the waistline was a beautiful pouf of red silk. What a long, freezing walk home with the wet ruined dress flapping against numbed legs! Into a bucket of warm water went the feet to recover. The awful, pleatless, shrunken dress had to be worn till warmer weather.

One of the mailbox's most troublesome aspects did have to do with mail.

North, up the highway, miles and miles past the school, lived the Pookes. South, five miles, was the town of Benton on the Canadian National Railway. This railway went across Canada, from east to west. For anyone living far to the north or south this meant great distances had to be traveled to reach a town.

The Pookes, of course, lived on a farm. Mrs. was a well-built, pretty woman with a beautiful, clear complexion, almost white, a rarity there with the dust and dryness and no lotions or creams. She sewed and embroidered with skill and to us was the only lady around. Mr. Pooke seemed like a foreigner, a bad word out there, though half our neighbors were foreign born. Only the English were considered to be the *correct* and superior race. I don't know what Mr. Pooke was but we thought perhaps a Russian. All people of dubious origin were put into that category. Sometimes he had lots of brown whiskers and sometimes he had none. Always he wore a big handle-bar mustache, which he fingered. He was tongue tied.

He was not a very successful farmer and became mailman for the extra income. He was the mailman, but we didn't know when he was or when he wasn't because there were such irregular gaps between deliveries. Perhaps he only worked when he got paid. Anyway, he was hired and his job was to pick up the mail in Benton and drop it into various people's tins along the highway on his way home. It had been his suggestion and that's how it happened that we got a mailbox.

Many times he came by as we were getting out of school and he'd hand each family's mail to their kids to take home. We tried to avoid him. He always had lots to say, perhaps even a message for the parents, as he was a friendly man, but we could never understand a word he said. If we asked, "What?" (we'd not heard of the phrase "I beg your pardon?"), he'd repeat the sounds all over again, only louder. I wished for enough nerve to ask him to write it down but was sure that wasn't the thing to do. More than once he told Dad that he'd sent a message of some importance. It was our one regular bout with embarrassment which we found no way to solve. Dad made no suggestion as to how we should handle the situation, though he got mad about it often enough.

Mr. Pooke soon gave up the idea of carrying mail.

But long after it had any use, the tin with its lid forever stuck out stayed nailed to the post until it finally rusted away. Still, it was called the mailbox and it was a special place.

Sketch from Reta's Art Notes book, made in eighth grade

 **Chapter 3**

THE TALBOT QUARTER

Dad rented a quarter section of land (160 acres) north of the Othens, known as the "Talbot Quarter." It wasn't very good ground, having been poorly cultivated, and was full of unpicked rocks, but Dad wanted the extra crop it might produce if properly handled. It had been rented by others. Dad first started out to pick rocks, and sometimes he took us with him. We could help, and he never made us work too hard. If we got tired, he didn't push. We were always keen to go.

It was a fair distance from home, so the first time was a big adventure. When Dad got thirsty and stopped work to go to the nearest house for a drink of water, we met two mighty interesting neighbors. Ben Moore wasn't very near the field, so we went to his place only once, but coaxed to go again. Outside Ben Moore's front door was a neat little pile of dozens of small tin aspirin boxes. This was why we were so anxious to visit him again; we wanted those boxes! Such treasures! "Think of all the fun things we could do with them." During one visit, we talked over how we might get them. We didn't feel free to steal, and wouldn't dream of asking for them. We just hoped he'd think to give us a few. We decided to stand beside the pile and look at them hard, but he never caught on!

Ben Moore was fat and old, or at least he seemed old to us. A bachelor, he lived in a black tar paper shack that smelled of tar when the sun shone on it. Slats of wood were nailed on the paper here and there, helter-skelter, to keep the wind from blowing it off. "He ran a very poor farm," said Dad. This usually meant that the man was lazy. He was someone the grown-up people whispered about. We later learned he was Richard's uncle but his family didn't "own up" to him. He was a drunk.

Ben Moore had a bad time getting up out of his chair and limped a little, no doubt from his drinking. We'd heard the ladies talking. Maybe some of it was from drinking, but Dad said he had arthritis.

People felt sorry for his sort but strictly avoided his kind. Morally, however, confirmed drunks were tolerated more readily than the men who took an occasional drink. The latter were considered sinful.

There was another tar paper shack near Benton - and one man there too. Drunks must live in tar paper shacks and alone, we reasoned.

There was a pool hall or some sort of saloon in Oyen, strictly a man's world, and wives were never told who might have quietly slipped in there, if only for a chat. We thought it was mostly for transients, such as the harvest workers. I believe some of the shopkeepers in town used it too, but most farmers had little money to spend on such things. The people who did go there were not our kind!

For years, Dad kept a bottle of whiskey high in the kitchen cupboard, as medicine. I never saw him touch it but it was there "in case."

On the other side of the field, and across the road from Ben Moore's lane, lived Old Joe Hunslick. That's what he was called. He was a short, gnarled sort of fellow with a growth of pepper-and-salt whiskers and a dirty cap. There was a perpetual wad of chewing tobacco in the side of his mouth, in a little round lump. He looked grizzly. He always seemed to be at home - not in the fields. Dad liked to talk to him so that's where we usually went for our break, except for the one visit to Ben Moore's.

I think Dad wanted to befriend Joe Hunslick. Dad was sure Joe could stand improving. He put up with Dad because no one else bothered with him. And no wonder! He was grouchy and used fearful language. We kept out of his way because he didn't like kids, and he could aim accurately and squirt his tobacco juice on our bare feet.

The floor in his tumbledown barn was raised, since he never cleaned out the manure! We wondered how the cows and horses ever got in the door. The cows bawled around the yard because he milked and fed them only when he felt like it.

Mrs. Hunslick was certainly a good catch for him; such a willing worker and pleasant woman. For extra money she raised hens, helped the neighbors and cooked for the threshing crews in the fall. If they were too far away from her house, she went in the cook car that followed the machine. Her house was neat both inside and out. She probably did the milking some of the time, but when busy figured he could do it. She earned more than her keep, for she was never idle.

Old Joe, in defiance, kept dirty clothes to wear that she mustn't touch, not even to sew on a button. His suspenders were held up with a nail across the missing buttons' holes. He didn't like going alone to shop in town, but she wouldn't go with him unless he'd shave and put on clean overalls so he looked half decent once in a while. He owned no Saturday night suit. We learned such things standing beside Mom's skirts at the grocery store, while the women talked.

Their house was small but had a bright, biggish kitchen. While Dad stood and talked near the pump one day, we noticed a room at the back of the house with the windows all boarded up. We ambled that way and climbed a ledge to take a peek through the cracks. Out of a door on the corner popped a real live witch! With a black shawl on her head, she was bent way over and the wind blew voluminous black clothes all about her. She was covered with wrinkles. In her hand was a cane which she intended using on us. She limped and, from the time she appeared, was muttering away in some strange language we figured was, as always, Russian. I wonder if our thinking the Russians were such bad people had something to do with the grown-ups' reactions to the Russian Revolution, not many years past?

After running a safe distance and getting over the first fright, this was fun, and we wanted to see her room more than ever. Was it all creepy and dark? We'd try again. So while Dad visited we gave her a merry chase that afternoon.

We found out that she was Mrs. Hunslick's mother and they kept her shut up in that room with a big hook on the door. It had been accidentally left unfastened that first time.

Next time we went, the door was locked and when we tried to

peek, she banged her cane on the floor and jabbered at us. It was a game. Dad never caught us but her daughter nearly did when she heard all the noise the old lady made.

The Hunslicks had a daughter, Lizzie, a number of years older than I, who seldom showed up in school. She was the wife's daughter. People surmised it was one of *those* situations: Old Joe was lucky to get a Mrs. and she was only too glad to have a permanent place to roost.

Dad said Lizzie Hunslick was no good. She "painted" (wore rouge and lipstick), which was a sign she was a loose woman. She also went to dances all alone! Square dances were the one social event. We couldn't picture grouchy Old Joe Hunslick wanting to go to a dance, so we felt sorry for Lizzie.

Mabel and I liked her because she talked to us, if and when she was at home. Besides, she had a horse all her own and we wanted so much to ride. One day she took us into the pasture to see her horse. She hefted us up on his bare back. Mabel was on behind and wrapped her arms tightly around my middle. We were frighteningly high up and half hoped to get down again. Lizzie called, "giddyup," but nothing happened. We even rocked back and forth to help him get started, without effect. She whopped him a couple of times and he still wouldn't budge. Finally she went around behind him, picked up his tail and gave it a hefty twist, like a crank. She was a big girl. The nag took off, straight up in the air. I remembered the feeling of going up and up and seeing how far away the ground was getting. The next thing I knew, I was trying to sit up and Mabel was still hanging on to me. I remember wondering how and when we'd hit the ground! I was sick all over for a while.

Somehow or other I never trusted Lizzie again, though I felt she'd meant no harm.

A DRESS FOR IRENE

One afternoon, when I could find nothing amusing to do, and wished I could, I got a bright idea. I had never thought of it before. I'd sew! Make something! I went hunting around the house.

We had a sewing machine, the now very old-fashioned treadle

sort, which could only sew straightforward seams. Mom used it once in a while to mend such things as torn flannelette sheets - very once in a while!

Dad mended all his own overalls. He'd very painstakingly shown us how he did it, and we were much impressed. Dad gave us the feeling he was never stumped by anything. Out would come his large, treasured darning needle and a length of heavy black yarn.

He threaded the needle, tied a knot in the thread, and finished his mending in a jiffy. It was under with the needle on one side and over on the other, pulling the raw edges together. That was all I was taught about sewing!

I found a small piece of blue-and-white-checked gingham and the idea jelled into a dress for Irene. The piece of cloth was large enough to fit the little girl. She hadn't started school yet, so if the dress didn't turn out very well she'd not have to be seen in it. Mom knew nothing about sewing so was no help at all, though I asked her a number of questions.

Then I remembered a paper-doll cut-out dress of Dolly Dingle's I'd seen in a magazine. I copied the idea, with an added wrinkle, putting a few gathers on the side of the skirt, which I forgot to measure for, and they ended up too near the hem line!

Along with the gingham was a strip of yellow sateen that could be used for trimming. It was cut into narrow strips to be sewed around the edges of the sleeves and neck. These straight yellow pieces went on around the sleeves just fine, but what bumps and gathers to get it around the neck!

Ever since seeing those pink rose buds of ribbon on Eva's burial outfit I'd thought them a pretty trimming. Now was the time to try one. It took painstaking effort with needle and thread to go in and out along the edge of a yellow strip of cloth. Even then the stitches were nowhere near even, nor would they stay in a straight line. However, when finished, and the thread pulled tight, there was a wonderful flower. Even with its raw edges and unjoined ends it looked lovely. Instead of being a tiny rosebud, it looked more like a flat sunflower! I made two and sewed them on at the waistline.

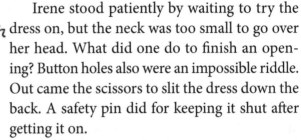

Irene stood patiently by waiting to try the dress on, but the neck was too small to go over her head. What did one do to finish an opening? Button holes also were an impossible riddle. Out came the scissors to slit the dress down the back. A safety pin did for keeping it shut after getting it on.

The sleeves were a bit funny, too narrow and too long. Irene managed to get into the dress and then complained that the sleeves were uncomfortable. She wore the dress for only about one hour, but I was very pleased with how it looked.

I was tired! My shoulders ached too. It was disappointing when Irene didn't want to wear the dress, and I felt the material was wasted, but I'd learned a lot and wished for more cloth for another time. It was a great beginning! Mom said she thought I had a "real bent for sewing." Such a remark was encouragement and had far-reaching effects. I did learn to sew and loved it. In later years I was to spend many productive hours designing, sewing, embroidering and ruffling gowns for schoolmates, friends and relatives.

PARENTS

After years of taking parents for granted, there comes a time when children stop, think and even take stock of them.

We were different from anyone else. We had a special religion and Dad said this made a "whale of a lot of difference," and he saw to it that it did! We weren't allowed to play with other children. We couldn't go to their houses and none of them came to ours. Once, when I was older, I begged persistently to be allowed to go to the Moores' after school. Richard had invited me because they were going to wallpaper part of their house and from somewhere had acquired a beautiful book of samples. Besides, he'd talked with much enthusiasm of a new player piano. I wanted very badly to see both these wonders.

Permission was at last granted. Wouldn't you know it had to go wrong? During the afternoon, someone brought out a cardboard doll they'd made, with a dress cut from the wallpaper sample book. The doll had surprising labels back and front. The words were unfamiliar but their positions and the giggling that went on told me they weren't nice at all. It was a shocking experience. It made me feel alien. The visit was ruined and Dad was proven right, somehow. I never told him. That was the only time I ever went alone to visit anyone in all of elementary school.

Dad asked what happened each day in school. Of course we were only too glad to tell him, in much more detail than he wished to hear, and he'd get a bit impatient, why, we weren't quite sure. He only wanted to keep tabs on us, not to hear a long tale.

If Dad had anything to say, it was to the point. If he punished, it was quick and sure, "a good licking." Only once I added my two cents when he and Mom had one of their arguments. Before I knew it, he'd broken an apple-box board over my knees! That clearly meant no more interfering! Seldom did he warn and never did he take time to explain until afterward, or most often not at all. Usually, when we could figure out his reason for punishing us, we thought him fair.

There was one set of circumstances I did consider unfair. This was when he gave orders we didn't understand and we'd be scared. It could be something as simple as an order to get a tool whose name we didn't know and he'd insist we "go get it." I'd always take a chance on bringing back something. If it was not the right thing I might get a licking. That was just one of those things! I excused Dad since he was always in a hurry and had no time to explain, I thought.

Talk was scarce at home, which made us feel lonely. It consisted of everyday orders like "Hustle and get the horses," "Run to the tool shed and get me the hammer" or "When's dinner ready?" There was no everyday humor, but a predominating feeling Dad gave us of hurry, hurry. He never walked, but almost ran.

His main thoughts, as to things of this world, were for his land. I suspect he would have understood the satisfaction Scarlett O'Hara got from owning the "good black earth" of Tara. Perhaps he loved the "good brown earth" of Alberta! He looked forward each year to a "good big crop." His fields were kept clean, free of weeds and stones. It was a matter of pride.

Another thing that Dad was proud of was that he never swore or used slang. He pointed this out to us because he believed that to swear was to break the Commandments. The one expression he used, when completely exasperated, was "Land Sakes." There were times when he clicked his tongue instead.

Dad's presence and thinking were all-pervasive. Mom was completely submerged.

UNCLE NELSON AND AUNT KATE

Dad might announce, "We are going to Nelson's place." So on a few rare Sundays in our family life, we'd all get cleaned up to go visit Uncle Nelson and Aunt Kate, if the families were on speaking terms! There had been wars as long as several years. We kids never enjoyed it.

Uncle Nelson had been out West longer than Dad, living on his farm north of the Moores. He shopped in the town of Oyen and used it as his mailing address. Oyen was much bigger and better than Benton and further from his home. He even hauled his wheat there. He stayed a bachelor for years and so acquired many more things than Dad did, but his buildings looked poorer and had no paint. One winter he visited back East in Ontario and returned with a wife. She was a prim and proper English woman. She had once been a schoolteacher, which we found hard to believe. She was tall, old, and always wore a hat when outdoors. The hat was little and flat and fussy, anchored with a very long hatpin whose steel glistened beyond the hat's edges. It looked like it had once, long ago, been a Sunday go-to-meeting hat of finery. Now it was worn even to feed the chickens. I wonder if she ever admitted to her folks that she was a farmer's wife. She never mentioned them.

Her nose twitched. We took this to be evidence of her dislike for us. She called us brats. "When children go visiting, they sit on chairs with hands folded," she said, and we did. She took us outside and showed us how to play croquet, which almost made us want to go again. She set up all the wickets and stayed with us, but we made out poorly; her yard was on the side of a hill! Inside, her house was quite fancy, with a window cabinet filled with glasses she never used, for us at least. At home we had heavy white cups for everything.

Aunt Kate somehow managed to have just one little boy. She dressed him in pink silk suits till he was shockingly old. When he started school, she brought along his own little chamber pot. Poor kid, he took many a beating because of his "old maid" mother.

Mom would arrive home from a visit fussing and fuming. Aunt Kate had "lorded it over" her again, not only about how children *should* be raised but also about how she shouldn't have so many in the first place: "Then you could have a few decent things." Mom never got a chance to talk back.

There was one family Aunt Kate seemed to like. They came to live on a run-down farm right across from her fields. This Jackson family had three girls. Ida, the oldest, was older than I. She had soft long yellow hair done in corkscrew curls clear down to her waist. No other mother let their kids have such long hair, for 'twas "Vanity, too much trouble." Anything different in our section of the country was also suspect. When Ida spoke at all, it was so quietly you had to pay attention to hear. We other kids were boisterous, noisy and did any amount of yelling at play. I couldn't see what Aunt Kate saw in her. Now I can say, she was probably feminine and helpless looking, which Aunty considered ladylike.

Ida rode horseback. One day I was standing next to her while she patted her horse. I kind of wanted to make friends with her, so I patted the horse too. Then I noticed great big tears running down her face. No sound. I watched for a bit, then asked what was the matter. "The horse is standing on my toe," she said. With that I gave it a good swat and it moved away.

Her pink, tender-looking foot had a deep blue groove in it, right at the base of the big toe. We went into the school and the teacher fussed over it. I had no patience with her! Anyone who didn't have any more gumption than that wouldn't be any fun bothering to play with. Let Aunt Kate like her!

Dad said the Jacksons were mighty poor farmers. They only stayed a short while and then moved somewhere else.

Uncle Nelson became most interested in his garden. He grafted trees. He especially wanted to see if he could graft apple trees that would be hardy enough to endure the cold winters. His trees never grew very big. He was proud of his prize vegetables too. Once, when a visiting minister came to call, I was asked to hold a bunch of his oversized carrots in the group picture. They were freshly dug for that very reason. The expression on my face showed I wasn't flattered!

Uncle Nelson taught himself to play the zither, after a fashion. He could be counted on to bring it out and maybe sing (we said croak) along with it. Elders were notorious for what they couldn't do with singing.

He did a masterful job of weaving rugs of heavy wool done in dreadful color combinations. We thought them dreadful then; today they would probably be accepted. He sent me a small rug for a wedding gift and I hid it!

Uncle was as strong-minded and opinionated as Dad. He belonged to the same Swedenborgian religion. Dad didn't hold with Uncle Nelson's hobbies. He maintained what Uncle did in his spare time was a bunch of nonsense: "He should be reading the Writings more," and he told him so. To us, Dad said, "I've seen dust on his books, so I know they aren't read often enough."

MOLLY

Molly was a soft, white, furry cow who figured largely in our lives for some years. She was a particular pet of my mother's, who often saved the potato peelings for her as a treat. She enjoyed all the attention she got, and was a most gentle creature. I learned to milk her when I was only seven years old. Her milk was rich and creamy, better than that of any other cow we had. One thing hard to understand was the fact that she had the meanest calves of all the milk cows.

On the house side of the barnyard was Molly's little open gate, not very wide. On either side of it were tall gateposts, taller than the regular fence posts anyway. Dad had a very heavy wire, looped and twisted around the top of them, which he stooped a bit to get under.

Molly would come to the gate to await her treat and, it being an unusual gate, even came through it at times to wait nearer the house. This was not to be tolerated and she'd be driven back before she got what she came for.

The barnyard buildings were fenced in with access to the pastures. The house sat outside this enclosure and was backed by a big open wheat field. When the horses were brought into the barnyard fresh from the pasture, Dad ran this way and that waving his arms. The horses who were to be worked that day must be chased into the barn to be harnessed. They didn't want to work so they raced around and up to the fence to try to get away. The one low gate, which Dad used to come and go, kept back the horses. The cows *could* walk under it but rarely did.

One time I had a nasty experience with that gate and felt that Dad always expected us to know more than we did. The piece of looped wire at the top had a fair-sized stick in the middle. Every once in a while Dad twisted this tight. It gradually unwound again.

One day, when taking a pail of the peelings to Molly at the gate, Dad called to say, "twist the wire good and tight." While the cow was munching happily, I used both hands to turn the stick end over end to twist the wire. It was fairly easy at first, but then got harder and harder, but still was not twisted as tight as Dad would do it. After deciding it was done enough, because I couldn't turn it any more, I let go of the stick. The whole thing unwound on me! Wham! Stars sparkled all around and my eyes filled with water. But my nose: what had happened to it? Did I still have one or had it disappeared into my face? There was a horrible feeling where it should be. After a tentative touch, I found it still there. I was so numb that I couldn't be sure if it was flattened and blue. Just fingers couldn't tell. Mom ran out to collect the good pail the cow was bashing about (looking for more to eat) and to tell me I did still have a nose. Dad came along to say, "Why don't you keep your wits about you?" And I stood and thought how lucky it was my nose and not an eye!

MOM

Mom was a very little person who was most kind and gentle. She truly seemed misplaced out there and was anything but robust. But she was full of pluck. She had very little education, being an orphan from England and sent to Canada when very young, probably to help settle the new land. She said she had had schooling only through third grade. Where she grew up there were few rules about children going to school.

For her, writing a letter was a major undertaking. She learned her sentence structure by writing to us after we went away to school. I think she did remarkably well and she learned also how to get some of her thoughts across.

She had a most simple faith. We always said, "Now I lay me down to sleep," before she kissed us good night and tucked us in. Her favorite treasure was a beautiful picture of Jesus walking on the water, done in bright glossy colors. It was hung on a small bit of wall around the corner by the cellar door. We children enjoyed it with her as a pretty picture. Dad did not approve of it, made no mention of it directly to us, but let her keep it there. She did not understand all the views Dad went on about.

When he was in the fields, she spent many long hours standing with her back to the old kitchen range, dreaming off into space. I suppose her daydreaming was her only relief from endless days of chores, each day the same as the one before. The few good times were when she remembered some pleasant little episode from her youth.

Sometimes she had a smile on her face, but most often she was unhappy and ended up in tears. Either way it was disturbing and we'd go twitch her skirt to get her attention or just to stop her from crying. She might be impatient then, which wasn't pleasant. Ordinarily she was very patient, listening to our small doings and problems and always ready with a hug. After grabbing her skirt and asking, "What are you crying for?" she'd say, "You don't understand." And we most certainly didn't then. When pressed she'd give us an answer like, "There are no trees or anything pretty here," or "I wish I could fix the house up." I grew to feel that the few beautiful things she wanted were good. It was sad that they seemed so unattainable. She had a great desire to better herself in every way, but didn't know how. If only she could have had a few magazines, it might have helped. She did struggle to read anything that came into the house. She could be a cheery little person, and had much more of a sense of humor than did Dad. He seemed to have none.

She rarely mentioned any personal belongings. When her one cotton dress was worn out, she'd search the Eaton's catalog to see what might be found to replace it. Being so small she could never get one to fit. In those days they came only in sizes like small, medium and large. There wasn't the vast category of sizes there are today. So Mom looked for "something to cover her back," as she'd say. There was little pouring over styles. A house dress was a house dress! They had no style but there were a few choices in color.

Once when I asked her what was the matter she said, "A baby is coming." That was a real surprise! She'd never talked about anything like that to me before. She must have felt I was old enough to mention it; there were at least a half-dozen kids by then. I'd never been curious about such things or even noticed when a baby was due. I accepted the fact that a new baby arrived at our house periodically without question. Perhaps Mom's oversized house dresses concealed the evidence. When I thought about this, I felt sorry for Mom. She had enough work and worry without having babies!

I came to the conclusion that fathers were domineering, just as she often said. Before I thought about it, I hadn't paid any attention to her statement. Mom spent a lot of time arguing, but never seemed to get anywhere.

She did love her babies and Dad was proud of how fresh and clean she kept them.

Mom had a terrible time with discipline and we knew we could count on many threats before any action was taken. Most times we just got away with it. There was one eventful and shameful time I recall when she must have been determined to give me a well-deserved licking.

She had really gotten mad and I knew she was right. When I saw the size stick she'd picked up, I wasn't taking any chance. So, still giving her an argument and keeping out of reach while edging for the open door, I ran out. She wasted no time in following. Across the front yard we ran, headed for the pasture where the gate was open. It was a joke. I could run much faster than she, so I stopped a couple of times till she almost caught up. Then I would dash off.

Once I heard her say (I thought laughingly), "Wait till I catch you." By this time, I was tired of the fun and waited for her. This sort of thing had happened before, in a lesser way, and I'd give her a hug and all was forgotten. But not this time. Wham! That stick came down with a vengeance. Such mixed feelings. First I was furious as I'd stopped and given her the chance. At the same time, I was sorry to have led her such a chase. She looked exhausted.

Dad was largely responsible for our attitude toward her. He paid little attention to what she said and less to her wishes. We were torn between her affectionate hugs and Dad's way of thinking. He thought her impractical too, and in a sense he was right, but now I understand her reasons. An instance of this was shopping for food.

We'd be standing at the counter in the Grocery and General Store, with the food all collected to be added up while Dad did errands elsewhere. Mom had finished going back and forth considering carefully what to buy. This besides taking a quick look and wishing she could buy a nice new patterned oilcloth for the table, or some such, in the dry goods department. We looked on hopefully, wishing she'd pick out a goody to take home. There were open wooden buckets of candy and cookies. We knew better than to ask for something on the spot.

While waiting, Mom would be fidgeting and looking worried and every so often we sensed why. The storekeeper might appear a bit uneasy too; he'd been through this before. In would stride Dad and look everything over. Sure enough, there was a pail of strawberry jam instead of the usual cheap plum jam. Back it would go on the shelf. Sometimes any jam went back. The poor storekeeper just stood by and we kids felt like hiding.

The storekeeper, S.A. Miller, as everyone called him, was a pleasant, reserved and rather sensitive man, very much on his toes. He was lively and quick and, I might add, handsome. All the ladies thought so, with his blue eyes and curly blond hair. He was the most successful grocer Oyen ever had due to a fine blend of shrewdness and kindness. He kept his store as neat as a pin, no small feat with so much mud brought in on the men's barnyard boots. He liked Mom and once in a while would slip in the better pail of jam for the same price. Then we'd have a pleasant ride home anticipating the piece of bread with nice new strawberry jam on it.

Dad was a good customer in everyone's eyes because he paid his bills. Farmers could have an awful time paying for things some years. Others went broke and moved on, leaving unpaid bills behind. S.A. Miller made a good living, seeming to know how much credit to give each customer. After a bill ran up to a certain point he would sell only the barest essentials. Thus no one would go hungry, but the squeeze was on and both parties were aware that the bill must eventually be paid.

So, with Mom tied to her round of drudgery in a small drab house, with an odd grocery trip as pleasure, and with Dad lost to the outside in his world of wheat, we were left to our own resources to grow up as we would. My favorite saying about it is, "We grew up like the prairie flowers, wild and free."

OUTSIDE OF SCHOOL

We were often happy, often forlorn. There was no comfortable middle ground. We had no play "things" and when we ran dry on ideas, we were very dry. We knew better than to ask, "What can I do?" We'd be put to work. I even kept out of sight when large chores were imminent since play time was stolen time anyway.

Even the school readers were drab; they had no pictures, which we badly needed. There was so little to brighten and broaden children's lives. Our readers did include good literature, both poems and prose. We learned to recite many poems, almost none of which we understood. "Horatius at the Bridge" is a prize example because we'd not the foggiest notion of what it was all about. Today I get a thrill rediscovering some of these same familiar bits and pieces, and enjoying them. To draw a map in a geography class and be allowed to crayon it in color, with all its blue rivers and purple mountains, was a joy, so that was a favorite subject.

At home during summer, when the wheat was growing and the days were long (it's far to the north), we'd wish for something to play with. Anything! I can remember being sent to the woodpile to collect something for starting the fire for cooking supper. It was called the woodpile but never, never was there a pile. An old railway tie sat as a chopping block with a man-sized ax beside it. Dad *tried* to keep firewood there, such as an old apple crate from winter (the only time we got fresh fruit: apples! And then very few), but he didn't always succeed.

On the way to the woodpile I got the feeling of the forever and forever prairie. The slanting rays of the sun and long shadows were haunting. The long, long afternoons never seemed to be over and tomorrow would be exactly the same. Overhead was a perfectly round bowl of blue with rarely a cloud and another bowl, dusty colored, that was the ground. Nearby was short dead grass.

It seemed so lonely. Who could imagine what lay beyond that far distant horizon? It was easy to picture the bareness going on forever!

Maybe the Raleigh man would come! This happened once, maybe twice, a year. The highway east of the house, running south, was where he'd be seen coming. A trail of dust would catch our attention first. While watching, it was possible to see little specks. These grew and became cars, or teams of horses. They dropped from sight when they climbed over a hill then showed up again. If they got big enough, and came in the road by the mailbox, they were coming to see us! We often watched to see if this would happen, but visitors were rare.

If we saw anyone coming to our house we ran to warn Mom. It could even be this year's hired man walking in to help with the harvest. Mom's hands flew to her hair, making sure the hairpins were tucked tight, holding the bun at the back of her head, while rushing about to begin picking up. It was hopeless. At the same time she'd be talking away about what a sight the place was and all that should be done. We kids stayed glued to the windows until the last minute and then rushed upstairs out of sight. After a bit we'd quietly creep back down again amid giggles and creaking steps. By fighting, pushing, pulling, the lucky one got the last step and stuck eyeballs past the doorjamb to report everything seen and heard back to the rest.

The visitor must have heard the scuffle and Mom invariably said that her children were shy, but she did nothing about it. We knew she didn't like brazen young ones so ended up not knowing how to behave. Besides, we looked a sight in what old clothes we had and Mom believed people should be all tidied up when seen. If it was someone known and Mom had gone to the gate to greet them, we came out and followed to watch at a distance. After they left, another thing Mom might say was, "You children should have some manners," but there again we didn't know what manners were! All the word meant was some sort of behavior different from ours!

The Raleigh man came with a horse pulling a black buggy, different from the usual kind. It was not open and flat but had a big, black, boxy look to it, like the ones the Amish drive in  Pennsylvania. He got his name from his chief ware, Raleigh's Liniment, good for all aching backs and muscles. He carried an abundant supply and found ready customers to keep his business thriving. There were other boxes piled inside too, full of interesting things. Some were good smelling and one was pretties.

After trying hard to sell Mom a bottle of liniment, out would come boxes of spice and vanilla. From another place came small round green tins of ZamBuk, a green salve, good for all cuts and bruises, which brought cries of "Mom, can I have this one when it's empty? It's my turn. She got the one last year." In other boxes were snaps, books and safety pins, but we held our breath when he reached for the last one, filled with ribbons and laces. Mom fondled them and put them back. Altogether it was a varied and colorful collection and such fun to see, even if we couldn't buy. Our list, if we had one, was perhaps a precious darning needle for Dad, the ZamBuk and some wide flat elastic for garters, to hold up winter stockings.

His wares changed over the years. As the local grocery store became better stocked, some items were dropped. Some things he could depend on selling this time or next were washers. These were small, round, flat discs with very short bolts. Cooking pots and pans were made of enamelware, which easily became chipped. These chips quickly turned into holes which could not be soldered. These washers were bolted in the holes and the pots could then be used for a long time. There might be a slow leak but they were still usable. The big copper wash boilers that heated on the stove cost a lot of money and were saved the same way.

The Raleigh man came to know his clients and for that reason showed up at our house well before dark or early in the day. He depended on people to put him up and share a meal. This went for his horse too. He knew he'd never be invited to stay at our place. Just once we let a new one stay for supper because it was so late.

We never entertained anyone. Company always sent Mom into a swivet and Dad didn't know what to do with them. Besides, there were too many kids and traveling people weren't trusted much. From just one experience, I'd say justly so. When Mabel and I went to show this new one where to feed his horse, he was as fresh as could be and grabbed at Mabel. Mom was smart to have sent the two of us.

Dad felt and said, "If kids don't know what to do with themselves, put them to work." He also said the same thing when he found us quarreling. Such easy but unwanted tasks as feeding the hens turned into fun unconsciously. After flinging a mad handful of grain from the bucket, we'd be off to chase the roosters, who seemed too greedy. The mother hen must have her share. The newest fuzzy chicks were chased and caught to hold and feel. While we were on an unhappy trip to the woodpile, a rare hawk would circle the barnyard and scare the chickens, who rushed, with wings flapping, squawking into or under the buildings.

Our dog, Purp, always jumped to follow and never failed to be good company. He invariably made us feel that *someone* was worse off than we were. He looked so hopeful but didn't have a good thing happen to him from our point of view. Dad refused to let him into the house, whatever the weather, and no good food was spared for him.

In lean years, we felt the parents' anxiety. Life was a mixture of hopes and fears, but we grew up with very few "don'ts" and learned much from Dad. He had no poetry (aesthetics) in his makeup. He believed in no foolishness and any child who showed imagination was scolded roundly for "lies." He did teach a practical approach to life and perhaps a person can learn the impractical more easily later on in life.

It took many years after leaving home, and reading about other people's reactions, before I was able to form any sort of perspective on our life out there. My conclusion was almost the same as sister Irene's, who said, "It was a good place to be from." To me, that included Dad. His impatient hurry, hurry attitude created tension. A few playthings, at least in winter, would have helped the bleakness. A better relationship between the parents would have made the greatest difference and improved the parent-child relationship. If Dad had been told about this, I'm sure he'd have considered it unnecessary.

COYOTES

The Raleigh man's buggy reminds me of coyotes. The only other person with a strange buggy was a straggly man who hunted coyotes in the late fall when the animals' heavy new winter coats were at their best. This buggy wasn't so handsomely kept. It was no more than a large homemade wooden box on wheels with a door on the back. No paint.

I don't remember hearing or seeing coyotes in summer. Probably there were plenty of gophers and wildfowl to keep them happy in warm weather. But when it turned cold on dark clear nights, we heard them howl very close to the farm buildings. They ran in packs this time of year and hearing them howl brought to mind the tall tales of hungry timber wolves who were said to be much more dangerous. No one had ever been attacked by coyotes, but the grown-ups believed it was possible if they were hungry enough. Hearing them howl nearby naturally had us thinking they were very hungry!

In cold snowy winter, it gave us a shivery feeling to be wakened in the dark by their yipping and eerie, long drawn-out howlings. On moonlit nights we could see their silhouettes on the hill behind the barn. On occasion, our dog Purp would point his nose in the air and join in.

The government paid a bounty on them and their winter coats

sold for good money. That was why some stray men, usually the foot-loose variety, would take to stalking them and hunted them down for days at a time.

Once, when one of these men stopped in our yard to water his horses and ask if we'd seen any coyotes, we had a close look at his buggy. We'd taken for granted that the big box was for piling up skins, but, when he opened the door, out jumped several long, bony grey-hounds. These dogs hunted for and ran down the coyotes so the men could shoot them. Even though I didn't like coyotes, I always hoped after that they would get away.

Those dogs looked to me to be more of a menace than the wild coyotes!

IRENE AND I

Irene, lively and quick, was two sisters later in the family than I. She was the one most apt to be persuaded to come get the cows with me, if a promise of *something* was good enough. She got away with more than anyone else when she was young. Mabel, the sister between, was slow and careful and much more frightened of everything than I was. Irene seemed to have no fear whatsoever. After misbehavior, she more than once said to Dad, "Go ahead and lick me and get it over with." Somehow or other, she was never whipped as hard then, if at all. I remember she stamped her foot and told Dad she'd "never milk a cow," and she never did! It was as simple as that, for her.

There was a long skinny slough in the south pasture, running the whole length. It was the only one on our property to have water, at least in parts of it, during summer. Wherever it dried up, first came slimy mud then a crusty alkali whiteness that looked and tasted salty. Nothing at all grew in the alkali stretches, but the cows took a lick now and then. The perimeter of mud grew wider and wider around the sloughs, but the cows continued to brave the sticky stuff to reach the water's edge for a drink.

The water became smelly too, with floating islands of green algae which the frogs used as hiding places. They hid from the ducks who nested on the bank of the slough. This condition discouraged children from getting anywhere near the edges of the shallow water when summertime made wading feasible. We never waded; floundering in the mud was too unpleasant.

This slough was different; it had a variety of fascinations, and I was a little in awe of it. I recall being there once with Dad. He was mending his fence that ran right through it, and the fence was beside the highway that ran through it too. The slough continued on the other side of the highway into a neighbor's pasture. Under the road was a round corrugated iron culvert. That part of the slough was high and dry when Dad chose to repair his fence posts.

While he was working I climbed from the road down the short bank to look into the culvert, and decided to crawl through it. After getting partway I felt scared; the other end was still so far off and the sounds of Dad's hammering so "funny." I tried to back up and got stuck, probably from sheer fright. I screamed. At last Dad came to the rescue. He had to climb up over the road and to the other end to call orders in to me. Then he went back to the other end so he could grab my ankle to help me out. To this day I don't even want to look in tight places where men might have to work or repair something.

From springtime on we were always wanting to get into water. What child doesn't? One day Irene and I had the opportunity and inclination to try. We'd gone early to get the cows for milking. They were right by the slough. Along its edge there was a bit of bank in one spot. We stood awhile by a marshy place just to look. The grass was sharp-edged on our bare feet but maybe a bullfrog could be found. Water bugs were fun to chase. A duck might scurry into the water from nearby, out of reach, with young ones following. Purp gave them a good barking. The water was very green-looking with spots of soft fuzz floating on the top. It had the characteristic slough smell. Here and there were very small weedy-looking plants. When stepped on they gave off a sharp strong fragrance, better than wild peppermint. Years later and far away, a friend handed me a little plant of this. With one whiff, I was transported. Smells bring back such vivid recollections. I've often thought, and felt then, how few things there were for us to see and do. As a result of the lack, a most keen interest was taken in the smallest details and happenings.

As Irene and I looked at the water, we wondered if it was *very* deep out there. Mom had said, "Never go near the sloughs." By this time we were on the very edge and pretty soon one foot went in. While talking and laughing, in went the other. "Let's just wade around a bit by the edges." Underneath was very uneven ground due to the cows drinking and milling about. It was full of mudholes. One slip and we were soaking wet. Oh dear. Now we felt free to enjoy it and had a gay time bobbing up and down. "Didn't it feel good?" we asked each other. We'd never been for a swim before, nor did we know how.

After staying only a short while, or so it seemed, we began thinking of ways and means of getting back into the house and upstairs without Mom seeing us all wet. "Maybe we'll dry out on the way if we walk real slow," or we'd tell her, "We fell in getting the cows." It was the first time we'd ever been so bold. I had a terrible time over such things, being so conscience-ridden when disobedient. Irene never seemed to share those feelings.

We'd no sooner made it successfully into the house and up the stairs when an awful itching began! We looked at ourselves and saw red spots. Soon there were big red splotches all over us. There was nothing to do but call Mom.

She carried on for a bit and then called the doctor. "Into a tub," he ordered, "along with a box of baking soda." By the time a decent amount of water was carried in for the tub, and Mom had sloshed us around in it, we felt better. That put a damper on doing anything "we shouldn't ought to" for a while. Besides it was enough excitement to do us a week, at least.

THE SEASONS

Spring

Instead of gray, the sky is so blue. One day there comes the slightest feel of spring. The air is different. There are smells again. It might disappear but not for long. When our weather decided to do something, it did it! Rain, shine, blow or snow and it was over, not like the uncertain East. Dad's first talk of spring was about the Chinook winds that had come. They seemed to melt the snow with a warm blowing.

It lost all powdery whiteness and sunk down into bumpy unevenness coated with ice that glistened in the sun. Sunrise reflected rosy hues turning to many prismed colors as the sun climbed higher.

Bare spots showed in the fields and on the hillsides. When an ear was put to the ground the sound of running water could be heard under the deep snow in the ravine. This ravine divided the east pasture in two and had to be crossed to get to school. We watched it carefully. It made walking home something to worry about. Could we make it safely across or would Dad be there to meet us if we couldn't? It was in sight of home.

When it was grassy, it looked safe, but when the snow began melting off the hillsides and the runoffs met under the ravine, water ran fast beneath. We could count on crossing safely in the early morning because the nights were still so frosty cold that much ice would form and the snow would be crusty firm too. As in all other springs the inevitably dangerous day would come after a thaw or two. That day, on the way home from school, the snow was no longer crisp but soft and squishy – at least the top layer was. We'd reach the ravine and wonder what the water had done underneath the snow. Hesitating, we'd wonder if it was still firm enough to quickly run across. After a step or two, and feeling the top was giving way too much, we'd be scared and run back.

Some years we'd arrive to find puddles of water showing. When we couldn't be sure what lay beneath, we'd stand and wait for Dad. If he'd bothered to think about it or happened to know the water was actually running, we'd be met. But we couldn't count on him to be aware of our needs. Whenever he took time to help us out, we were most grateful. He was a very busy person doing more important things, we felt. This certainly helped us to learn to be independent.

If we got to the ravine and found open water that looked fierce and deep, we shouted, jumped up and down, waited, hoping Mom would see us and send Dad to the rescue. He would be at home because no farm work could be done yet. Dad would hitch a team of horses to the stoneboat, which looked like a crude sort of sled. Then we would watch him zigzagging towards us. He tried to hit as many patches of snow as possible to make it easier on the horses. Then we anxiously watched him choose the best spot to cross over the stream. The horses might even have a bad time. When he got safely across we were so glad! Then we'd jump on and huddle next to him, hanging onto a pant leg with one free arm and holding books and the lunch pail with the other. If it was safe, we'd sit down. The stoneboat was very small and Dad always stood in the middle, trying to keep his balance. If water was rushing beneath the holes of the horses' hooves it was more frightening than open water. With open water we just floated across like a raft.

If the horses only left holes in the snow, with water beneath, Dad would be sore (to use his own term) because he'd wasted time when we could have crossed ourselves. It was hard to judge sometimes. Being the oldest, I had to make the decision and was as bothered about Dad's reaction as I was about the safety of the stream. Then there were the occasions when Mom didn't see us or Dad didn't come because he was sure it was safe enough. After waiting what seemed an endless time and with much debating, we'd take a chance. Getting wet feet could be accepted as it wasn't far from home. But to get halfway across and suddenly be plunged into icy water up to the middle, and have to go on, was a panicky experience with thoughts of, "What if...?" A young sister might have hung back crying, too afraid to follow. There was nothing to do but go back and carry her piggyback.

We all survived to tell tales of our scares without even a case of pneumonia, though Mom did plenty of worrying about us at the time. It was good to have that part of spring over with.

Next there were earthy smells with small unclean bits of snow, the only sign left of winter. Everything looked wet and mud was everywhere. Roads were impassable; wagons could sink to their hubs in the low places and some sloughs rose over the roads. Horses were whipped more than usual by people trying to get them to go somewhere.

The birds had a new song and every slough was brimming full of water. Many newly arrived ducks swam happily there. The water was a most beautiful blue and was rippled by the constant wind. Now there were black fields of summer fallow, soaking wet and soft. The short brown grasses were flattened in the pastures. Old stubble fields were a washed out pale gold. Strawstacks had turned darker and flattened out. Where cows and horses had nibbled away at the edges, many stacks were left looking like mushrooms. If eaten in too far, they became a hazard to the animals. The heavy dome above could collapse and smother them.

The first bit of greenness showed up around the edges of the slough. An occasional peep could be heard from a frog and we were out to hunt him up. The wind became warmer and didn't blow so hard. The horses had all come back home from their winter foraging.

The sunshine was warmer, and before long the hillsides were covered with crocuses. On first appearing, the tiny buds were so heavily furred they seemed still to be wearing a winter coat to keep warm through the chilly nights. As they swelled, a bit of lavender showed between the fingers of fur. Very short-stemmed, out of the way of the wind, they opened into startling white beauties with pointed petals.

Summer

The days, which were very short in winter in this Northern place, became longer. Pastures turned green and it was summer. Horses stood, two at a time, nudging each other's shoulders to help rid themselves of the last bit of their heavy winters coats. The short new fur glistened in the sun. Perhaps they took a romp around, kicking up their heels while still able to enjoy a bit of freedom. Tails swished while they were lazily cropping grass, keeping the swarms of horse flies at bay. Now the cows lived outside completely. Even they ran about for a bit, especially when a thunderstorm was brewing. The ground dried out; seeding time was past.

Mirages danced on the horizon. At these special times, tall grain elevators of the unseen town of Oyen seemed to be dancing in the sky. Big and little whirlwinds of dust suddenly showed up as funnels on the clean summer-fallowed fields.

One summer, Dad planted a row of sunflowers behind the house that grew taller than we could reach. We loved sitting under them. The birds did too. They spent a long time chirping and chattering as they settled to roost during twilight. By sitting quiet and still under the lowest big leaves, we could reach up quickly and grab a sparrow. He was held and petted a bit before we opened a hand to let him fly away.

A summertime chore each day was to hunt up the cows for milking. Many times we were sent to drive home the horses too. Dad had a great many horses, perhaps as many as twenty at one time. He kept extras to rotate when others became tired and sore from too much work. We were half afraid of the horses, or afraid of half the horses, I don't know which. It depended on the situation! They were such big, heavy creatures. Rarely did any of them want to come home when we went to get them.

Our constant companion was that small black and brown collie sort of dog, Purp. He grew up with us. When I visited after four years of high school, he was still very much alive, though blind and sorry looking. Purp, who never went near the cows because Dad had whipped him for it, was delighted to help chase the horses. He was good for barking and starting them up but we'd keep a close watch, often having to hang onto him when the horses got mean. Several times he came too close to those flying hooves and nearly ended his life. He'd gone sailing into the air after being kicked, and suffered broken legs and ribs. Once it had been a badly battered head and he was sick a long while with an open wound. Experience taught him to be wary and quick.

In desperation, when a horse stayed busy eating grass or only raised its head and stubbornly stood its ground, we'd let Purp have a try. When he saw us yelling and waving our arms at a horse, he'd zero in. Barking all the while, he'd first run way off to the side, turn around and race back past their hind legs. As he went by, he took a quick nip slightly above the hoof, a very tender part. If nothing happened, except the inevitable kick, the same procedure went on past the horse's nose. This was sure to get a reaction. Having already had the harassment of being bitten on the ankles, most horses would give up and start for home. Stubborn ones went back to eating. Purp would be back again, more daring than ever, and after a second or third bite on the nose the horse angrily chased after him. This was the moment we'd rush up to keep them moving towards home.

There were no horses we could ride, although this would have been a pleasure in summer. Dad stated, "Horses like that cost money to feed and are no good for work." Among all the dark ones there was a big, gentle, white horse, with gray shadings, known as Tom (we had a Dick and a Harry, too!). He was the despair of us all but the favorite. He'd allow us to climb on his back, but he wouldn't go anywhere. If his sides were kicked long enough and slapped hard enough, he might walk a few feet and stop again. More likely he'd turn his head around and bite our bare legs if they weren't tucked up out of reach.

Stretched flat on our stomachs along his back, we'd try again. This was a joint effort of more than one of us. If he chose to take a short walk, a hand was reached out to cover this eye or that one, to set him in the direction desired. When the right eye was covered, he'd go left and vice versa. It wouldn't last long. He'd walk into the barn or up to the nearest fence, but this gave us minutes of amusement.

The surprising thing was that Dad kept him when he was so lazy. He was the horse who could be counted on to hold back and never pull his share of the load. The whip was used on his back more than on any other horse we ever owned. I believe Dad liked him too, because he was so smart.

He got into more trouble for investigating the next pasture, the buildings or the oat bin, and took checking up on constantly when at home.

As the wheat ripened and the grass dried up, Tom looked around for more tasty fare. He was the one horse who managed to get over the barbed wire fence, paying little heed to cuts and bruises, and he kept an eye out for an open gate. He'd even get into the field of mouthwatering green oats planted especially for the cows (to replace the lack of green grass). He even committed the worst sin, raiding the wheat field. A horse can die from eating too much ripe wheat. If they get into the wheat, be it field or granary, they are in trouble! Besides, trampled wheat cannot be harvested. I remember at least one close call for Tom. He'd left a trail of havoc and must have been in the field some time before being discovered. His belly puffed up dangerously. He lay down and was so sick he came close to having to be punctured. This is a dangerous procedure, but the only chance a swollen animal has to survive. Tom was lucky. He managed to pull through, and lived to get into more mischief.

The farm had several Rube Goldberg set ups. One was a gate that separated the house area from the pump yard. This crude, homemade wooden gate was set in the barbed wire fence. On the center back of the gate was fastened an old logging chain, the other end of which was wrapped around another post standing alone just inside the fence.

Hung in the middle of the chain was an old wagon wheel axle. When the gate was pushed open, this pulled it shut again. Dad made it so's he could carry two big buckets of water from the well, kick it open and not have to stop to close it. Being quick, he could get through before it swung shut again. We kids had to put all our weight against it to squeeze through.

Tom quickly learned to push against it the same way we did and get through to crop the green grass around the house. He was also interested in the open wheat field that lay directly behind the house.

On one side of the barnyard was a chophouse that posed another problem for him when in quest of munchables. The door was held closed by a wooden peg screwed to the door jamb by a single screw so's it could be turned to open the door. A leather strap was nailed, top and bottom, on the door, to pull it open. Tom learned to turn the button with his teeth and to pull the strap to open the door.

He stepped through the open door freely, helping himself to the fresh ground wheat done for breakfast porridge, or the pile of ground weed seeds and shriveled wheat which was chop for the pigs. This chop mixed with milk grew delicious pork.

wooden button screwed to wall used to keep door closed

Door

leather strap nailed top & bottom - for a door handle.

When working in summer, the horses had to be watered morning, noon and at suppertime. Dad pumped the water from the well while we watched. As each horse was unhitched from the implement being used, their reins were flipped over their backs. Free, they headed straight for the watering trough, covered with dust and soaked with sweat. Just as soon as they were finished, we were there to drive them into the barn. If there were too many to drink at the same time, we were just as busy driving them back from the trough to wait. Otherwise they'd be down rolling in the soft dust of the pump yard, breaking their harness to pieces.

Every horse knew his own stable in the barn and there were two in each. In front of them was a manger kept full of straw from a hole above in the hay mow. While playing in this loft, we had to be careful not to slip down these holes.

In the front corner of the manger was an oat box. This was the horses' big interest after work, a treat they enjoyed exceedingly. I wonder why Dad didn't fill this box ahead of time? It was quite a chore with so many horses, and they were so impatient and nasty. I guess he did not realize that a little organization would have saved him a lot of trouble. He was a hard worker who never failed on the big jobs, but detested details of any sort.

Speaking of horses, my mother never knew when he would show up for meals. He went "by the sun," but there were times when he wished to finish the last bit of a field before quittin' time. Mom tried to keep a look out to see if he was headed home from the fields. If she was busy with something, her first inkling he was coming might be the sounds from the barnyard. When Dad got in, he didn't like waiting; he was hungry.

When Dad got home after quitting time at night, he usually called for a helping hand. If we were in the house, Mom shooed us out there. The horses needed to be watered, the oat box needed to be filled, and Dad needed help unharnessing the horses. Horses get as cross and as impatient as people when they are tired. We knew it was dangerous to take a measure of oats up to the two horses. Dad said, "Always go up between them," but that didn't work. They'd put their ears back, stomp their feet, bite and bump each other. And they towered above us. As quickly as possible, Dad tied each to the stall with a short rope to avoid a free-for-all. They even tried to kick each other in that small space. This was due to one having to be fed first while the other waited. All the rest would be whinnying and kicking up a fuss while waiting for their feed.

While Dad carried the oats up between them, he called their names steadily, gave one a push and said, "Over there," and kept them calmer. I couldn't do it! I was so afraid I could only squeak and they paid no attention. Scared of being stepped on, bitten or squashed after getting past those dangerous hind legs, I tried devious ways of getting around the problem!

Dad would loudly holler, "Go right ahead and don't hesitate," but it didn't seem quite that simple. If the timing was right, when Dad was feeding in one stall, the horses in the next one might momentarily perk up their heads to listen and I'd dash in to dump the oats. But getting back out? Even when eating they were wary. Perhaps I'd climb the partition and crawl along the top of it to safety.

This was tried in reverse with a pan full of oats. Stalls get taller at the front end and shimmying along the top was slow going, using only one hand. Besides, pouring the oats way down into the small box becomes a long chance. When he saw this procedure, Dad would be disgusted: "Oh go do something you *can* do and be useful." Certainly I felt less than adequate when I knew he needed help so much. He looked as dusty, damp and tired as the horses.

After feeding time, all the horses had to be unharnessed and turned out to pasture before Dad's day was done. Later, watching those horses lazily cropping grass and looking so peaceful, it was hard to remember they were the same creatures who were so nasty an hour or two before.

Once somehow we got a package of glossy-orange California poppy seeds. Dad had plowed a narrow strip in the front yard along the fence, hoping to grow a vegetable garden. The family, meaning Mom and the kids, would take care of it. We happily planted the row of poppy seeds but that was all. He'd left the soil quite lumpy. The poppies came up and were pretty all summer, though we were disappointed they didn't survive when we picked them. When the seedpods ripened we collected them and shook out the seeds and saved them. The next year, without touching the ground, we sprinkled them over the same patch and again it became a vivid bed of color. They were a delight! They cross-pollinated and grew in many sizes and colors. Each new flower was a surprise. After the third year we had a shoe box almost full of seeds, and many had re-seeded themselves. We'd done precious little weeding, so by this time the bed needed to be plowed again. At about this time the novelty wore off, we lost interest and the weeds took over.

Dad often mentioned pansies as his favorite flower, but we'd never seen any grown. No one liked gardening, due no doubt to the big potato patch that took enough gardening time. But each spring when the pansies bloom, I'm reminded of Dad. Mom's favorite flower was the rose and she claimed she was named after them – Rose. She was most pleased when we wrestled a few from the bushes of the wild pink ones as a surprise for her. The stems were thin and wiry, almost red in color, with thorns so close no finger could get between them. The bushes grew short and tangled in the pastures. While getting the cows we collected a few and in the fall enjoyed eating the bright-orange fruit around the seeds.

Roses are my favorite too.

Fall

Harvest time comes, then fall is over. The seas of rippling wheat, once green, are now ripe and brown. There is no green left anywhere.

The grass had long since turned brown and dead. Most sloughs had been dry all summer. The few left were no longer clear and blue. Our one was an opaque tan with greenish tinges, dirty and old looking with pockmarked holes by the water's edge, left by the cows.

The first load of wheat was taken to Benton to sell for long-awaited necessities. There we could peek into the monstrous, tall grain elevator. Even now I would like to see the inside of one! We never did. Dad made us jump down off the wagon before he drove in and we ran to the wide-open doorway to watch.

Just inside the doorway was a big jiggly platform that made the horses nervous. They walked across it to the solid plank flooring, leaving the wagon on the platform. First it was weighed and then emptied. Off to the side were heavy beams and dark endless-looking spaces. After the elevator man weighed the wheat and marked it down, he set noisy gears in motion. One end of the platform went down and the back of the wagon tipped. Wheat poured over the top, disappearing into a dark cavern below. Dad, still on the load at the front of the wagon, shoveled out more at the same time. This all looked very dangerous with the wagon tipped so far, and the wheat slipping and sliding away so fast. When about half the wheat had gone, the tail boards were taken down so the last bit of grain could run out. Then the platform was leveled and Dad collected his receipt. We stepped around inside the corner.

Looking straight up the building, no wheat could be seen. The middle of the building was hollow clear up to the roof. A few sparrows twittered there by the tiny windows. Perhaps the grain was stored in its fat sides!

This time of year, before snow fly, Mom took time to consider the beds. Mattresses were made of striped ticking and stuffed with straw.

Some might need to be redone. If the ticking needed new patches, an order was sent to Eaton's. Once Mom actually made a new mattress with Dad's encouragement and much of his hand sewing. When they finished sewing, he took it out to the strawstack and filled it with the fresh, fragrant straw. He came back looking like Santa with a large pack on his back!

Now came a time we loved; the parents were not quite so enthusiastic. The bed frame was a flat wire affair with a few poor excuses for springs on the ends. It was more like a hammock than a set of springs. Dad dumped the filled mattress on this and we gleefully jumped on it. Tramping it down was allowed, and then we were called off. Standing around, we offered suggestions as to where it looked bumpy and what corner needed some more straw pushed into it. We lay down on it a time or two and tried to wiggle a place to make it comfortable. After it once set with covers on, this couldn't be done so easily. After Dad let us work it down and try it out, we were chased out of the way so the opening could be sewed up and the bed made with flannelette sheets.

Collapsing into the first night's softness there were still squirmings to make it just right, sometimes complaining. If humps and bumps settled in the wrong places and couldn't be remedied by pushing and pinching, the ticking had to be reopened to level it out. More straw for Mom to sweep up afterward! After a time it was smooth and flat with no give at all. Worst of all was having it turn out to be too thin on a sagging bed. With two sleeping in every bed, this spelled trouble.

In the late fall most of the horses were turned out to forage for themselves. They disappeared until spring. Poor things! It was very quiet in the barn. The floor had a deep, fresh layer of straw. Only two horses remained. They were needed for driving to town for coal and other essentials.

The cows moved inside and lived almost entirely there, until warmer weather. They were quiet. Though never tied up, they claimed a stall of their own where they spent much time down on the straw, with feet tucked under them, chewing their cuds. They disliked going outside for a drink of water. When the ice had to be broken on the trough, they didn't like that cold water. Dad tried to make them drink more so they would give more milk.

Gone were the endless summer twilights. Shadows became very long as the sun moved south. I didn't like this. It was depressing; I felt lonely. I don't know why.

Winter

Cold.
Snow.
People and every creature spouting steam.
Blizzards raging in the night.
Clear, still, beautiful nights.
Coyotes howling.
Winds whistling and shrieking around the corners. Heads down and shoulders braced to face it. It is surprising how much noise the wind makes. The poor, small house creaking and cracking. How glad we were to be snug in bed!
Animals with their backs to a storm.
Snow piled up on them. Mom hopeful the horses had found somewhere to shelter. Dad putting coal on the fire in the middle of the night. Would any animals be dead?
Waking in the morning to utter quiet.
Finding everything downstairs in the kitchen frozen.
Back to bed, until the house got a bit warmer. The windows most beautiful, thick with velvety frost from top to bottom. Jungle pictures. Studying them awhile, before huffing and puffing to blow a round circle and see what had happened outside. Snow gently drifting, or bright sunshine peeping over the edge of the pasture.
Such stark white snow, powder fine, drifting like sand dunes on the level places. Tall snowbanks around the buildings with bare places between. Outside to hear the snow squeak as we walked or to build an igloo of snow blocks, more likely a house with partitions, or to tunnel into a snowbank, taking no time to wonder where our feet had gone. They were numb.
Inside, chilblains. "Why did I go outside?" Sitting Buddha fashion on the floor while holding a foot, rocking back and forth saying, "Oh Mom, can't you do something?" Dad shoveling a first path to

the "little house," with room so we could open the door. Such short days and long nights. A big issue: who would go with you after dark to this same little house?

The heavy wagon box was mounted on sleigh runners for Dad's odd trips to Benton for mail and so on. After a long time, watching and waiting, he would come home again.

The first little Atwater Kent radio came one winter, looking like a church window. We listened through the static to country music and cowboy songs. Once we heard Texas! In summer, the static was worse, but we didn't listen much then as there were other things to do.

Around the time when Mom had her fifth baby she felt poorly and the doctor said she was to have help for a week. We watched Dad leave for Benton to find someone. Home he came with a black-haired girl called Anna Hannavitch. She understood very little English and we were sure she was Russian - even Mom thought so. We never did find out where she came from. In the back of the wagon Dad brought her trunk.

Of our three bedrooms, she was to have the one upstairs around the corner, newly portioned off from another. Dad had nailed beaverboard over most of the bare 2x4s, but there was no "water paint" on the wall yet. The woodwork around the one window stuck out several inches from the wall. Either the window casing was too wide or the walls were too thin!

Anna was quiet. She gave us the feeling she very much disliked children. While getting supper she wielded a butcher knife and looked like she intended to skin us alive if we got too near. After work she disappeared into her room. We were most curious as to what she had in the trunk and what she did up there.

One time, when she was busy downstairs, I sneaked into her room. On the bed lay a *True Confessions* magazine. That looked interesting, and I'd heard it contained wicked stories, so I was afraid to touch it. Beside the trunk was a Pandora's box to be explored quickly now that an opportunity had come. It sat under the window. After carefully opening the lid, so no squeak could be heard, I saw a tray several inches deep, full of things. What caught my eye first was a narrow white rectangular box. On the top was an oval picture of a beautiful lady, only her head and shoulders. When I lifted the lid, the smell was utterly delicious. Little chocolate candies nestled in crinkly dark-brown papers. After several smells, I put them back.

There, in one corner, was a bright-red, soft-looking flower. I saw nothing else! Lifting it out, my thoughts raced on: what did one do with a lovely silk rose? It was very pretty to look at anyway. I wanted it badly but knew I shouldn't be in her things. After a moment's thought on the subject, I decided to hide the flower. If she didn't remember she'd left it in the trunk when she left us it would automatically become mine!

There were no dressers or other places to hide things in our rooms. We wore almost everything we owned, at any one time. In the end I shut the trunk, stood on it, and reached the top of the window to hide the flower behind the ledge of the window frame that stuck out from the wall. Anna came along and passed me before I got downstairs again but did not catch me in her room.

Then I became bothered.

Those first minutes afterward were bad, but, as time went on, my feelings got worse. Time dragged. I remembered some of the dire things Dad had said about people doing wrong. A time or two I almost rushed upstairs to put the flower back. I didn't, because then she'd know who did it.

After a bit, Anna came rushing down out of her room talking loudly, with the word "stole" clearly discernible. Mom looked blank and couldn't figure what was the matter so asked no questions. I knew some way had to be found of putting that flower back where it belonged, without getting caught.

By this time, I'd convinced myself it had only been borrowed so's I could have another look and feel before putting it back. That helped, some. Everyone sat down to supper without my having that chance. Anna kept a cold eye on everyone through that awkward meal. I was so hot and cold and feeling pink and purple, she surely couldn't help but see who was the culprit!

Finally, everyone got up from the table. As she and Mom were busy stacking the dishes, I hurried upstairs in the dark, climbed up on the trunk, grabbed the thing, then quickly down to lift the lid and throw it in.

No one ever said another word about it. I felt most lucky and would never, never steal again.

Sketch from Reta's Art Notes book, made in eighth grade

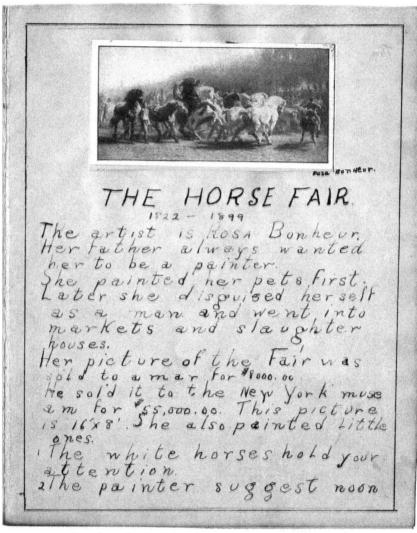

THE HORSE FAIR.

1822 – 1899

The artist is Rosa Bonheur.
Her father always wanted
her to be a painter.
She painted her pets first.
Later she disguised herself
as a man and went into
markets and slaughter
houses.
Her picture of the Fair was
sold to a man for $8000.00.
He sold it to the New York muse
um for $55,000.00. This picture
is 16'x8'. She also painted little
ones.
1 The white horses hold your
attention.
2 The painter suggest noon

Page from Reta's Art Notes book, made in eighth grade

Photographs from Reta's childhood

Reta Evens at nine months

William Arthur and Rose Pearce Evens

Mabel and Reta Evens

Mabel (left) and Reta (right) Evens wearing bows, with siblings

Margaret, Irene, Leslie, Bill, Ted and Reta Evens

Reta Evens in front of barn with dog named Purp and siblings upstairs

Purp with Mabel and Reta Evens

Wavy Plains float in the 1927 Canada Day parade

Wavy Plains school children in the 1927 Canada Day parade

Mabel, Irene and Reta Evens in costume for Canada Day 1927

William Evens in his field

Reta Evens at age 14

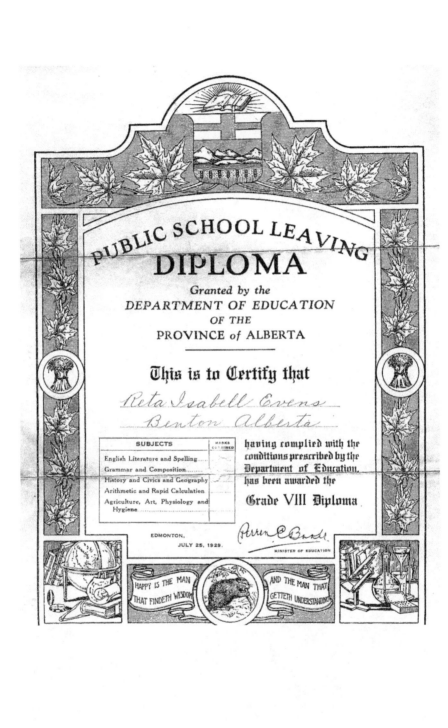

PUBLIC SCHOOL LEAVING
DIPLOMA

Granted by the

DEPARTMENT OF EDUCATION

OF THE

PROVINCE of ALBERTA

This is to Certify that

Reta Isabell Evens

Benton Alberta

SUBJECTS	MARKS OBTAINED
English Literature and Spelling	
Grammar and Composition	
History and Civics and Geography	
Arithmetic and Rapid Calculation	
Agriculture, Art, Physiology and Hygiene	

having complied with the conditions prescribed by the Department of Education, has been awarded the

Grade VIII Diploma

EDMONTON,

JULY 25, 1929.

Perren C Barde

MINISTER OF EDUCATION

HAPPY IS THE MAN THAT FINDETH WISDOM

AND THE MAN THAT GETTETH UNDERSTANDING

 **Chapter 4**

THE MIDDLE YEARS

Now we'd come to the middle years at home and for me at elementary school. We knew the families we went to school with, all the way down to the youngest. Most had stopped having children, excepting us. None of them was proud of a large family.

At school, there was plenty of opportunity to know what subjects were to be covered in the class ahead to finish our learning. We heard the others everyday as we did our own studies. They held no charm. It was routine, and time to be gotten through.

Busy times were spring and fall, and there was always too much work left undone if we stopped to think about it. One glimpsed what the parents were faced with, and growing up didn't seem like something to look forward to.

The stove was stoked up on Saturday night. All doors in the kitchen were closed to warm up the room for baths. We helped. Buckets of hot water simmered on the back of the stove. The big round tin tub was dragged in from the shed and set on the kitchen floor, close to the fire, to warm up. That tub was not as much fun anymore for us bigger ones. Our knees had to be doubled way up in order to sit in it all at once.

Baths started with the youngest and we dried them as they came out. The last couple of kids might beg for a change of turns, which I always allowed. No one wanted to bother drying the last one's back.

By that time everyone was anxious to be away, romping around. Baths went on for hours.

Mom would be hot and flushed from scrubbing, pouring rinse water over hair and supervising. Dad had to be around to haul out the dirty water once in a while. Such a blast of cold air came in as he went out the kitchen door! Baths started out leisurely but we became quite impatient toward the end to finish up. Dad had already begun his romping to help stir up the blood so's we'd go to bed all warmed up and tired out. Mom wasn't too pleased to have us overexcited at bedtime because as often as not it meant a few lickings before we were through.

On such a night, after we got upstairs, Dad might put his long black fur coat over his back and, on all fours, crawl up the stairs to play Bear, growling as he came. It was kind of frightening at first and everyone scuttled under the nearest cover. The only light to be seen came up the stairway from the kitchen. Many times he just appeared and we'd be scared and leery of the monster. But we knew it was Dad all the time, and soon we'd be out and after him to take us for a ride on his back. We shrieked when he dumped us. Truthfully, the game was more like Bucking Bronco than Bears!

Settling down after this took some time. Mom would come up the stairs to call a halt. First she would ask him to settle us down. Then she'd give up.

'Twas the best night of the week for going to bed. Clean sleepers fit snug and soft. After crawling under covers it felt warm and sleepy even though the bedrooms were frigid.

Dad at one time decided we needed a bigger tub, so acquired, I don't know from where, a long tin one painted white inside. It stood on four short legs and was put at the end of that used but still unfinished bedroom. It was tried a few times, mostly in summer as it turned out. Not only was it a chore to haul water all the way upstairs but also it was too cold up there. Emptying the thing was a panic and had to be done with teamwork. Only a small wash basin would fit under the drain. Some one of us lay flat on her stomach to watch this, while another stood above to pull the plug. When the one underneath hollered "the basin is full," the other had to quickly put the plug back in again. The water was dumped in a pail, carried downstairs and emptied outside.

We weren't very adept at filling that basin. Errors occurred in landing the plug squarely in the hole. Added to this was the problem of pouring the wide basin neatly into the narrower bucket. Lots of water was spilled on the floor. Some kids went to bed with wet-footed sleepers.

This new-fangled thing exasperated Mom, so we gave it up and went back to the old round washtub on the kitchen floor.

I'd never given up the desire to ride a horse. Now I was pretty big and sure that, if I were given the chance, I could ride. One morning the big boy with the stiff arm came by on his horse. He was, and still is, my picture of a cowboy. He'd finished with school and was working on his father's farm. This early morning he was out on a round to sell vegetable and flower seeds for extra money. Mom purchased nothing, but she asked him if he'd mind taking me to school on his way home. The idea of riding with company didn't appeal much to him; however, he boosted me up, jumped on in front and off we went.

What a wild ride.

At first I grabbed him around the middle and hung on for dear life. Luckily I had a good grip, as the hold became more and more precarious. I managed to maintain some sort of grasp on him. Once it was only his collar.

His horse streaked across the pasture. One minute I'd come down with a thump on his haunches. Next time it might be halfway down his other side. Between times, I was out in space. Tom seemed oblivious to my predicament, yet he must have felt pulled half to pieces. He was lucky to still have a shirt at the end of the ride. Perhaps he was annoyed he'd wasted his time or perhaps he was going to teach a girl she wasn't going to ride with *him*.

When I caught a passing glimpse of the ground it was a blur. The school seemed a hundred miles away, and he never uttered a word. I was dizzy and shaken when we got there, but glad to be able to walk safely into school. That was the end of that fond hope.

For a long while, I was most uninterested in horseback riding!

CHRISTMAS

Sometimes, as a Christmas treat, Dad wrote away for Japanese oranges. They came in small, almost white, wooden crates, neatly made, unlike the rough apple boxes. Black Japanese lettering marked the top. Carefully wrapped in white paper were a couple of dozen very tiny Mandarin oranges. On that happy morning we got ribbon candy, nuts, and one of these oranges in the toe of a stocking. These were gifts from Santa, in whom we firmly believed!

Once Mom said, "This year you each can pick out something from Eaton's catalog for $1.00." We searched and chose, over and over again. I loved dolls and wanted one more than anything. I had no qualms about wanting a doll, even though I was older than the rest. Girls played with them until a much older age then than they do now. A full-page illustration showed one with "composition head, painted hair and eyes," and it looked nice and big, about 15 inches tall. On the opposite page was another, a beautiful one with "china head, real hair and eyes that slept." I wanted the second one! They were both $1.50. That was too much money but I wanted nothing else.

When the order arrived safely before Christmas, the packages were tucked away on the shelves above the cellar stairs. These shelves were made on the undersides of the steps going up to the bedrooms. The parents considered this place safe from little peekers. The cellar door was just around the corner from the kitchen stove where Mom usually worked. Also, the cellar door latch was noisy.

Every time we went down cellar we gazed longingly at these packages. I came to the conclusion that one oblong box with a lid on it must be the doll. The shelves were treacherously hard to reach and a slip meant falling down the cellar steps. Overcome by curiosity, and feeling very sneaky, I maneuvered the box into position for a peek! All my dreams were dashed! It wasn't beautiful, it didn't have any hair – it was the composition doll! I couldn't hold back the tears. Mom had sent me to get something in the cellar and noticed later how unhappy I was. When she came near I cried harder than ever and she was most solicitous: "Whatever is the matter?" And I couldn't tell her!

Christmas morning, when Mom expected squeals of delight, she was instead faced with glumness. I didn't want that old doll. It was such a disappointment, and what seemed awful to me was that the two dolls cost the same amount! I thought of how Mom was being practical again and, no doubt, the composition doll would last much longer! Mom must have been discouraged; I'm sure she tried to make it a very special Christmas! She'd looked forward with such pleasure to this happy occasion. Our parents never gave themselves Christmas presents.

I had little to do with that doll. I'd looked forward to sewing doll clothes but now wouldn't be bothered. Nor did I ever peek again. I could hear Dad say, "You got just what you deserved."

Something unexpected and wonderful happened one lean Christmas. Dad was going to the big town of Oyen (big only in comparison with the nearest town, Benton). He needed something at the hardware store and I went along. This store was filled with heavy big things such as large oil cans, barrels, plowshares, logging chains and harnesses. The whole place had a strange smell, perhaps due to stacked piles of binder twine balls and other things that had been treated with creosote. Dad usually went to town to buy a machinery part, but at this season of the year there were more interesting things to be seen. It was such fun to look at shiny new things. This time there were several pretty things for the home arranged on a table. They were conspicuous because they appeared so dainty among that heavy stuff.

Outstanding was a most beautiful, pale-yellow alabaster clock. Of course, I didn't know what it was made of, but it was translucent, as if the sun shone through it - a fairy's clock. I went to find Dad, who had disappeared somewhere into the back of the store. After a while he was persuaded to come see the clock, and I ventured, "Wouldn't that be nice to give Mom? It would look so pretty in the house." He'd never given her a Christmas present, but this seemed like a better approach than asking for it for myself. I did want it for her, but was also anxious to persuade him so we'd have that pretty thing at home. Dad said, "No," as expected, "It's an extravagant thing."

We kids were always quiet when in the stores, only whispering to each other, or to the parent if the subject were very important.

On this occasion the storekeeper apparently overheard my plea. Before we left, he came from behind the counter, picked up the clock and after turning it this way and that said to me, "Would you very much like to have it?" What an astounding question! I'd never in my whole life been offered even a candy bar! When I managed to squeak out, "I'd like to give it for a Christmas present," he rolled it up in brown paper and handed it to me. I carried it home to hide. Many times before the big day, I took it out and admired it. On Christmas Mom was all smiles; she too thought it was beautiful.

For a change the small shelf beside the kitchen stove was cleared of all clutter, so the clock could stand alone in all its splendor. There it stood for years, long after it stopped running. Even when the little pillars fell apart and it got tarnished on the edges, it was still kept on the shelf as a reminder of past glory.

I'd like to have seen that man again and told him how much his thoughtfulness meant, and what long-lasting pleasure that gift produced. For years it had made the corner of the kitchen beautiful!

THE ESKIMO SUIT

I was twelve when something came along that left me with mixed feelings.

After harvest Mom asked for money to get something for us, something decent and warm for outside play. It could be worn to school before Christmas and she hoped longer. The something turned out to be what we called our Eskimo suits. The outside looked like fine brown flannelette and the insides were lined with heavy mackinaw. They were double-breasted and had wonderful knitted cuffs on wrists and ankles, which kept out the snow. No one had seen anything like them; this was before the days of snowsuits or ski pants.

These suits didn't ordinarily come in a large enough size for me, so I was measured and a special order placed. When it came, I didn't want to wear it. It made me feel big and awkward. In those days girls and

women wore only coats and
skirts. But it was so toasty
and warm compared with
the old coat!

Snow drift

We had just discovered
a new sport! Attached to the
barn was a large chicken coop, with a one-way sloping roof. On the
ground was a big snowbank piled up with a pocket between, caused
by the wind when the snow drifted. After crawling to the peak of the
icy roof, we slid, lickety-split, down on knees or seat, on across the
canyon, if we were going fast enough, and landed at the bottom of
the snowbank.

We'd had much trouble with Mom about wearing out the knees
of stockings! After buttoning the top button under the collar, she
warned these new suits were to be taken care of: "Watch out for nails
while climbing in the hay loft," and so forth. Outside the door, we
said to ourselves, "These suits are just the thing for the chicken house
roof." Now with all that padding our knees wouldn't suffer from the
bumpity edges of the shingles. I was the oldest and I didn't like my
suit anyway, so I chose to disregard her orders. The others followed
my lead. It didn't take long for knees and seat to be worn thin. I'm
sure Mom didn't know about the snowsliding. I heard her say one
day she'd "never buy any more of those suits. The material must have
been poor."

DAD'S KNITTING MACHINE

Dad was never idle. He didn't help with most household chores. I
didn't see him wash a dish or even hold a baby. In winter he could
have. The one exception was hauling water, but even this was sometimes done by the women folk.

During the cold months his one routine was doing the animal
chores, night and morning. Kids had to help with these, largely as a
matter of principle. Our usual job was to climb up into the hayloft to
push straw down into the manger. He sprinkled some of this around
for bedding to keep the barn floor fresh and clean.

A pair of horses were kept in the barn, but the rest were turned loose to roam and forage for a livelihood as best they could. The two horses and the three cows had to be watered night and morning. The horses were used to pull the sleigh to town when groceries and coal were needed. If we owned a homemade children's sled, which wasn't always, we might hook it on behind the sleigh and see how far we'd get. Snow flew in our faces and the ride was fast and bumpy so it never lasted long. We'd be upset and Dad was in a hurry to be gone without watching out for us.

Cows were milked night and morning, the most tiresome job of all, but the most important. If it hadn't been for the cows, I'm sure we'd not have gone outside some bitter cold nights. Blizzards were fierce. They blew out the lantern and not a thing could be seen. It was possible to get lost between house and barn, if there was no fence to follow! The barn was so warm and filling a pail with foaming fresh milk was so rewarding!

The house always needed painting and sometimes a little got done. I decidedly got the feeling there were some things Dad just didn't like to do. He never said so, but painting was one of those things. Towards spring he hauled in the harness to go over it piece by piece, to oil it and mend it. He still had a lot of free time during the coldest part of the year, probably enough to have done the painting!

From somewhere, he ordered a knitting machine. It clamped on the table like a meat grinder and the handle worked the same way. Fastened to the clamp, on the upper side of the table, was a two-foot-tall wire, with a loop on the top. The bobbin sat under this and the wool fed through the loop. Each winter, fat black skeins of wool came in the mail. One of us stood impatiently holding a skein over our hands, for what seemed to us like hours and hours. Dad wound the wool on a tall wooden bobbin. It could be bought ready wound, but Dad saved the few cents this way.

Out of a box came dozens of tiny needles

to be fitted into slots on the round cylinder of the machine. A steel spring encircled it to hold the needles in place. For ribbing, which was the same effect as purling, a flat round disc was laid on top, also full of needles.

Stockings were always ribbed; they fit more snuggly. We each had a choice as to how the ribbing was to be done: knit one, rib one, or knit two, rib one, etc. Having different kinds of stockings helped in sorting out the wash. There wasn't a choice in width. Little kids just pulled them further up their legs for fit.

When the first very cold spell hit, Dad was inspired to begin his task. We'd be very happy over the prospect of nice warm stockings. By the time winter was over we hated the itchy things. They'd be tight from washings, sometimes matted, and full of darns.

Dad did the darning and it wasn't always smooth. I tried my hand at it to see if I could do better. The dyes in the wool were poor. Sometimes, by spring, we'd be afraid our feet would be permanently black!

When Dad was ready to begin his knitting, he threaded it all from a small spool of white thread to test the machine. After a few rows, the black wool was knotted on. A heavy ribbed cuff came first, then our choice of ribbing for a long stretch of leg. When he did the heel, foot and toe there was much fussing and changing of needles. He made short back and forth motions of the handle. Short needles were slipped out and wool slipped onto longer ones on the side cylinder. After he knitted a few inches, a weight was hooked on to stretch the sock down tight out of the way and allow a smoother job. If a run occurred from a faulty needle or bumpy yarn, another needle was pulled out to "crochet" it up where it belonged. When a stocking was completed, the white thread was used for a few rows before starting the next one. After several were done he cut them apart where the white thread was. To be thrifty, the thread could be saved with care, and rewound back on the spool to be used again. The stocking now had a slit across the top of the toes, to be sewed up with the big darning needle. While Dad worked on this, he taught us how to lace the sewing so there would be some give.

When stockings were mastered, he learned how to knit mittens and our toques (stocking caps). Our family could easily be spotted, since we all wore black hats, black mittens and black stockings! Mom wore them too, all but the toque. She didn't consider this dignified on a grown woman. It was a lot of work knitting for so many, and Dad would say very tedious, but he was proud of his accomplishments. I feel he was proud not so much because of what he'd done, but because the family had warm things to wear. I thought of Mom's repeatedly saying, "He *is* a good provider."

Those thick stockings with ugly shoes laced well above the ankles did not make a girl feel very feminine. They were practical. Dad had to be practical, even in his thinking. What else mattered anyway? Black didn't show the dirt, wool was warm, the thicker the better, and boots protected feet from all things. The average woman wore opaque lisle stockings of a brown color. The not-so-sheer silk was for very best, but who anywhere around could afford them?

I'm sure Dad would be happy today, if he bothered to think about it, that city women, after years and years of wearing sheer nylons (a waste of money to him), are now wearing sensible warm stockings, very much like those he knitted long ago on the farm.

THE ROD WEEDER

Rocks in the wheat fields were a major hazard. Rocks meant implement breakdowns and that held work up. When Dad rod weeded, each day was a gamble. Such an impossible piece of equipment with rocks! A rod weeder was a 2x2 inch square rod, 12 feet long. It was mounted on wheels so that it turned as it was towed. A lever lowered it, to turn round and round in the soft summer-fallowed field to kill the weeds. Dad kept his fields "as clean as a whistle," to quote him. Weeds took moisture and there was so little rain.

It took nine to twelve horses abreast to pull the rod weeder. If this machine ran into a submerged rock of any size the rod snapped in two. Work was stopped, and the horses were unharnessed. Taking the rod out was a mean chore and then it had to be hauled to Oyen to be welded. It always put Dad in a bad humor because it took too much time and money.

One day I went out to meet Dad coming down the side of a field near home. I jumped on behind, amid much dust and the noise of the many horses. It was scary getting up there, but a ride on anything was fun. Dad sat on a small high seat and I hung on behind, like two kids riding a tricycle. In a minute he spied a rather big but movable rock, way off to one side. As he jumped off, he handed me the horses' reins and said, "Just drive to the end of the field and stop." Boy, what a responsibility! Dad had apparently decided to move the stone to the side of the field that was already cultivated, but he didn't take the time to say. With the horses abreast, they spread way out to either side. When I first climbed onto the seat, the idea of driving so many horses seemed exciting. The thought soon turned to panic!

We came to the end of the field with a barbed wire fence across it. I pulled back as hard as I could on the reins and yelled, "Whoa," as loud as possible. Nothing happened. Those creatures kept right on going! Dad seemed to be miles away and, after yelling for him with no results, I got a bright idea at the last minute. Pulling desperately with both hands on one rein the horses turned, just in time, with the last two crowding close to the fence and looking skittish. When Dad arrived we had turned in several circles!

Whew! What a scare! To think of what could have happened! The picture of the frightened horses, the fence and the rod weeder, was too awful to contemplate! Never again did I want to do a job like that for Dad. He expected too much sense in young people. I suppose it taught us to be resourceful and we did survive. Mom argued often on such matters, to no avail. I heard Dad once say that the way to teach a child to swim was to throw him out into the water. Shivers! I was glad we had no ponds nearby. I heartily disagree with this method.

There were skills that looked easy. For example, I watched Dad straighten nails, using a hammer on the anvil. When I tried, the thumb and finger holding the nail were hit as often as the nail. Still, to my way of thinking, this was a safe chore.

In the case of the rod weeder, I knew I could have jumped free and left the horses to run into the fence, but the consequences were too terrible to face! If there had been only one or two horses, they would have stopped of their own accord in front of the fence. But when there are a whole string of animals pulling hard at work – and that weeder pulled very hard – they don't seem to see or be aware of what is ahead of them until it is too late.

ROCK PICKING

In summer, while the wheat was growing, Dad picked rocks. In the fall, when he had finished, there wasn't a rock to be seen. During the winter, new ones worked their way up out of the ground. These were the big ones. Small ones, easy to see and remove, showed up during plowing and cultivating.

When Dad decided it was a good day for rock picking, he hitched a team of the heaviest horses to the stone wagon, which had big wheels with loose planks across them. This was done on the clean summer-fallowed fields, so was a dusty job. The inevitable wind blew dirt up with every step. Horses and wagon made their way slowly back and forth across the field until there was a load. We children went along to help throw on the little rocks. When we got tired, we walked home.

Dad disliked the sight of rock piles on the fields. Some men filled their sloughs and hollows. Instead, Dad had a plan that did away with this problem and gave him an unlimited place to dump them. He discussed it with the government, by letter, and was granted permission.

Half a mile west of our farm ran a main road to Oyen, north and south, along the edge of one of our fields. This road ran across three coulees. A coulee is a deep gulch in the prairie. These weren't very big and, for most of the year, they were only a minor nuisance. In spring time they filled with water and became impassable. The hills were steep for a team pulling a load of wheat to town, any time of year.

Beginning with the

biggest and nearest coulee, Dad hauled his rocks, layer upon layer of them, year after year, to raise the road above water level. It became a solid stone bridge. At the end of each season, when he stopped for the year, a few loads of earth were sprinkled over the top, otherwise the ride over them would be awfully bumpy. When one grade became a few feet taller, he'd work on the next one. They became wider too, as time went on. Neighbors who used the road weren't always charitable about the process.

After the first year, the government sent him a check. They would have done this again if he'd reported all his work, but he found such details too much trouble.

Perhaps I should describe how a stone wagon was used. Instead of using a wagon box on the wheels, loose planks were laid lengthwise on the frame. These were piled on for driving to the field. After arriving there, Dad laid them out flat with a couple of inches between each, for the dirt to fall through. When fully loaded, the wagon was driven to the coulee. The rocks on top of the load were rolled off by hand, to either side. Dad was able to unload the last few rocks by manipulating the planks so that they fell off. We jumped off and got out of the way. He walked to the end of the wagon and, taking hold of the outside plank at its end, pushed down and pulled to roll the rocks. The last few rolled off when he turned the board on its side. When one side was clear he went around to the other side of the wagon. Gradually the planks were worked to each side, leaving a pile of stones still in the middle. The spaces widened and then suddenly, when a last one or two were moved, there was great thundering noises of them rumbling and thumping through the two widened spaces. They bounced and crashed over one another, some rolling all the way to the bottom of the coulee.

The big rocks that barely showed a corner above ground were a different matter. These were discovered while picking the smaller ones, and Dad then marked them. Dad might remember where some of them were when he'd disced or plowed. Those below the surface caused the damage to the plows and rod weeder. Any stone Dad couldn't pick up had to be dug around with a shovel and pickax, then pried out with a long, heavy crowbar.

Sometimes he dug and dug, which was exciting. How huge would it turn out to be? We thought, the bigger the better! Maybe it would turn out to be so big Dad wouldn't be able to get it out! He was so tenacious that this never happened. Somehow he didn't seem to share our feeling of excitement about the rock! A few very large boulders took a couple of days each to remove. Never was there one as gigantic as we'd hoped, like the one in the buffalo wallow. Dad dug the earth away from what he figured was just past the middle of the rock. Then he dragged out the heavy logging chain with a hook on the end and fastened it as tightly as he could around the rock. The horses were hitched to the opposite end of the chain to pull the rock out. Dad stood ready with whip in hand, poor things, as they strained to get it out. The whip was to keep them pulling steadily ahead once the rock started moving. We were right there to roll in small stones, sometimes shoving them with our feet as the big one inched out of the hole. With particularly large rocks this step by step procedure was always necessary. The horses had to bring these up in stages. After each step, the big rock rolled back on the ones we shoved in, with rests for the horses between steps.

There were hazards. The chain or harness might snap in two and the rock could roll back in an unexpected direction and be a danger. Or the horses simply might not be able to budge it, and give up in sheer exhaustion. When that happened, Dad had to do more digging

Stone Boat. — 4ft —

logging chain

fence posts
steel rim from an old wagon wheel.

and go through the awesome maneuver all over again. When a field had all been dug it was dotted with odd-shaped stones.

Dad made a stoneboat to haul rocks to the coulee. It resembled a flat runnered sled and was hard pulling over the field. If the rock was too heavy, it stayed where it was until there was just enough snow to make the pulling easier. When this was done, if it was safe, we sometimes stole a ride on the rock. Most rocks were fairly round. More often we trailed behind while Dad walked, driving the horses, to warn him if the rock showed any signs of rolling off.

After working the rock onto the stoneboat, the hole had to be filled up without leaving a hollow.

This was hard work.

HARVEST

For farmers, fall was the high spot of the year though the children thought spring was more fun. No one seemed to do anything about Thanksgiving, although it was mentioned in school, where a feeble effort was made involving some sad drawings of turkeys. But everyone loved harvest time!

After summer ended, or should I say when Dad thought the right time had come, harvesting began. Dad's long period of freedom to choose his day's work ended. He could no longer decide between weeding, rock picking or carpentry, or new granaries, or patching the old granaries. The big important day of harvest had come. It was time to cut the Talbot Quarter, or else the field north of the house, usually the one seeded first.

Dad would be off to town to get oil, grease and many five-pound balls of binder twine. While there, he also spread the word a hired man was needed. At this time of year transient workers rode the freight trains into prairie towns to find harvest jobs. Many of them were uninvited guests of the railway. Many were recent new immigrants. Some were bad men; all were open to question. There were those who hoped to find land and stay. If they were liked, the farmers encouraged them to do so.

At this time the binder was made ready, the sickle bar freshly sharpened, and the canvas stretched tight

sickle bar

binder

on the platform to catch the wheat as it fell. This canvas belt revolved and carried the loose stalks along to one end. There they were miraculously tied into sheaves. As each sheaf was tied, it rolled onto a carrier of curved steel rods, like a big table fork. When three or four collected, as many as it would hold, Dad squeezed a lever that dropped them to the ground.

It was wizardry itself to watch. Walking beside it, we wondered how the cogs and chains knew the right amount to take each time, to make such neat tight sheaves. The carrier was fascinating too, with its shining steel rods. The rest of the binder looked rusty. We'd sneak on, to slide smoothly off with the bundle of sheaves. Dad's all-seeing eye was there in a hurry and a threat, "Don't you do that again..."

Round and round the big field Dad would go, for days, cutting a six to eight foot strip each time. Longer and longer rows of sheaves lined up on the sides of the field. The wheat left standing became a tiny strip and looked so fragile. Once it had been a sea that rippled in the wind. We liked to be there when the last bit of wheat was cut; if not, we felt we'd missed an occasion. It was a little sad too, then, that the field was so bare.

The hired men were often late. They usually hitched a ride out from town and walked in from the road, which took time. When this happened, Dad got busy himself and stooked (bundled into shocks) the grain. It was very important this be done promptly, to dry out the wheat for threshing and to shed water in case of rain. Actually, the heads of grain must be ripened fairly hard at this time; if not they would shrink after cutting and bring a lower price.

Stooking was back-breaking work. Dad wanted us girls to help, but Mom was against it. We could barely drag the heavy sheaves to Dad. When brother Leslie came along he did not get off so easy, at the same young age. Many children were kept home from school to work at this season.

A stook consisted of five or six sheaves carried to a spot and stood on end teepee fashion. All fields must be done well before the arrival of the harvesters, so the stalks would be dry

Stook

enough for the threshing machine to handle and not gum it up. If the wheat was left standing until it was ripe, the heads shelled out and the stalks broke in the wind. Little field mice collected round the stooks. We too liked to crawl around on all fours inside these tentlike structures to play Hide and Seek.

Some enterprising farmer in each area owned a threshing machine, and made plenty of money with it. He collected a whole retinue of men who followed him from place to place. Many were local farmers, out to make a bit extra or at least work long enough to pay for their own threshing. Dad never did this. Threshing crews worked as fast as they could, using all the available daylight. They wished to get everyone's crop harvested before snow fly, and keep down the cost of the hired men's wages. Weather was forever the master, but fate was rarely unkind at harvest time. Threshing wet grain was impossible. Snow could arrive anytime, and then a day of thaw would cause a wait till the wheat dried out. At best, this meant harvesting a poorer grade of wheat. At worst, it could snow heavily and destroy the entire crop, meaning the loss of a year's work. I never knew of anyone having a total loss but did hear of a last field not being finished. The owner of the threshing machine did people's farms in the order of their asking. The last ones took their chances with the weather.

On the day the threshers came there were sights to see. The tall, lumbering threshing machine forgot the roads and came on the levelest route possible, straight across pastures or highways. It wasn't possible for the horses to pull this heavy thing up steep hills, so these must be bypassed. The cook wagon arrived promptly to get dinner under way. Often it was the first thing to come, and then we'd be on the watch for the big machine's safe arrival.

The activity was so exciting, we hated to leave for school that morning. Creaking hayracks came from different directions, converging on the scene with jingling harness and snorting horses amid bustling men. The whole atmosphere was keyed up. Dad had decided what field should be done first (the one promising the best yield) and where the strawstack was to be. One near home did for

ladder

the winter bedding in the barn. A granary was already placed and waiting.

These granaries were moved all the time. They looked like tall one-room shacks and were good-sized, each holding an average of at least 1000 bushels of wheat. Up high was an open window on one end, at wheat level when filled. Some farmers boarded them up for the winter but Dad didn't bother. If snow drifted in, he'd shovel it off, several times if necessary. Once I remember going with him and seeing many little frozen sparrows on top of the wheat. I felt bad. If the snow wasn't removed and later melted toward spring, any seed wheat, or wheat that was still left unshipped, could mildew or sprout in the bottom where the dampness had seeped. So you see, Dad's lack of attention to detail sometimes cost money and trouble.

The threshing machine was pulled to the granary and maneuvered so's the grain spout was inside one of those high, open windows. Thus the straw could blow out the right direction into the wind, away from the machine and the granary. The further away the strawstack was put, the better. They were a fire hazard. A spark from the machinery could set them off. In warmer weather, lightning could strike on those level planes and burn up the granary. The greatest danger from fire was during threshing.

Next came the big moment we'd waited for. Our hands were clamped tight over both ears in readiness. Men had been scurrying about and suddenly the monster machine started off with a roar, then settled down to run till lunch time!

In the meantime, the bouncing hayracks had scattered to load up on sheaves. Two men went with each one. One man worked on the ground pitching the sheaves up to the other on the load. He would catch them with his fork and try to make a well-stacked load. With practice, they became very adept. When the rack was loaded, they brought it to the threshing machine. If there were delays, they were considered a poor crew. When greenhorns, or young fellows, came in with a poor load they were bawled out for wasting time. As the teams worked, the stooks got further and further away from the threshing machine. The straw came out in billows, like smoke from a chimney, to pile up and up, in a big soft stack. From the spout, into the granary, poured the year's effort. Dad climbed the ladder of sticks nailed to the side of the granary, anxious to catch a handful of wheat. He wanted to pour it through his fingers to see what grade of wheat he'd raised that year. From a smaller spout at the back of the threshing machine, ran weed seeds and shrunken grain into a small pile on the ground. This was later hauled to the chop house to be ground up and fed to the hungry pigs.

Lunchtime came. The watering trough was filled. The men took turns pumping to keep it full for the endless line of thirsty horses. After the horses drank and were fed there was a great splashing, shuffling and joking of the men around the pump. Some carried off a bucketful, others took turns under the pump collecting double hands full of water to burble over tired, dusty faces and heads. When they washed their black faces, they were seen to have turned bright red from the wind and the chaff.

Off to the cook car they went, always sounding happy at the prospect of food and jostling over one another in the line. This car was a Gypsy wagon on wheels. Watching the smoke come from the chimney pipe, we thought it like the Gypsies because it was so exotic. Delightful smells and much laughter came from inside. We children were never allowed near any of these operations, but watched from as near as we dared to go.

Threshers can eat mountainous amounts of food. The cook spent the whole day cooking meat and potatoes and baking rows of pies.

Once I crept to the bottom of the little steps on the back of the cook house for a peek and the cook shooed me away. Probably she felt kids would only be after food. Along one wall was a long flat counter with a bench under it. Most of the other wall was the same except for a stove in the corner. When there was a big working crew, like at our place, they took turns eating.

At sundown the workmen who lived nearby would go home. The

extra hired men bunked in a granary or even in our hayloft. I don't remember anyone supplying beds for them, and Dad didn't like them in the hayloft at all. Part of the reason was that some of them carried flasks and smoked.

If there was any wood, they might build a bonfire in the evening, out in front of the granary. This would keep off the chill while they swapped stories in the firelight. They told stories of how they rode the freight trains and didn't get caught. Some train crews were lenient and didn't look under the box cars or on top. They rolled into the ditches to spend the nights, if they didn't find an empty box car. In lean years, they rode further west and worked in the lumber camps. Someone invariably had a mouth organ to end the evening. We watched from our bedroom window and went to sleep with reflections of their flames dancing on the ceiling.

The hired men were mostly foreigners. I remember a Lithuanian who seemed to be left out. I never had heard of that country before. He couldn't speak a word of English.

At the end of the day these men usually went to sleep with some piece of clothing rolled up as a pillow under their heads, tired out, clothes and all. No man out there owned such a thing as a nightshirt or that newfangled thing called pajamas. When at home they slept in their longies, a thin set for summer and heavy fleece-lined ones for winter.

After two long, long days the fields would be bare. It seemed to us it was over too quickly. Afterwards, if we listened, the threshers might be heard at a nearby farm. All that was left at home were stark yellow fields of bristling stubble, and the tracks of the wagons crisscrossing over the hills. The big fluffy strawstacks were left too; they soon would be fun to play in.

I couldn't help reflecting on the ends and beginnings of things. So much of living seemed to be freezing up with the cold and coping with the snow. Winter was not a calm white stillness, like down East. There people cozy up to a pretty fireplace and enjoy peacefulness. Out here it was a fight for survival. Anyway, now the men were all gone! It had been a jolly, sociable time. There seemed nothing to think about but the long quiet winter to be spent indoors.

Dad considered when to haul the wheat. Some had been taken at once for ready money but as much as possible was kept. If it were held back until the market wasn't so flooded, prices might go up. At least they got a cent or two extra per bushel, for storage, for keeping it past flood tide.

In the wake of harvest good things might be in store, depending on debts and this year's yield. For one thing, a new hair ribbon to replace the string usually worn. Best of all there were sure to be good things to eat! A can of tomatoes was a tasty dessert. Perhaps we might even buy one of those tins of strawberry jam. That topped the list of grand things, we ate so much bread.

After the stubble was covered with snow, and the granary emptied and moved, dad set fire to the extra strawstacks. They made glorious big bonfires but always scared us too. If a granary was far from home and was to be left on the field, a chance was taken, on a well-chosen day, of burning the straw anyway. Neighbors, seeing the smoke, hoped everything was all right. If Dad didn't get this job done until late spring, he'd have to go to the bother of plowing a strip of furrows and hope for a windless day. Sparks were a hazard, and he'd be afraid a prairie fire might be started in the dried-out stubble and dead grass.

In that dry atmosphere, things don't decay as fast as in the damp coastal regions. It was surprising to see bits of straw dropped on dusty wagon trails a couple of years back, still there, but broken into minute bits and pieces.

This form of harvesting has been gone from the scene for many years now. Gone too are all the horses. Tractors do the work. Even the barns are obsolete; farmers now buy canned milk. It's sad to see these changes come, but easier for them.

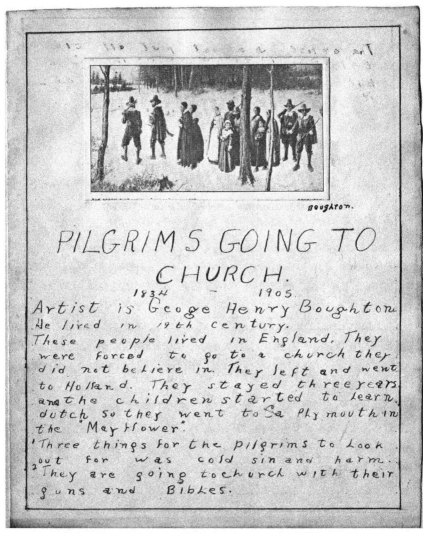

Page from Reta's Art Notes book, made in eighth grade

 **Chapter 5**

PLAY

There came times when we had new ideas for play. This might keep us busy for hours, even days. We could only get away with this if we kept out of sight. Otherwise the parents would see all that energy going to waste, and put us to work.

In early spring when the snow was no longer fun to play in, we'd go to the haymow. The straw was low from feeding and bedding down the stock all winter. We'd dig into it and move it about with great expectations. It was full of mice, and at this time of year, nests of little ones. Pussy cat followed, hoping to get her fill. She was a help pouncing on some just under the straw. Our idea was to capture them, to see how many we could get, and not be bitten in the process.

Mabel, my next younger sister, was most adept at grabbing the big ones by the tail. When they tried to bite, she'd give them a flip that kept them quiet long enough to get them into a box or pail. Dad was a problem. If he found out what we were doing, he'd come and kill the mice we had caught. With so much noise and hollerin' during the process, it wasn't hard to tell where we were if he was outside. If he didn't butt in, we counted the catch and let them go, to build themselves another nest for more mouse games later.

When we were through mouse hunting we found a broom. Arm loads of straw were carried to the outside edges, and the middle of the haymow swept clean down to the boards. Some of the straw had to be carried to the sides, ready for pushing down the mangers, or Dad would be mad. The rest was piled as high as possible at each end of the mow. From the middle, we'd get a good running start and try to get all the way to the top of the straw pile, to touch a rafter if possible. The fun ended with straw fights or Hide and Seek in the barn.

When tomorrow came, it was, "Let's play it again," until we ran out of mice. The hayloft was wonderfully dry and warm and this was the best time of year to play there. When it was too full, play was difficult and the steep sides could mean a slip and fall to the mangers far below.

Having only younger sisters and bits of brothers to play with was a drawback; any kind of sport or game was hard to play. Being the oldest, I could outrun and outsmart them and there was no pleasure in that. We had to think of other pastimes, and even then it was a constant effort to explain. I also had to watch out for possible accidents and try to guard against them. If the younger ones were crossed, or given too many orders, they soon lost patience and would mess up long-range plans. They might even threaten to get into my things.

I wasn't the teacher type, being much more interested in learning and discovering things for myself.

When some shallow sloughs dried up in early summer, they became carpeted with the softest, finest green grass. This soon died, leaving only cracked mud.

There was a slough behind the barn, a short distance into a wheat field. It was almost perfectly round. Our first barefoot escapade would be to try out its soft greenness. The ground was still very chilly, so we kept our shoes on until we reached the slough. Then off they'd come!

Before we got to the slough, we had to make paths through the wheat. Today's wheat is hybridized, having much shorter stalks. In those days, it grew very tall. To us children it seemed like a forest and, near the slough, the wheat was taller than we were.

When we got near it, we would circle, looking for the slough. After finding it, the shortest route was chosen and we tramped back and forth, following the leader a time or two so's it could be easily spotted next time without knocking more wheat down. If the path was a little roundabout, t'was all the more interesting to follow.

One day Dad discovered his wheat trodden down. He let us know that one path was one too many! That was the end of that game.

A favorite game we played was named Town. When the weather was dry and warm, the dirt became soft and dusty in the fenced barnyard by the watering trough. The three or four inches of dry earth felt like talcum powder to our bare feet. This was the right time to play Town.

A big area was raked over to make it smooth and level. Next a garden hoe was hunted up. The hoe didn't seem to have a regular storing place. Often it was to be found leaning against the back wall of the house, where it had been used to chop weeds near the kitchen door. Taking turns with it between our legs, we'd drag it from here to there, leaving a bare path behind. These were make-believe roads. At the end of a road would be a town. There'd be streets, stores and houses. These were made by mounding up the dust, with doorways, etc. All the dust was removed from the floors.

No one was allowed to step over walls. There was much slapping each other when this rule was broken. Each one could own a house in a different town or out in the country. He could fuss with it as much as he liked, making mud pies in the kitchen, etc. Then when he felt like it, he'd hop up and follow a road to visit someone else's house, perhaps for a make-believe supper.

One pretended to be Mrs. Brown in the country. Another was Mr. Miller at the grocery store in town.

Some estates became quite elaborate when we found string and sticks to make fences. The younger kids always got bored and ended the game. Sometimes the paths and houses were ruined by carelessness. This might be done on purpose, if someone didn't like a rule.

They were always game to play it another day!

GRANDMA EVENS

One day we came to believe that we had a grandmother. Once or twice Dad had mentioned a farm in Penetanguishene, way back East in Ontario, where he grew up. They lived on a "great bay of clear water on an even bigger lake - Lake Huron, very good for swimming," which he very much enjoyed. He made it sound so good that we wondered how he ever could have left it. He didn't say anything about the people there. What he talked of mostly was the fruit that grew on the trees. How he liked fruit and missed it! Apples were his favorite and he told of how he "could never wait for them to ripen and sometimes got a stomachache from eating too many green ones." Many kinds of plums, crabapples and grapes grew there too.

Dad told little of his family and what he said wasn't happy. Once and only once, as I remember, his mother sent a package. It was then that he told us that his mother was our grandmother. He didn't tell us anything about her. But a package arrived! Here it was an ordinary day, not Christmas or his birthday or anything! That package was a wonderful thing!

 On top were a half dozen scarlet ribbons for our hair. Under that were a few muffin sized candies that "tickled" Dad and set him to telling stories of his home for the first time. The candies were the shape of big flat stars made of refined maple sugar. He explained the process, from cutting the trees to boiling the sap.

He was happy that his mother had thought to send him his favorite treat. He carefully wrapped them up and put them away. Dad had a very sweet tooth but rarely indulged it because "it was not good for your health."

On the bottom, of all things, were two crocheted hats. One was for Mabel and one for me. They were done in little bumpy designs of dark-ecru open work. There was nothing for Mom. The hats had wire around the edge of the brim, otherwise they were soft and collapsed in a flat circle. Vivid pink satin ribbon was sewed on around the crown. They looked handsome. But, oh, how they fit and felt! The crowns were so big they came down to our eyes. The brim drooped and bounced up and down, like jelly, when we walked.

Mom kept hoping she could do something with them so we could show them off in town. She didn't know the first thing about knitting, sewing and such. Those hats would have posed a fitting problem for anyone. We did try wearing them to town once anyway but ended up just carrying them.

So, it ended up we wore them for fun around home and especially for playing Town. We kept in step with the bounce, on the way a-visiting, and felt the part of fancy ladies. We even played that Aunt Kate had come to town!

Imagine Grandma sending us something! It made us feel good all over!

GETTING THE COWS

One job Dad insisted on our doing regularly was seeing to it the cows came home night and morning for milking.

If they went out to the pasture after the evening's milking, they usually came back before morning, so we didn't usually have to get them in the morning. They never came home for milking in the early evening in fine weather.

There was no tight schedule as to when they had to be milked. Maybe before supper, maybe after, because the time for supper varied, depending on Dad. If he was tired, he came in to an early supper and afterward went out again to work until dark. If he wasn't tired, he stayed out till dark before eating.

Dad's rule was that the cows must be brought home before dark. Who knew when it was going to get dark? Naturally we'd wait as long as possible. Mom might remember to prod us; Dad never did.

If the cows were in the south pasture it wasn't so bad. There was a nice dusty path that led that way, good for bare feet. There were many hazards for bare feet. Wild roses and short tough buckbrush could be seen. There were young thistles, painful to bare feet, and toes were stubbed on jutting rocks. We simply did not own shoes in summertime, so we stuck to the path.

The east pasture, with the ravine, wasn't so good for several reasons. If the cows were over the hill, we'd not see what direction to head for. Besides, all through it, and the ravine particularly, were many prickery things. The reason certain land was chosen as pasture had to be its problems and slopes. The better acres were cultivated into fields.

In general, we hated getting the cows. There were arguments with each other as to whose turn it was. When that was settled, there was a spell of coaxing, threats and bribes, attempting to get someone to come along as company.

Purp was the only one happy to go. He was a mongrel, a small black and brown collie-looking dog who lasted all my life at home and then some.

One memorable evening, we realized it was getting dark. We'd waited too long to get the cows! At first we rushed down the hill to the south pasture where the cows had been the last several days. As luck would have it, they weren't there. We hurried back home to tell Dad we couldn't find them. He showed no mercy: "It's your job to get the cows. You'd better hustle and find them." Tears did no good nor did Mom telling him it was pretty dark. We were all afraid of the night. Even our faithful dog Purp had deserted the scene.

Bawling, out the door we went. Those cows must be in that awful east pasture! After going a short distance from the house we felt hopeless, so went back to the lamplit kitchen. Again pleading uselessly, we asked, "Then PLEASE could we take the lantern?" "Well, yes you can," said Dad, but Mom argued it was dangerous. We might fall with it and have it catch on fire, but we listened to Dad!

We tried to persuade Purp to go with us, which involved dragging him by the collar. The hassle was time-consuming and slow going. As soon as we let go he went back to the shed to sleep. We felt alone, left to the terrifying dark. Shadows popped up all around and we stumbled on the grass lumps. Every tuft of grass left a long shadow. Somehow, it seemed, there might be *things* just beyond the moving edge of light. Who knew what kind of unknown terror. There were nebulous, frightening *things* to scare and chase us. No use to run, we reasoned: "They'd still be out there and they'd run too." We ran just the same!

We realized we'd have to come right up to the cows to see them, and the pasture had no end. We couldn't know in the dark where we'd been. The more we talked about it, the worse it seemed: "Maybe when we got to this corner, the cows had walked over there..." We called them all kinds of names, like "rotten cows." Mostly we were busy keeping our eyes on what dangerous things might be all around us and hearing *sounds* (you can't imagine a place quieter than the prairie on a summer's night).

We talked less and less, and watched more and got more scared. I spent a good part of my young life being scared. We'd covered some time but little distance, I felt sure, when we saw something on the hillside.

It was a skunk!

We'd been studying skunks in school. The teacher said the stuff they squirted on people was so awful, the only thing you could do was bury your clothes. I wondered why you couldn't burn them. What would a person do, then? We each had only one set of clothes.

In fact, there was a whole row of skunks. We'd never get past them to go on! We stood still to think. If we turned around and ran, they'd chase us, but we took the chance. After falling down a few times and nearly extinguishing the lantern, we decided to walk. It was a very fast walk; we were relieved to be headed in a safe direction. I never saw a skunk in my whole life at home, so guess I doubt that we saw any that night.

When we were nearly home we had qualms. Dad had to be faced. Seeing as how we'd been gone for "hours and hours," surely he'd be lenient. He met us at the door: "Well, did you get the cows?" Of course we wondered why he'd asked when he knew we hadn't. Looking up at him, we told how we'd looked and looked until meeting up with this awful line of creatures. He seemed skeptical but let us in. We skittered right out of sight and sound to the safety of upstairs, leaving him and Mom going strong at one another.

No cows got milked that night. In the morning there they were, standing in the barnyard, near bursting. It was a big long job of milking.

I remember no punishment. I guess we'd learned a lesson.

After that the cows were brought home while there was plenty of daylight!

MISS KILBERG

When I was in seventh grade, a new teacher came from down East and stayed for a year. Her name was Miss Kilberg. She was Swedish, which was something new and different. She had blond wavy hair and we thought her beautiful. She wore such pretty, dainty dresses that she was femininity itself. She was full of ideas. Jim, Richard and I were now the oldest in school.

What an impact she had on all of us! In her quiet, pleasant way, she accomplished wonders. On almost her first day of school (maybe it was) she taught us the word "perseverance." She wrote it in big letters across the blackboard and we learned what it meant and how to spell it. We were thunderstruck at learning such a big word.

There were lively spelling bees with two or three classes at one time. There were so few in each class, this made it fun instead of long drawn-out sessions for each group. We were lined up along the side of the room. When the first person didn't get the answer, he went to the end of the line and the next one tried. Times tables were handled the same way. We loved it.

She fired up the boys especially, with patriotism, while she read to us such classics as "O Captain! My Captain!" Good sportsmanship was also included: 'twas, "Play up and play the game."

She gave a short, entirely new class that the girls very much liked. It concerned special pictures painted long ago that had made the people who did them famous. She'd ordered small 2x2 inch copies in black and white of each one she told us about. We then made a small booklet and decorated the cover. This was so popular that as a prize for being good for a month, we earned a big 6x8 inch copy of the picture of our choice. I remember taking such a long time to choose one. Richard had the same problem. He chose one of Sir Galahad looking for the Holy Grail, which I very much liked also. Feeling it was more for a boy, I settled for *The Age of Innocence*. We'd not had prizes before, and thought that Miss Kilberg was wonderful!

The annual school fair, with seven districts invited, was to be entered this year by our school, Wavy Plains. We hoped to make a good showing. Vegetable and flower seeds were handed out most school years, were taken home, and perhaps planted by the parents. This was the first year the children were at all interested. My well-started garden went to weeds, but the neighbor boys went on to win prizes, especially on their mangels. What they were used for I'll never know. They looked like giant beets.

Miss Kilberg brought bits and pieces of organdy and lace to school. These were left over from making her own dresses. They caused sparkles of excitement and smiles. They were lovely things with colors we'd never seen before. She set the girls to sewing whatever they liked on the list. What fun in school! Some even chose to do patches.

I made a yellow organdy doll dress, scalloped on the bottom and edged with lace. It won first prize, which was a red ribbon and a whole huge dollar.

Handwriting and geography maps were also entered. Not very good all-over patterns and lampshades were made too. We chose our own colors and designs. Green shamrocks edged in black were painted with watercolors. They were on a pink background that had also been painted with watercolors. To make the lampshades, we first cut the shades out of blue paper and then we cut iris shapes out of black paper and pasted them on. Paste was dreadful stuff then.

The schoolroom was a beehive of activity any time we could spare from lessons. The girls cooked and baked at home and boys raised animals to enter in the fair's competition. We won many prizes for our school!

green shamrocks painted on a pink background. Edged in black.

Paste was dreadful then.

for pasting

Blue background
Black paper iris-
narrow black strips
folds.
(Jorked a mess - from
white paste putting
on such narrow black
strips!

The biggest thing that year, 1927, was to be a parade to celebrate Canada's Diamond Jubilee on July 1st. When our projects were under way, Miss Kilberg announced that nothing less would do than for our school to enter a float in the parade. We sat dumb and wide-eyed over the very idea.

Looking back, I realize what an inexperienced lot we were, acquainted only with the simple things of home. All the children I went to school with were first children who were very naive compared with those who followed later. They fought, but there wasn't the bad talk and the cheating and lying that came to the fore when younger brothers and sisters went to school. The parents were still young, busy, and full of enthusiasm for the West. We heard them call it the Golden West and puzzled over this. Why? Certainly there was no gold. Was it because of the fields of ripening golden-colored wheat? Perhaps it was.

Miss Kilberg chose "The Gateway to Canada" as our title and rounded up all the help she could get from parents in collecting things. She was tireless herself, and a wonder to watch. She got a big truck, from goodness knows where (I'd never seen one before), and we decorated it all over with strips of white crepe paper. This had to be fastened down very well because of all the wind. Even so it gave us no end of problems during the parade. Toward the front of the truck body was a big white arch with our title across it. Behind the arch sat Florence, the oldest and prettiest girl in the district. She was no longer in school but the teacher borrowed her. Dressed in all white, flowing cheesecloth with a golden paper crown on her head, she represented Canada.

All the rest of us stood in front of the arch. It was pretty hard standing there with the truck bouncing over Oyen's unpaved street. That street was only a mud road full of dried ruts. Sometimes we almost fell on our faces. We ended up bunched together for security. Miss Kilberg had thought of this, and had drawn chalk circles on the floor of the truck with our names on them. After a bad bump we rushed around until we found our proper places again!

We were dressed as Germans, Swedes, etc. I was an Irish gal, Mabel was Dutch, and Irene was Chinese, or was it Japanese? We represented immigrants coming to Canada. Two boys in white sailor suits, with guns over their shoulders, marched in front. Behind were two more, dressed in World War I soldier suits.

You can scarce believe the amount of work that went into this undertaking. People didn't have the things at hand that we now do.

Teacher hunted far afield for some items and took money of her own to pay for them.

She first sent to the city, a couple of hundred miles away, for the white crepe paper. Even seeing it was a new experience for us. She had trouble getting the golden paper for Florence's crown. It came from even farther away. Such fussing over the precious price and the careful planning before it was done! Nothing else was bought except some string to tie down the crepe paper. Nails were no good and Scotch tape hadn't been invented yet.

As for costumes, everyone hunted through his scant belongings and enough material was found to make what was needed. White aprons helped, made from 100 lb. sugar sacks, and most peasants seemed to be wearing them. Mabel wore one, her Dutch cap was made from one, and we used what was left for others. Some cloth was dyed by teacher. It was good only until washed, and often not then, as it streaked so in those days.

My green satin jumper was laced at the bodice. It had been someone's treasure from the old country. The blouse for it was the top of a woman's old nightgown. Irene's costume was a piece of curtain. With teacher's help, I made all of Irene's and Mabel's costumes. Parents helped too, but Miss Kilberg made many.

Teacher called our entry a "float." Wavy Plains had never done anything like this before, so we sure surprised everyone, including ourselves.

We won first prize, a silver cup. The beautiful thing was to stand from that day on, atop a specially made bracket at school, for all to see. We were very proud of it and so the first feelings of school spirit were born.

It was *such* a big day. We were glad when the attention-getting parade was over so's we could enjoy the fair.

THE FAIR

The school fairs were held in Oyen, which helped make it an important town. Little more than a spot of ground, vacant anyway, was set

aside. For all that, it was a very small town. The few stores were hud-
dled so close together, they appeared to be keeping each other warm.

A wide muddy area was known as Main Street. Stores lined it for
about half a block. Running in front of most stores was a wooden
sidewalk, reminiscent of a miniature railway track upside down. One
side ended with a garage, its old tractors and other rusty machines
drizzling out beyond. The last building on this side of the street was
the Picture Show, open on Saturday nights. Cars could park beyond
it when it wasn't too muddy, and of course horses didn't care. Behind
the stores were the houses of the store owners. Beyond them were the
far reaches of prairie, with space for anything, and that's the way it
was for years and years.

The fairgrounds were on the edge of town, to the south. A crude
wooden building, very long (to us), marked the spot. On counters
running its length were displayed the year's efforts. The dusty patch
next to it was the racetrack with its grandstand of sorts (benches).
Pens of barbed wire were hastily put together for the show animals,
pigs and calves. Wavy Plains had few entries in that category, probably
due to the fact that Miss Kilberg didn't know anything about animals.

It was all like the typical country fair, often written about, with
a decidedly western flavor. To participate in this, the year's biggest
occasion, was a rewarding experience for a young one. I'm sorry for
those who never did!

Where did all the people come from? Whole families arrived with
lunches and baby bottles. Each family claimed a spot to park cars
or wagons as a home base. Smaller children soon forgot where they
belonged, as everyone trailed off to visit and look around. If a child
became absorbed in looking at something, the next minute the family would be lost and there was a moment of panic until someone
recognizable was found. As the day wore on, we gave up. The parents
weren't going home yet, so we'd mill around on our own. Any one of
us might bump into a lost and crying younger sister. Mabel loved to
pick up and comfort the strays and spent most of her time this way,
but I was off to see all that could be seen. No other time was there
such freedom. Other trips to town were spent standing beside Dad.

He refused to waste time looking for anyone. He said that if one of us got lost, he'd go home without him.

There was Florence, so dressed up in her prettiest new pink dress, pushing and patting her bobbed and marcelled hair and eying the boys. I know because I saw her on a street corner and asked what she was waiting for.

One of our own school boys, most often Richard, would come along and ask if I was going to run in any races. He talked me into a bit of practice for a three-legged race, which we almost won. Sack races were most fun to watch, but hardest to get contestants for. Our school wasn't too interested in racing. When we did, we always came in with that large middle group.

Best of all were the horse races. Everyone or anyone entered and that went for the horses too.

The finale was hilarious, drawing the crowd and cheers. It was a relay for men. They chose sides and the two groups lined up on either side of the field. When the whistle blew, one on each side jumped on his horse, raced to the other end of the track and jumped off. On the ground was a pile of ladies' clothes: some very old fashioned pantaloons, and big hats and dresses. The fellow had to dress in these and race back down the field. Off came the clothes and on to the next one till the race was won.

The long low building was bursting with things to see, mostly from schools. The large majority of goodies, pies and cakes and canned food, were in the mothers' section at one end. Every kid there wished they'd been judges for the day to sample all that mouthwatering food. The place had been closed all morning for the judging, while visiting and racing went on. There was even a little bronco riding and a few games of chance. The balloon man did a thriving business. It was at this fair I saw the first balloon on a stick, people eating ice cream cones, and bananas for sale.

When the building finally opened, all were eager to see what had been shown and who had won. Children pushed to reach the counters, among the grown-ups, to be able to see. Who were the lucky ones to win the red, blue and yellow circles stuck to the now open tags? Dad gave me a nickel to spend for a treat. We didn't have pennies. The ice cream was easy to pass up; there was lots of cream at home! The balloon seemed like fun, and I would have chosen it if there'd been a chance of hiding it until we went home. Always being hungry anyway, the banana was chosen. Afterwards, I wasn't so sure the taste had been worth my first spending money.

MOM'S TREAT

The following year Mom was sick during the school fair. I felt she must be most disappointed to miss the big, important event and wanted to do something for her. The fair didn't turn out to be nearly as exciting as the one the year before, with one exception.

Dad, for the first time in my life, gave me a whole quarter to spend! It was also the last time. I never did spend it all. I carried it in my hand the whole day, considering what to do with it and thinking I could take it home, to save with my things.

I remembered a necklace made of glass beads that had hung a long time in the tiny Chinese restaurant window downtown. I'd never been inside and there wasn't another piece of jewelry for sale anywhere. How often I thought of that necklace and hadn't dared to hope of having so much money.

Now, with the quarter in my hand, I left the fairgrounds, anxious for another look. I was afraid of the Chinaman so walked back and forth past the window. No one else was around. Scarce anyone was ever seen going into the place, and he never came out! Maybe it was a saloon.

I didn't dare ask Dad, for fear he'd take the money away. I felt sure he expected me to buy something sensible with it. While pacing the sidewalk, I wondered what I'd do with a necklace. No one I knew had one. It would be conspicuous.

I left and went back to the fairgrounds. There was Dad treating the family to ice cream cones. What a surprise! What a treat! We took delicious little licks to make them last as long as possible. Poor Mom, missing such goodness! That was just the thing - I'd take her some. Without letting Dad know, I went to look for a box to carry the cone in and found somewhere a large Magic Baking Powder tin.

I went back to the ice cream man, who was all alone now, and bought a cone. It wouldn't stand up alone in the tin so I bought another cone. The can was carefully put in the back seat of the car until we went home. I felt good now, having spent my money for someone other than myself. I anticipated how happy and surprised Mom would be, and was impatient to get home.

When we piled into the car to leave, the kids next to me wanted to know what was in the tin I was so carefully holding upright. I shushed them and in whispered secrecy told them of the surprise. They were excited too.

We arrived at home. Leaving Dad behind, I jumped out of the car, with the rest following, to find Mom. We gathered round to watch her take off the lid. She opened it and stopped. We all took a look and when I did, what a shock to see a puddle of white liquid with stuff floating around in it. Without hearing a word from Mom, who wondered what she had been given, I ran to my room. How stupid, not to have figured it out. I didn't want to be seen. I wonder why I never thought to take Mom the necklace?

THE GYPSIES

Fair day began with everyone very serious and busy, getting the entries from home in the right spot and tagged. Then grown-ups were meeting and greeting each other and speculating as to the outcome of what they'd brought: "The son's calf looked pretty fair." They discussed everything from crops to politics.

By the time the judging was over and the displays had been well studied, the day gained a carnival aspect. The happy winners felt like celebrating, and the losers were happy to forget their losses. Dad wanted to go home at this time, but we persuaded him to stay. It was lucky we did as a band of Gypsies came late and we watched them encamp. Seeing their wagons and bright-colored clothes added a touch of the unusual to our lives. They all were black haired, with bright black eyes. Some wore kerchiefs. They were talkative and lively. I got very close to a girl my own size and she wore earrings. She was beautiful!

We children had discovered the Gypsies' arrival first. We ran back to tell the parents. We said that their wagons were parked beyond our own, and told everything else about them. With stern faces the parents warned us to stay away from them; they weren't good people but pickpockets and thieves and "would even steal the clothes off your back." Mom called them light-fingered.

Soon, some men said they'd lost their wallets and had not known how. We didn't know whether to believe this or not, but it made the Gypsies seem all the more exciting!

Richard came running to say I must come with him. He wanted me to see their wagons, which they'd left to set up a game of chance. I'd never seen him so courageous, so went along with him. Many people were afraid to have anything to do with the Gypsies.

We sat on the ground nearby. Tethered to the ground were many horses and only a few wagons. Richard speculated on this. Probably the men rode the horses, and only women and children rode inside. The wagons looked like houses with rounded roofs. We judged that one must be for sleeping, and one for cooking. Another must be some-one's house because there were little white curtains at the windows. We waited some time for someone to come out of the door, so we could get a peek inside.

From there, we went to watch their booth. A counter in front was covered with numbers, and there was a spinning wheel. Hung around the sides were brightly-colored prizes. Best of all, I remember the little Kewpie dolls with red feathers glued on them for skirts. Made with paper-thin pink celluloid heads, they didn't break, but could be dented with the merest pressure of a finger. How I wanted one! They were so cute, with round black-painted eyes and wide smiling mouths.

Richard and I often talked of how cozy it must be to live in a little house on wheels and to be free to go wherever you pleased.

For years, I wanted to be a Gypsy.

GOPHERS

Something else Miss Kilberg did was to bring law and order out of our gopher tails. These little creatures were all over the prairie. Some lived alone. Others lived in groups. Each group dug extensive tunnels, leaving a sizable mound of dirt. There were holes all over the top where they could pop down at a moment's notice. They liked to sit up and look around, while their busy little tails thumped the ground. They looked like tan squirrels, and not at all like the fat prairie dogs in the zoo, with their saucy and cheeky ways.

Wheat was their favorite dish, so they were a problem to the farmer. The Government considered them a pest and paid a bounty on them. Every parent tried encouraging their young ones to catch them. Children were sometimes forced to do this. When they got too numerous around home, Dad mixed up poison and grudgingly went after them himself.

Once there was a near disaster. Dad mixed the poison liquid in the kitchen, ready to pour over a bucket of wheat. This sort of thing was usually done at the well. A couple of us came in from outside, saw it and went for the big white cups. It looked exactly like lemonade. I poured some in my cup. Mom happened along in time, leaving us shaken by her outburst. Mostly she was mad at Dad. I felt sick all afternoon while helping spoon the liquid down the gopher holes. I was sure I'd die of gopher poisoning, even though I'd not touched a drop. That's what imagination can do for you. I was so scared of how close I'd come to drinking that cupful.

There were various ways we children caught gophers, depending on what was at hand. Catching them could be fun, but not the killing. We thought they were so cute! When pushed to get rid of them quickly, we used the two spring traps because they were the easiest and quickest method. Not pleasant though because they always hurt the poor creatures. I must admit, we became more immune to their suffering as the summer wore on.

The slowest method was the favored way. A long, soft piece of string was best, but binder twine often had to do. A slipknot was made on the end and carefully laid around the hole. The rest was run straight out on the ground, with us flat on our stomachs, holding the other end. Either there was another slipknot on it or it was wrapped several times around fingers for a firm grip. When the curious little gopher popped up for a look, with a quick jerk we'd have him around the middle. He was pulled out, complaining bitterly.

The game to play then was Horse. With the string slack, the gopher expected his freedom and took off. We'd go galloping after wherever he chose to run until Dad might see and holler, "Get busy." A careful lookout kept him away from other holes to run down, otherwise we'd never get him out again.

Gophers living by a slough had a bucket or two of water poured down to drown them out, poor things. They came up blinking and sneezing or in puzzled wonderment, all soaking wet.

After they were caught and killed, we put a left foot on them and pulled off their tails to take to school. The teacher counted the tails and sent the figure to the Government.

Other teachers had done this casually, but not so Miss Kilberg. Every Friday afternoon was count up time. She called each child in turn to come up front to her desk. Out of the boys' pockets, girls' baking tins and paper bags were brought the tails, to be dumped on the desk. The number was written down on a chart after each of our names. Each pile was then taken to the furnace at the back of the room and burned. This did away with losing them to be found again, swiping, and cheating by counting the same tail twice. Boys loved to tease girls by trying to get their gopher tails.

Miss Kilberg was thorough. She sent all names and numbers caught in to the Government. Other teachers had never been very conscientious about this. Everyone who caught over 200 tails got 50 cents. I did, and such wealth was happily hurried home and given to Dad. He never said anything, but we felt he was pleased and needed it.

One year the neighbor boy, who was mean and lazy, pulled the tails off his gophers and then let them go. He was sure they'd grow new ones. He maintained that when his father made him go out next year, he wouldn't have far to go for a catch.

Imagine his surprise next year when he had to catch them all and had nothing to show for it!

THE SCOTT DOUGLAS PLACE

We walked home from school one way, no straggling, but together. That was a law. In late springtime we older ones weren't in such a hurry, unless Dad had made a point of "getting right home." Younger ones hurried home because hunger got the best of them. Coaxing didn't work too well or for too long.

In our east pasture, in sight of school, was a weather-beaten house looking more like a granary. We were told to stay away from it. The windows were boarded up tight and it had long been deserted. Periodically, we briefly explored it. By the side of the house was a square of heavy loose planks which could be lifted up. They covered a well. Within was a rope on a rusty pulley and a wooden bucket tied to the end. The rope was intact but there was no bottom in the bucket, so that wasn't much fun. Besides, I was afraid of wells.

Behind the house a piece was a small, broken-down building with a row of rhubarb beside it. We sometimes picked this to take home, feeling like thieves. I don't know why, since nobody lived there. It was delicious and Dad loved rhubarb. This was seldom done or he'd know where we'd been and there'd be questioning. We liked to please him and he was placated by the rhubarb, even though he did want us home on time.

This building was called the "Scott Douglas place," and it was shrouded in mystery. We often tried to pull one board off a side window, but ran each time. It was spooky. Perhaps it was partly due to Mom, who used to singsong a little verse, "Hush thee, hush thee, my little bay-bee, so's the Black Douglas will not get thee." Know any Scottish history?

Near the end of my grade school days, Dad bought this place. We found that he had been renting the east pasture from the Government. The old house was to be towed home and used when we had a hired man. Dad hadn't said a word to us about this. Someone at school one morning looked out the window and saw activity at the Scott Douglas place. This story was whispered all over the room. Behind teacher's back, we popped up to chance a peek. After telling us to sit down on several occasions, she discovered the reason for our curiosity. When the few somethings went by on the road, the same thing happened. The minute lunchtime came, the children could stand it no longer. All swarmed over to that old house, leaving lunch untouched. Teacher rang and rang the bell and finally had to come herself.

The place turned out to be as interesting as we'd anticipated. It was not empty. Inside, all dusty and cobwebby, were many things to see and wonder about. It looked to us as if the people had gone out, nailed the door shut and never come back. There were even pans on the stove, with remains of food, long since dried up. A homemade wooden table sat in the kitchen. There were odd bits of heavy white china and one pretty plate in a makeshift cupboard, besides a few wooden chairs. On the walls were several yellowed calendars. Magazines lay in a corner with laughable, old-style people pictured.

We rushed into the other room in the house, where stood two dusty beds with tall brass rods at the head and feet. Only one bed had a mattress and there were no covers. When we touched the mattress, out rushed startled mice. The children squealed. In one corner gaped an open hole in the ceiling. Below were slats of wood nailed to the bare 2x4s, as a ladder.

Nailed shut in the attic was a large potbellied wooden barrel filled with clothes. Out of it came ladies' long dresses with braid all over them, and big, big hats decorated with faded flowers and puffs of silk.

Teacher gave up fussing, but she hurried us through looking things over. We speculated as to what became of the people. Why had they left everything? Had they intended to come back? Or was it because they'd come to give the new West a try, decided it was not for them, and had left while there was still money enough for a ticket? We'd never know.

Too bad not to have kept a memento or two!

BEN HUR

I cannot think of the book *Ben Hur* without recollecting a pleasant episode. Not that I remember anything about the book but a boring story (with the exception of a chariot race) that went on for pages.

Miss Kilberg pushed for some reading in the 8th grade, but we didn't much like the idea. She hit upon *Ben Hur*, and knowing we'd probably never read it at home, assigned it at school. Little money again was the problem. The government supplied readers, geographies and history. Any other books were bought by individual schools. I never once heard our grown-ups talk about books. School was for learning the three R's. Teacher managed to get a copy of this special book somewhere, with a limited borrowing time, and came up with an idea: we would all read it together.

What a lark that turned out to be.

At designated times, fat Richard, Jim and I moved into one seat, usually mine. Someone was always left struggling to keep from falling off the edge. The boys thought I should sit in the middle so I didn't have much of a problem. Richard and I raced through the page and forgot it about as fast. We then had time to whisper until Jim finished and the page could be turned. We did our best visiting then. Usually I couldn't stand him!

Teacher doubted many times the wisdom of this experiment and even threatened to end it. "No," we promised, "we'll be good." Deep down we knew she wasn't the sort to have us start something and not finish it. Next, we'd have to take it home to read in a hurry. It was a hard book and she'd not be there to explain the difficult words. After we were all through reading, she gave us an exam on the book.

Needless to say, it was a failure!

CHRISTMAS CONCERTS

School ended each year with a Christmas concert and all the parents came. These were looked forward to with much excitement, but also misgivings. Everyone who could possibly be talked into it must stand up front and do something. The usual was a poem, taken from a Reader. Some singing was done by classes. I can't remember anyone not being self-conscious. It was misery! Perhaps classmate Jim didn't feel awkward, but he sure looked it!

Miss Kilberg, with her usual uninhibited outlook, set about to put on something different. She succeeded in making the affair quite entertaining.

These concerts were usually held at our own school. This year the word must have gotten 'round that it was going to be better than usual because we were invited to give it at Benton Hall. The Hall was only a year or two old. It had been built by the farmers to hold such things as meetings, typically to discuss forming a wheat pool in the hope of getting better prices.

"Why do we have to go to Benton?" we asked the parents. Benton Valley school, one mile south of town, would be there too. Richard had been told that because of our success at the fair, people wanted to see what Miss Kilberg would do with Christmas. What she did was great, and Benton Valley scarce had a showing.

A bumper crop had been harvested, the first of two before the Dust Bowl era struck. Dad had money for new machinery, and Mom went all out to make us special Christmas dresses. She ordered all the material and gave it to Mrs. Pooke to make dresses for the three girls. I can still see how happy Mom looked as she unfolded them. First came white cotton petticoats and then almost sheer, thin white silk dresses with gathered skirts and puffed sleeves. They were most impractical! Best of all Mrs. Pooke had added a surprise of her own. Above the wide hem was a row of sparkling silver tinsel. It created that once-in-a-lifetime fairy-princess feeling and we made the most of it. I almost forgot my hair was straight and ugly!

I remember too when we got dressed to go out, how drab Mom looked in her dark tan house dress. I tried to think of something to do to fix it. The thing didn't fit. It looked awful, and I felt sorry about it. But she said to "Never mind." She didn't enter into things but smiled from the sidelines. She said she hadn't the energy, and didn't know how to take part.

The whole affair was overwhelming. I forgot half my lines in the poem I had to recite with Richard. Besides, we were big then and I didn't think it funny to be dressed in little boy and girl costumes, and to hold hands to recite a poem together. But the audience loved it!

With me in that pretty dress, after the concert was over, Richard was a pest. He couldn't stop talking about my appearance and trailed around after me.

Next came the good part. When the children were all seated in the audience, a grown-up stood on the stage and handed every child a bag of candy. For some it was the only gift they got that Christmas; there was none at home. That year balls were added and other things. I got my heart's desire: a beautiful little china-faced doll. With my sparkling dress and the doll, it was a joyous night.

After the children's part was over, the chairs were noisily slid across the floor, back against the walls, and the blanket on a wire (the stage) was taken down. Wax was sprinkled on the not-so-perfect floor. Grown-ups chattered and debated as to just the right amount of wax, while we bounced about impatiently, waiting for the fun to begin.

Social affairs brought out the smiles. Everyone looked as excited and happy as kids. There was much joking and laughter and everyone did have a wonderful time. Benton Hall had an upright piano and someone to play it. The fiddler tuned up and when the caller clapped his hands the square dancing began. We children had a glorious time, sliding across the floor, in and out among the dancers, eating cake and pie, and being pests in general.

We were so tired that night we fell fast asleep in bed without a chance of savoring that happy feeling.

THE CHRISTMAS TREE

What an outstanding year that was!

Dad thrilled us the same Christmas. I felt the teacher must have inspired everyone. Two days after the concert – only two days – Dad seemed to be puttering about in and out of the house and it was so cold outside.

The lamp was lit and Mom was cooking supper at the stove when we heard Dad call from outside, "Open the door." Someone ran to open it. Looking pleased, in he came holding the oddest thing. He had to tell us what it was. We could understand better after he stood it up. Before our eyes stood a brand new 2x4 about five feet tall! About every foot, first on this side and then on that, was nailed a slim – one might say wispy – branch of short-needled pine.

It was a Christmas tree!

The noisy kitchen was hushed while we took it in. Then we ran pell-mell to smell and feel the green branches. Wherever did he get them? I still wonder. I never saw, before or after that time, a sprig of pine in Oyen.

One good thing starts a person thinking of more. Next we wished for some decoration to cover the tree's bareness. Some colored paper chains like we'd made to hang on the school windows would be perfect. It needed something for decorations.

Then I remembered the little china doll hidden safely away after the concert. Everyone thought it would make a nice decoration. Christmas was a long way off, and I was afraid the younger ones would not leave it alone. After bringing it downstairs I decided it would be safe if I hung it high enough.

No sooner had it been hung near the top of the tree than it crashed to pieces on the floor! Need I say more?

Photograph of lampshade made by Reta in Miss Kilberg's class

 Chapter 6

HISTORY

Miss Kilberg made us conscious of history, not only world history, but also our own. Like all children who know only their own small corner of the world (and ours was a bare corner), we were not aware things had ever been any different than they were.

The pretty places and houses that appeared in the rare magazines that we saw, were as unreal to us as "Jack and the Bean Stalk" or "Little Miss Muffet."

This teacher from down East asked many questions and we didn't know the answers. Questions such as: "Where did your parents come from and when?" and "What did they do before that?" Then she told how the pioneers settled the West. She told each of us to go home and collect all the old pictures and stories we could from our parents.

They were the settlers she had talked about!

Imagine their story being history! Up until then, history class had seemed like musty old stories. It always seemed to be about people fighting, and the worst part was that we had to memorize the dates.

Looking into our own history turned into a major project, and was absorbing for everyone. We wrote down all we were told at home; now I wish I could remember all that we learned. Teacher laughed over some of the stories. In the end, there were writing and painting contests and the net results were collected into a booklet to be kept at school. My sister Irene later told me that most of it was in my handwriting.

Today the little country schools are gone, along with that record and the silver cup. Miss Kilberg's idea was that they should be kept, but no one cared.

This was the time when I learned that Dad and his older brother Nelson had heard of the "land of opportunity" and decided to try their luck homesteading on the prairie. Men took the train west, traveling as close as they could to available land. Then they spent their money on a wagon and team of horses. They drove during the day, tethered the horses to the wheels at night and slept under the wagon. They looked for a location that suited them before choosing their 160 acres (a ¼ section) as a homestead. It cost Dad $10.00, he thinks, to settle it with the Government for the land. After three years of working the land, it became his. In Canada, the farmer only owns the top nine inches of the land. Everything below that, including oil rights, belongs to the Government.

There is a P.S. of interest to this issue of land rights, from something that came about years later.

Very abundant oil fields were discovered in Alberta. The big Turner Valley oil wells are west of us. The Government decided to drill around home to see what they could find. They did not find enough oil to mention, but in the process ruined the well water in the area. Just enough oil seeped into the water strata to make it unusable for drinking.

The town of Oyen dug a new, very deep well. So Dad and others must go to town for their drinking water, a round trip of eighteen miles over country roads for Dad.

We had a friend who farmed near the oil wells, and he had a sad story to tell. After the wells went in, the Government paid a pittance for surface damages on the bits and corners of the fields where they sunk their pumps. From each pump, a little pipe lets out the natural gas, which burns in a bright flame. From a plane at night, this area is something to see; the burning gas jets look like the stars overhead. One feels entirely encircled in stars!

In recent years, schools have been consolidated and farmers have moved their families into town to live. The men travel out to their fields from there. The workhorses are gone; everything is mechanized. The farmer's children drink canned milk from the stores.

It is people like Dad, left on the farms, who consider twice before digging a new, deep and expensive well.

The air everywhere around there smells polluted. The farmer still burns his coal to keep warm and light his lamps. It is hard to understand.

Back when Dad and Uncle Nelson were homesteading, if he had the money a new farmer could buy any surrounding land he wanted. For most of them this took many years. In the meantime, any ¼ section the individual needed could be rented for a small amount from the Government. I always wondered why they didn't live closer to one another, but I hadn't taken into account their need to expand.

The country consisted of endless waves of grass over slightly rolling hills and small plateaus, dotted here and there with sloughs. From the air, a person saw a surprising number of these small ponds. Buffalo trails were also still to be seen.

The very first settlers' dwellings were sod huts. They were made from oblong chunks of sod, stacked up the way bricks are laid. They don't sound practical. In the East, the dampness would quickly destroy them. Out there, where the rains were sparse and the sunshine frequent, they lasted a long time.

There was a sod hut still standing on our land when I was young. I never liked it. It was our tool shed then. Dad had put a thick wooden plank shelf along one wall. On this he piled his hammers, wrenches and other tools. The dirt floor was worn to a hollow in the center and in spring was full of water. A nasty place to slip and fall, to become a muddy mess. There was not enough light to see well. One small open doorway and a bit of a square without glass, as a window, faced northeast so early morning light was possible.

I was sent out there once to get a chisel or some tool. I first asked what tool he wanted, to which he said, "Oh go and get it," loudly. Perhaps he was impatient, but he called it "being in a hurry." I didn't know what tool he wanted, but rather than stand and take his wrath, I went back. I'd hoped to recognize it, even in the dark interior of the hut.

I didn't! This held him up, so I was hit for returning empty-handed. We learned to keep out of arm's reach.

Giants in the Earth is a graphic book. It tells the story of pioneer struggles very much like ours. My mother, in particular, lived through great difficulties in those early times. Dad never lived in that sod hut. It had been built by someone before him.

This is as good a place as any to retell Uncle Nelson's stories about his first years. He often told about his adventures with his younger brother (Dad), whom he called W.A.

There were nine children in my grandparents' family. Because the older brothers bought the home farm in Ontario, and all the adjoining acres, Uncle Nelson felt there was no chance for him. He went to visit an aunt farther north in Ontario where he learned to saw logs. While logging, it occurred to Nelson that he might try gold and silver hunting in Gowganda, still farther north. He'd heard the men talk about it.

While there he also heard about fishing and gave it one try. It was too early in the season and he caught nothing, so no fishing for him after that. Being brought up to work, this probably seemed like foolishness. It would have seemed so to Dad. Waiting for a fish to bite would be a waste of time.

In the meantime, he went back to visit his aunt and happened to talk to an elderly neighbor who asked, "Why not go out West and get a homestead?" He decided to take the challenge, at least to go out and look. His mother had ten brothers and sisters, and one of their children, a cousin, had gone to live in sight of the Rockies. This foothills land was better and more settled than the wide stretch of prairies farther east.

He went there, stayed with the cousin and got a job with a neighbor cutting hay for the summer. The neighbor had a young nephew coming west in the spring. "Why not come out then and help him move his settlers' effects?" said this neighbor. Nelson went home for the winter.

Little did he guess this fellow would turn out to be a scoundrel! Uncle helped him move to land in Canada that he'd chosen blind.

Uncle looked around for a piece for himself and found one. It was ten miles from the future town of Oyen, Alberta, in far Northwest

Canada. The railway had come as far as Alberta's border, a distance of sixty miles from Nelson's ground, but the roadbed was planned further. He spent his first night in someone's tent at the edge of an alkali slough near what became the very little town of Benton.

Then came one of Uncle's favorite stories. Next day he set out walking to look for a place to stay. Tramping on the prairie, he met a man with a team of horses. Figuring he might have a place, Uncle asked him if he could accommodate him. The man hurriedly drove on. Next he discovered a sod house where the owner, Mr. Falls, took him in. After several weeks, a visitor came and was telling Mr. Falls about meeting a hobo who wanted to stay with him. "Yes, I know all about that," piped up Nelson, having been the hobo. In Uncle's words, "The man felt cheap from embarrassment."

By June, Nelson had a team and wagon and was staying on his own homestead. He slept in the wagon box with a door over the top. He awoke as late as June third to find the ground covered with snow. It was freezing cold. One of the four precious horses belonging to his host of the sod hut, died of the cold. Probably the animal was half-starved.

He soon borrowed a team of oxen and a sulky plow, with one share, to get a little sod breaking done. The plow was weighed down with stones until heavy enough to cut the sod. Oxen were able to live on the tall grass and do without the heavier feed of oats that the horses needed. They cut the horns off these beasts of burden and the blood spurted out. It's a funny thing, but people who live a hard life seem to take much interest in gory things. Perhaps it's the only change from the ordinary.

What neighbors he found, near or far, helped each other and shared whatever they had. He'd been able to borrow the oxen because of helping the owner pick rocks off his place. He said, "There were no trees far or near, only some stones to bother." He had help another time because he'd given the man some tobacco.

The year was 1909. For the next couple of summers he lived on his land and, when winter came, moved farther west to earn money. He worked in lumber camps large (one having over 100 men) and small, cutting trees and hauling them with horses and often oxen. They were cut into ties for the future railway.

The railroad bed made good traveling for as far as it went. He acquired a bicycle and rode this from his land to the Saskatchewan town of Kindersley, sixty miles east, for food. Teams with loads of lumber used it too. Sometimes the trip was too long to make it all in one day. He'd stop to spend the night at a partly built shack of lumber where he'd be sure to meet a few kindred souls doing the same thing. It was too cold to sleep much, but at least the shack kept the wind off. While staying in town, they managed to sleep in someone's stable loft. Whoever went to town brought back mail for everybody they knew and enough grub for themselves to last a long while.

The settlers took time off, regardless, to help one another. And here Uncle told another tale. Mr. Falls, whose guest he'd been at the sod hut, wanted a load of settlers' effects from town. He would send his own team and wagon. Uncle offered to do the job. When it began to get dark, he stopped at someone's place. The gentleman said, "Never mind hobbling the horses," so they were unhitched and let loose to feed. When morning came, they were nowhere in sight. Uncle walked to track them down and found they'd gone back home!

Next day Mr. Falls set out to pick up his wagon. It was gone. He heard a few days later another man had borrowed it to haul a load of lumber. The man had put on a big load and fallen off, being drunk. He had managed to crawl back up on the wagon again, and again fell off. He didn't fare so well the second time. Someone else came along and found him and took him to the hospital where he was expected to die.

Unusual things had to be ordered from the East. The men out West were not the sort to waste any time. Logically, with a man in such bad shape, they sent for a coffin! But the drunk fellow gradually got better, and was asked to pay for the coffin. Says he, "I will not. I'm not dead," and he lived for many years.

The wagon went far afield and took some time before it was claimed by the rightful owner.

There was little trouble getting lost on the prairie in the daytime, even if there were no roads. You only had to find the direction you wanted to go and follow a trail of some sort.

Uncle Nelson put up a lumber shack, 10x12 feet, boasting one window and a door. The roof was made of "car boards" and covered with tar paper. He successfully dug a well and became the principal well digger in the area.

In 1910, Dad finished two years of Agricultural College at Guelph, Ontario, and decided to join his brother on his homestead. The steel was being laid for the railway and places had been spotted along it for stations. Dad arrived at the nearest city, more than two hundred miles away, where Nelson met him with his team and wagon. Dad apparently bought himself two small horses. With Uncle's two heavy horses hitched to the wagon and Dad's lighter ones in the lead, they loaded up Dad's little worldly goods and headed home. They reached the Red Deer River, forty miles from their destination, and stopped to eat some food before crossing on the ferry. By the riverbank they found a good hatchet somebody had overlooked.

They had picked a trail to follow, and by the time evening came they stopped at a homesteader's. He had a house and barn of sorts and was a horse trader. Right away he tried to talk Dad into trading one of his newly acquired horses. Dad became interested because one of them had turned out to be no prize. Nelson maintained the animal must have foundered at one time because it was rather stiff on its feet and walked on its front toes.

The next morning the trader was again after Dad to trade. He had a horse for him that would pull right up. By this time Dad was quite persuaded, but asked his brother's advice. Nelson would only say, "It's up to you."

Dad traded.

The new horse was smaller and skinnier than the one Dad owned before, but he did pull right up for the first mile after they left. After that, he gradually slowed down, until he got so bad, they had to unhitch him. "Now what shall I do?" asked Dad. "Well," said Nelson, "When I was back East, an uncle once told me it was lawful to trade horses back again, if no money has been exchanged. This must be done within twenty-four hours."

Dad stayed with his new horse until dark, while Nelson went on to their home with the other three. When night arrived, Dad went back to the horse trader's farm. Keeping carefully out of sight, he exchanged horses. Next day W.A. arrived home with his proper horse. "He was tickled," to quote Uncle. This should have been a hard lesson in looking out for himself. In spite of it, Dad was always too trusting of people he did business with.

Here is a typical example of what faced them when they were getting settled:

They needed a load of coal, so the two of them set out with the team and wagon. Goodness knows how far they went, as there was no coal nearby, nor within dozens of miles. The coal they got was light in color, being very near the surface, with only a couple of feet of earth on top of it. It was not very expensive.

On the way home with the wagon loaded with coal, it got stuck on a stretch of mucky land and they had to unload everything, pull all the gear out and separate the wagon. Piece by piece they carried everything across the wet land and then reassembled it before they could go on.

Dad told us how the grass grew so tall that it was hard to believe. Paths made by the buffalo, and perhaps by the Indians, could still be seen, running for miles. The packed dry trails last for many years in a land where there is so little rain. Beside them, bleached snowy white, were the bones of dead buffalo. I even remember seeing buffalo skulls when I was very young.

 Sometimes on the prairie, we would find a slough that was perfectly round. It would be quite small, with an unusually large stone in the middle. In fact, that was where we found the biggest rocks. There weren't many of these. We had two on our property, and I knew of only one other near home.

These were known as buffalo wallows. It was said that they were caused by the animals rubbing round and round the stone to remove itchy winter fur, and to chase off the flies in the summer. In time the wallows became steep-sided and deep. In our time, of course, no buffalo were left as they had been hunted to near extinction. Now the buffalo live on reserves farther west.

These old buffalo wallows had a special fascination for us growing up. They were treacherous after the spring thaws because of their steep sides. We were told to be careful around them. Mom said, "Stay away!" Usually we investigated all the other sloughs as soon as they filled with bright-blue water. We didn't pay much attention to the wallows. Sometimes we gazed at our own reflections in their depths, but they weren't very interesting. Rarely was there any life in them, and no plants grew on their edges. They held the deepest water anywhere and if a person slipped, into the water he went! Mom worried about this happening while there was still ice on them. The tall stone stuck above the water level. When a thaw came the ice melted around the stone, as well as at the edge, leaving a big doughnut of ice. Cows had to be kept away from the wallows since they too might fall in. Luckily they were the first water to dry up, which they did quickly, because they were on the highest ground.

Farmers gradually filled them with pieces of old farm machinery and weed seeds, if they had no pigs to feed the seeds to. Dead animals were dumped into them. One of our horses died and Dad dumped the carcass in our wallow. It was the first time any of us had seen how nature takes care of dead bodies. Worms! Ugh! Such a horrid sight! We were fascinated by them, and at the same time repulsed. We went back several times for a quick look. What interested us most was how quickly the animal disappeared, all but the hooves and fur. The ants came next and buried even these.

Many animals lived in the grassy wilderness. Coyotes traveled in packs and howled at the moon at night. Big fat badgers lived in deep dugouts, their holes treacherous to men on horseback. Gophers enjoyed their freedom. There were porcupines back then. Dad had a beautiful, round birchbark box, white on the inside and brown on the outside, made by the Indians. The outside was decorated with porcupine quills. All through the years Dad used this box to keep his two white celluloid collars and the little studs to fasten them onto his shirts. A string knit tie kept them company.

Most of all there were jackrabbits, great big fellows, who turned pure white in winter except for a small black tip on their ears. They throve in numbers and were killed for food. The weasel was another little furry animal that turned white in winter, leaving only the black tip on his tail. Both animals were so snowy white you could stumble over them before seeing them at all on the clean, abundant snow. Rabbits often hunched down in the snow. They waited until you were very near, hoping to be overlooked.

Weasels are most interesting animals because they are so curious. When we chased them in the summertime, they ran down gopher holes. They popped back up again before we had time to turn around, almost under our feet. We were too afraid to catch them. It wasn't easy anyway. Their winter fur is known as ermine and it brought a good price.

The weasel's summer coat is a creamy tan with yellow underneath. Farmers despised them because they were death to chickens. They killed wantonly! They attacked one chicken's neck, sucked some blood and went on to the next. Chickens are most drowsy at night, but when a weasel gets into the henhouse, they set up a noisy clamor and flap about. More than once Dad ran out in the night to find that a weasel had killed several hens.

There were brightly colored, striped garter snakes. Rattlers lived further south.

The most abundant birds were the ducks. Many more flew over than stayed. I remember clouds of them in the spring and fall. Dad kept his shotgun ready and, by running out the door and firing up into the flock, often brought down a couple for supper. That is the truth! Big Canadian Geese also winged overhead, but too high to shoot and they didn't land. Grouse and prairie chicken were good eating, but few of them survive today.

There were colorful little birds: Meadow Larks, Horned Larks, Red-winged Blackbirds and Bobolinks, all with pretty songs. One bird's song could be heard a great distance in the long, still twilight of summer, and so it is today. There aren't many small birds, due probably to the lack of trees. Brightly-colored flowers blossomed with delightful fragrances, stronger in scent than flowers in damp climates. The wild pink rose is a fine example, so beautiful compared with the small white ones that grow in the East.

Dad batched with his brother a couple of years and I guess worked on his own land. He built the same sort of square wooden building with rough 2x4s showing inside as all the second wave settlers did. They lived in these until they'd made enough money to build something better. Shelves across the corners were the only furniture. Curtains across these were added, if and when.

I don't remember living in ours, but my mother tells a tale of missing me once, only to find I'd climbed onto a bottom shelf behind the one curtain. I was busy licking my fingers and very much enjoying an upset pail of Roger's Golden Syrup. I was sitting in it and trickles were quietly oozing down the walls.

That syrup was the one sweet thing in the house when I was very young. It makes me think of Dad. He loved fresh buttermilk pancakes made right after churning, even if this was in the middle of the afternoon. The syrup was a must for the rest of us or we'd not care about the pancakes. Not so Dad. He rolled them up and ate them with his fingers, not bothering with the sweet. The small pails of syrup had handles and were saved to keep things in. When I started school, a shiny new one was my lunch bucket.

Every little thing was used till it wore out. Each piece of string, paper bag or scrap of cloth was saved and used. The parents often quoted, "Willful waste leads to woeful want." Today I marvel at all the waste in our everyday lives and remember those times.

Those first wooden shacks were so inadequate that I wonder how the people ever kept warm. Very few of the men were good carpenters. One boy came to school with a funny story about his father's attempts at building. It seemed that, when he'd finished his house, he could find no place to keep dry when it rained except under the kitchen table.

Some old bachelors bought tar paper and tacked it all over the outside. Lath strips were nailed on at random to keep the wind from blowing it off. Their shacks were low and squat compared with the family man's. The two bachelors we knew settled down in them to live out their lives. One was Mr. Fox, who

lived way down the road, south of us. His name was all we knew about him and he was never seen in town. His name suggested someone hiding out. There were no farm implements around his house, and we wondered what he did. I wanted to see the inside of his little place. It looked cozy with its low roof and tiny stovepipe, always smoking, when we went by.

I remember our shack standing next to the pump, with the shelves still in the corners. It was called several things:

1. The toolshed
2. The harness shop
3. The pump house
4. The chophouse

There was never any confusion as to what place Dad meant; he used the name that went with the thing he wanted! The "big bench," as Dad called the shelf, was the first thing moved into the shack, from the sod hut.

When money became available Dad bought a huge, funneled, noisy grinder. This ground the mixed grains for the pigs. Best of all, it ground wheat for our breakfast porridge. With an added attachment he could grind wheat into flour for bread. He came in after this chore a laughable sight. From the top of his straw hat to the toes of his shoes he was dusted white. The only color showing was his red mouth when he talked and his eyes, showing bright under the white-lashed lids. Mom shook and shook his dusty clothes outside and then needed to shake herself. Dad still used the flour grinder long after a flour mill had been built in the town and people could buy their flour at a store.

Dad put up a partition to separate the chophouse part from the rest of the shack. Next he added another noisy piece of equipment, a gasoline engine. Dad had long planned for this, to try pumping water at busy times. He dreamed up quite an affair to make it work. The gasoline engine was bolted to the floor next to the pump end of the building. A hole was cut through the wall for the belt to go from the engine to the pump.

When he was through, a little ladder was attached to the pump handle, with gears and wheels at the bottom. When the engine ran, the ladder appeared to be jumping up and down all by itself.

It was wonderful and saved all those backbreaking hours of watering the many horses. In winter and for ourselves, we pumped by hand. Mom and we kids would give the engine a hopeful try on a wash day. It had a big fly wheel. On the rim of the wheel was a small steel handle that flattened back into a groove when it started running. Not much leverage there! Then there was all the priming: "It must be empty. Where is the gas tin?" and so on. Chances were, it wouldn't start. Turning the wheel was heavy work. We kept at it until tired out, then gave up and pumped by hand. The one time the pump started easily was after Dad had just used it and it was still warmed up.

So this first wooden shack of ours had a long and useful life. Most first houses were used for granaries when that long-cherished bigger house, that was to be home, was built.

More people came west, and soon all the land was owned by someone. It took a large tract of land to raise a family because of the low yield per acre. The black soil was rich and deep, often 2 feet, but semi-arid with so little rain.

We asked Dad why he couldn't have gone farther west. There was more rain there, so the crops grew heavier. Best of all it was near the Rockies. The sight of them at all seasons would be a joy. "That land was taken first and cost much more," he said.

It is interesting to note that, since that dreadful Dust Bowl era in our section, the Government stepped back in to own land. As farms were abandoned here and there, it took possession of them. This was done to avoid over-cultivating the land. The new methods of strip farming and crop rotation helped. The Government called these Special Areas and they were desolate, uninhabited places.

A few places can be rented if regulations are carefully followed. Grazing land can be rented, with so many cows per square mile. In some instances, a farmer may rent a piece to cultivate next to his farm. A certain percentage of the yield is paid to the government.

WATER

Settlers could get water from a slough for the animals, but needed a well for themselves.

Uncle Nelson became so expert at well digging that he helped many neighbors. This way he earned some extra money on the side. He undertook the task of digging our well, sending up buckets full of dirt for Dad to empty. Looking down the well afterward we wondered how he could have dug so deep and in such a narrow space. Every eight feet he stopped to case it in with boards, called cribbing. Around the perimeter was built a narrow ledge used as a toehold. These should have been wider and every five feet to be convenient for climbing down. Probably the boards came in 8-foot lengths.

Dad located the place to dig our well by bringing in a man to witch for water. He still believes in witching. Our well was only 45-feet deep so perhaps it works!

The water looked mighty far down, especially when Dad had to go down for repairs. He disappeared from sight in the gloom below while we stood watching. We had to stand watch, in case anything was needed or something happened. If an extra tool was needed we let it down on a rope. If something happened we were to report to Mom. Climbing down the thing was an undertaking, and coming up was even worse. Loose planks covered the top. Dad once called up that the cribbing was caving in, and another time that he felt faint. We didn't know what to do. I'm sure he very much disliked going down in the first place. No wonder Mom stayed inside the house, where she couldn't see and wear herself out with worry.

Any food that was to be kept during the summer was hung down the well. It was such a chore to manage that it was seldom done.

Invariably it was a piece of meat, hung there for two reasons: one was to keep it cool and the other was to keep it out of the reach of flies. This problem was the chief reason we lived on eggs and chicken in summer.

Flies were battled fiercely. There never seemed to be so many around the barn but, regardless of screens, they plagued the house. Long sticky ribbons of flypaper hung from the ceiling and flat squares were used on the table. Out came the flit gun when they became impossible. The house was filled with fumes and we sat outside a spell. Then back inside to sweep the whole house clean of dead flies.

The worst part of the pump was its behavior in the winter. It often froze up. Buckets of snow were collected and put on the stove to heat. The hot water was carried out to pour over the spout and thaw out the ice. The trough in front of the pump also had an ice problem. This had to be chopped out so the animals could have a small area as a drinking basin.

In summer the trough must be kept full of water so's it wouldn't dry out and leak. Cows might come home any old time for a drink of water. If they found no water, there'd be less milk.

After Dad had a pump engine, he thought, "Why not build another trough to relieve the congestion?" He also wanted to use both troughs, he told us later, to freeze ice in winter. After chopping it, he would store it in a shed, heavily covered with straw, for use in the summer. Then the drink of water we carried to the fields could be nice and cool!

The ice quickly melted when summer came.

Instead of a trough, he installed a large galvanized barrel, five or six feet across and sunk in the ground. When filled with water it looked bottomless. A horse soon backed into it and died within minutes. Dad said this happened because of the horse's cramped position. Mom was very upset. She loved all animals. Next, Leslie, the oldest boy, all the more treasured after four girls, fell into it and by chance was discovered before he drowned! He was very young, but none of us knew the first thing about swimming.

That was the end of that bright idea! The barrel was dug up and stood at the side of the house. When Dad butchered, the squares of meat were dumped into it to stay frozen all winter. An ax was used to chop out a piece as needed. There were no such things as steaks and

roasts, just meat! Too bad they didn't try the same deep freeze for vegetables.

Many farmers built tall wooden windmills, for which there was plenty of wind. I wonder why Dad didn't. They looked so comfortable, quietly whirring away, and they added something to the bare landscape. Dad probably felt it was one more thing to fuss with and he didn't care for climbing any height above a few feet.

BARNS

After the people had a dwelling, the animals must have one. It's a wonder it wasn't the other way around. Everyone we knew spent more money on their barns than on their houses. Successful farmers were very proud of their large barns.

This is easy to understand because animals were so important on the farm. Without them people couldn't exist. The first beasts of burden for early settlers were oxen. Uncle Nelson plowed his first fields with them. They were easier to feed than horses because they could live off the grass. When told about them, it seemed hard to believe. None were left when I grew up and new settlers were still arriving. One reason could be their slowness, when such big areas had to be cultivated to make a living. Horses were then bought to replace them as soon as possible. The more horses to work the land, the bigger the farm could be. A cow was next.

Cows were important for food. As the family grew so did the number of cattle. No one had very many, just enough for meat and milk. This meat was a major source of food, together with eggs and chickens. We also depended on potatoes, which everyone grew in abundance. Then, too, nothing took the place of wheat and its flour.

Dad's first barn was made of two layers of wire with wheat straw between. The corner posts were of wood. The open doorway faced south. The roof was made the same way as the walls and had a tendency to sag. Straw was piled high on top, out of reach, for bedding and feeding. In the center was a hole to push it down. A wire ladder next to the open doorway was a means to the roof.

When the Raleigh man came one day I was asked to feed his horse. I was in a big hurry to get back to the house for fear of missing something. I fell down this hole with the first armful of straw and had my wind knocked out.

Another time, Dad built an implement shed adjoining the barn in the same fashion. It was the only time we ever had such a shed, and it didn't last long. It was good-sized and all the front was open, so the machinery rusted anyway. After it was first done, we kids got the dickens for climbing up the fence walls, which bent easily. Our sport was in running around on the roof as long as possible without going through the straw. Feet and legs going through were not a comfortable outcome, I may add. Besides, it was sometimes hard to get out. Once, small brother Leslie, who insisted on following, fell all the way through and hurt himself on an implement below. When the snow drifted onto the implements, Dad discovered the holes we had made.

There's one thing about this implement shed I like to remember. It happened the winter it was new, and it was glorious fun. We couldn't imagine what Dad was doing. He went to a lot of trouble, but, at first, we didn't understand.

On the front corner of the shed roof, next to the barn ladder, he built a small platform. From the ground up to this, he piled straw in a long slope. Next he unrolled a length of fence down this slope. He used the same sort of wire as the building was made of that came in squares. This was carefully covered with snow, which was plentiful. Next he carried buckets of water from the well, to pour over this as he tramped it down. On the final layer, we also helped by tramping up and down behind him to pack it solid. It was left to freeze overnight. We still didn't know what it was for!

Next day, a last thin layer of snow and water were added. Then Dad took a sled he'd made up to the top. Carefully he centered it and after a number of attempts made runner grooves down the slope from top to bottom. "Now don't go near it until it is frozen," he said next. After it froze, he was the first one down. He called it a toboggan slide! There were a number of nearly bad accidents because the sides dropped off into nowhere, and it took constant repairing.

When we started down, we felt on top of the world and the ride went such a long way after reaching ground level. Staying in the grooves, till at least half way down where the height seemed a bit safer, kept every ride exciting. For the first time, we even donned all our warm togs to go play in the moonlight and the bright starry nights until Mom called, "Come in to bed." We enjoyed it so much that we wore it completely out.

One warm day, Dad was told that a neighbor, seven miles west of us, was pulling out. This neighbor had built a big hip-roofed barn not long before. Dad went to talk with him and came back poorer, but he was the proud possessor of the barn. All he had to do was get it home! He thought about how for a long time and so did the neighbors. Much advice was given and some people volunteered their help. After harvest, the group went over to look at it and held lively hashes as to how to go about the task. They jacked it up bit by bit, first one corner and then another, and decided to wait for the first snowfall. In the meantime, men told Dad how it should be braced inside, or it would be pulled to pieces during the move. Dad said he couldn't see taking all that time and bother, so he didn't.

The first snow luckily was only inches deep and the wind packed it firm. Men set to work pushing and pulling a pair of sleigh runners off their big box sleds to replace the blocks under each corner of the barn.

On each of the two front corners, they hitched four horses. Looking at the size of the barn, this seemed impossibly inadequate. It was a hard pull for so few horses. They worked especially hard to pull up the hills. More horses weren't used because of the difficulty managing them. The success of the mission depended on the horses reacting promptly to orders. Dad drove four of the horses and someone else the other four. Several other sleds of men had come to watch and we older children rode in one of the sleds. The most anxious moment was at the start. No one was sure the horses could manage it. The two men driving the horses walked, keeping track of each other, stopping and starting at the same time, to give the horses a rest and going at the same speed. The barn creaked woefully at times.

They'd carefully studied the safest route home, and a chosen sled led the way. Barbed wire fences were cut and fence posts moved, but they almost forgot the telephone wire. They were upon it before someone hollered to stop. Some men surrounded the barn and walked along as it moved, shouting out any danger signals. With this community effort, it arrived safely at the chosen spot – safe, and almost sound. There were only a few minor repairs to be done.

It dwarfed our house.

I felt it should have been put north of the house, instead of south. To the south had been the furthest sweeping view, and now the barn blocked it. When Dad came around to this point of view, some years later and long after I'd gone, he moved the house!

Now that the barn was ours, nothing would do but to give it a nice bright coat of red paint with white trim. The house, of course, continued to stand neglected and gray. No use wasting paint on a house! When done, the barn did look beautiful and bright in all that drab expanse. All it needed now was to have the big haymow filled with straw.

That was the next job before the snow got deep. We were to go along, always, as a minor help and we never objected. The large hayracks were like a large wooden floor on wheels, with a board fence all around. Up in front was a small ladder used to climb in. While riding over the bumpy field we ran around or tried to stand still in the middle without holding on. First one to fall down was out.

The tall, fat strawstacks were such fun. We climbed all over them and slid down the steepest sides when feeling brave. Dad was busy loading the hayrack with a pitchfork. If a stack was a new one, we were restricted to very little climbing and never allowed to explore alone. They could be dangerous.

After aging and weathering, the straw in the stack became packed and safe, all except the crevices between the ridges, some of which never became safe. A good strawstack, in our opinion, had no crevices. When the straw was fresh and soft, a person could disappear into a crevice and be smothered in a hurry. Another hazard came about when starting down on a slide and having the straw roll along too, piling up. Suddenly we would find ourselves on the edge of a precipice about to fall over.

When the hayrack was being filled, Dad jumped on it here and there to pack down the straw. When he had finished his loading, he welcomed us aboard to do some good as weights. The straw ballooned far out and high above the hay wagon. It was scary on top. We felt way up in the air and stayed very much in the middle, most often flat on our backs in the nest of straw.

The creaking wagon wheels were muffled far below, and their bouncing over the ridges became a gentle roll way up there. Dad climbed up the narrow ladder in front, turned around and sat back into the straw, straddling the ladder where the reins had been wrapped. He was far below us and out of our sight. Anxiety kept us from enjoying the ride back if the load was big. This, of course, it usually was! I was very much afraid of falling off, over the edge, when we jounced on a bump.

The straw was very wobbly because it reached so far beyond the wheels. When Dad jumped on our side, the other side bounced up a good distance. I had a recurring nightmare about a fat lady neighbor. I daydreamed that she jumped on the full wagon and bounced us off into space!

When we got home we were entranced watching the slings that first year. They were used to unload the hay from the wagon, up into the gaping hole in the front of the barn.

Slowly the big bundle climbed, higher and higher, until it hit something that sent it swinging into the mow and out of sight. A trip rope released it to fall into a soft pile in the middle of the loft.

PEOPLE

In that country, most of the older people became rugged individualists. They had to be tenacious to stick it out against the problems of settling a new part of the country. Inconveniences of all sorts were endured. We could tell, even as children, that if someone soft moved in, he'd never make a go of it. Most of these people had little formal education, although a majority of our neighbors spoke English, at least. In general, they were a jolly, lively group when they got together. They could laugh at the time one had lost three fingers in a piece of machinery, or had fallen off of a runaway, only to limp from then on. There were so many that were maimed.

Runaways were the worst thing to see. There were many stories about them. The first one I remember happened when Dad was taking a boulder on the stone boat to the coulees. There was no gate in the fence he had to cross to reach the road. Instead he lifted three or four fence posts out of their holes and laid them flat on the ground, barbed wire and all. If and when we were available, we stood on either side of this makeshift gate to hold the wire down. When he was alone, Dad held it down with rocks. We stood, all set to run in case of trouble. Dad drove the horses over it.

On this one occasion, a horse stepped on a wire barb and jumped forward. The other horse balked and looked frightened, so we knew there'd be trouble. Soon the stone boat was caught in the fence and we ran, but Dad held on to the reins, we thought, far too long. The horses seesawed and then ran; the stone rolled off. Barbed wire squealed from the posts, snapped and curled in menacing lashes. More posts went down before it was over. We were lucky no one was hurt. The horses had a few minor cuts. When finally free, they ran down the side of the hill and stopped, still trembling and looking very nervous. Was Dad going to whip them?

Horses most often run only a short distance after an accident. I wondered if they had a feeling they'd done wrong. Dad often punished his horses, but on an occasion like this, he quieted them by talking more gently than usual and patting them. Then he coaxed them to get back over the fence at once. Dad never made pets of his horses, nor of any other creature. He cared more for their respect, and they knew to follow his orders promptly. He felt that pets slowed down the work or would get in his way. The cats even knew this and kept out of the reach of his boots.

Another time Dad went to work in a field south of the house, close enough so we could see him. When he worked a good distance away, he'd hook the wagon on behind the plow. At dinner time, or nighttime, he'd have the wagon to come home in, until the field was finished.

This evening, we saw him coming home with many horses abreast, the two middle ones being hitched to the wagon. He had to cross the south pasture, which contained a valley with a partially dried up slough at the bottom. He was on the further hillside when the horses started running. We could see him lean way back, pulling on the reins. Suddenly the horses with the reins jumped forward to keep up to the others, and Dad flew out of the wagon, in an arc, landing on top of them!

He was there only a minute and then disappeared down among their galloping hooves. He ended up on the ground with the wagon roaring over him, and was not even touched by a wheel or anything else. Watching it happen took so long before we saw Dad, who was lying prone, move and then sit up. The horses were out of our sight, standing by the slough. We ran down the lane and toward him. Dad was banged up a bit and some harness broken, but nothing major. As I recall, it was the flattened fence at the end of a field that touched off that runaway too.

People were hurt by kicking horses, gored by bulls, and hurt by falling from various buildings. Farm machinery was a constant hazard. Much later, there was a good Scotch doctor. He came out there, and stuck it out. He told us he had a dreadful time with his patients. No one called him unless they had an emergency on their hands. These emergency patients were already beyond help! The poor doctor was blamed when they died. One doctor covered a wide area. He lived a lonely life.

The busiest person was the midwife. One could be found not too far away. They were comfortable, capable women, usually from the Old Country.

I've thought much about these people, and often felt sorry for them. I learned that we can't judge them by our standards. Very few would even listen to new ideas and ways of living. Education, as such, was fairly scorned. They made an exception of the schoolteacher. Her training consisted of eighteen months of Normal School after 8th grade. Knowing her spelling and addition was good. Why did anyone need to know any more than that?

Women, at first, were scarce. Men went West alone to search out and settle the land. The married ones then went back East to fetch their women. As soon as there were a few women out West, others didn't hesitate to come.

The first social event I knew about was called a "Shivaree." I believe it was held for a young couple and was the equivalent of what we call a "shower" today. Anyway, they were often put on for a couple who had just moved into the district. Everyone from near and far would come. They collected after dark and encircled the dwelling. With dishpans, pots and ladles, anything to bang together and make lots of noise, they converged on the house and surprised the newcomers. They brought food too, and settled down to a get-acquainted evening. As many things as needed or could be spared were left behind to help the newcomers. Such things as a calf or a few chickens might be promised as a donation.

As soon as there were enough people in the group, they got together to barn dance. This was the "piece de resistance" of social life. All that was needed was a fiddler for music and someone to call. The repertoire wasn't large but it was lively. "Turkey in the Straw" got the biggest workout.

At first these dances were held in houses. A new barn was good, perhaps a little chilly, but any place big enough would do. The floor in some houses wasn't strong enough to take the downbeat. They danced with all their might! When they swung down at the same moment on "All the Men West," the floor behaved like rubber. When they swung their partners, they picked them right up. Such squeals from the girls when their feet left the floor! It was safer in a foursome, like "Sally in the Sugar Bowl," with hands held tight and arms up and over each other's necks for the swinging part.

Young people were very bashful with one another, but, when caught up in the spirit of these dances, who would notice? It was a meeting place. More than one romance blossomed after a dance. There were many more men than women so the gals were tagged first by one fellow and then another and were sure to dance all evening.

The young men awaited the coming of each new schoolmarm and kidded one another. One was sure to end up being sweet on her. They were wonderful prospective wives, if they could be persuaded.

The entire family went to these dances. Babies were put to sleep in baskets under benches. Young ones played around the edges of the room. They were often chased out of the way of the dancers, and away from the food, until they fell asleep, perhaps on a pile of coats. Everyone danced with everyone else, down to the youngest who knew how.

When schools were built, dances were always held in them. One of the first I remember well was held at our school, lighted by lanterns hung from the ceiling because there was no other place to put lamps. Dad didn't like us kids to mix, but he loved to dance, so we went and he forgot us. When a dance was held in some other school district, there was quite a trip ahead. Glenada was one, sometimes Fair Acres, but that was far away. Dances were held only in winter.

The long box sleds were half filled with straw, bunched up on the sides. The family piled in, facing each other, with the large Buffalo robe over their laps. Blankets were of little use as a wind break, so no one bothered with them.

There was scrambling and slapping as to who was going to be next to Dad. He stood at the front, in his long-haired black bearskin coat. The place next to him provided the most protection from the wind. "Who's got all the robe?" It was never big enough, so no one wanted to sit at the end of the line and fight for a corner. "My feet are cold already," and so forth, until Dad was ready to start. As he climbed in it was, "No more racket or you'll stay home." Mom was there holding a young one but practically lost in the shuffle.

Sometimes it was snowing and Dad wondered about going. Most

often he took the chance that it wouldn't get worse. If it got bad, he relied on the horses to find their way home. Rocks and sad irons (the flat irons used for ironing) had been heated on the stove, then wrapped in paper and rags to keep our feet warm. On beautiful, clear nights the stars seemed close overhead. They shine large and bright out there with no city lights on the horizon. Perhaps the Northern Lights, so often seen in winter, would dance and play across half the sky.

The women had baked mountainous quantities of cakes and pies, besides bread for sandwiches. A sandwich might contain only butter, but the children ate it happily if it was still too early for cake. Big enamel pots of coffee were put on the stove to boil all evening. When the time came to pour the coffee, there was the inevitable discussion as to how many eggs should be broken and dropped in to settle the grounds.

Everyone turned out for miles and miles around, and often arrived back home just in time to do the morning milking.

Men worked hard, but the women were the real heroes! Men more or less accomplished their dream: a piece of land all their own, horses and machinery. The women's wants came second. An attractively decorated home was a rare accomplishment, no matter how much the overworked wife might long for it!

Women had it good in one respect: there weren't enough of them, and so all were most popular. There wasn't an old maid among them! Some men would be happy to have a home with any wife they could get. When there was a choice, they didn't worry about romance but picked one out, Naughty Marietta fashion, by feeling their muscles. At the top of any man's list was, "Is she a good cook?" What else mattered so much? In those days women were the ones who died first, leaving widowers and children. With women scarce anyway, the widower had a problem.

If there was some big calamity, such as a barn being struck by lightning, all turned out to help rebuild it.

There was once a community project that we kids thought was awful. Dad and his neighbors decided there were too many of those big jackrabbits eating the crops. They planned a rabbit drive after the first snow. This sounded safe enough, but we had no idea of what was to follow.

A three-cornered open pen of wire was built in a vacant area behind the school. Men and children formed an enormous circle and gradually closed in, while brandishing sticks and hollering. The circle ended tight across the pen, and the men then beat and flailed the frightened creatures to death. It truly was awful. Many of the little carcasses were taken home for meat.

There were no churches. Music consisted of hymns sung by a few people in their own homes. Most of the hymns I heard sounded morbid to me. In Dad's opinion, old church songs were too jolly.

In later years a couple of Holy Rollers came to our school to lecture at night. They gained a number of converts. That sect had not been heard of before, only straightforward Presbyterians, Lutherans and Catholics. Dad wouldn't let us go and see them, but one night his own curiosity got the better of him. We walked over and stood outside in the dark to listen. We could hear them singing at the top of their lungs, while stomping and clapping hands. Dad certainly disapproved. He made us throw away the pretty Bible pictures they left at school. He didn't believe in pictures based on the Bible stories.

I think he was wrong.

We throve on cowboy songs, the sadder, the more popular. Perhaps we were lamenting for ourselves.

While we were growing up, a newspaper came once a week, the *Winnipeg Free Press*, from almost a thousand miles away. At one time, Dad got *The Saturday Evening Post*, which came all the way from the Curtis Publishing Co. in Philadelphia. Dad particularly enjoyed the big political cartoon on the last page, drawn by Herbert Johnson.

Imagine my surprise when one day I came to live next door to his place outside Philadelphia. Never had I felt that famous people were alive and real!

My daughter later married Johnson's grandson.

Photographs taken in Alberta in 1958

The Road to Benton

The House

The Barn

Benton

Oyen

The Stone Boat

The Buffalo Wallow
(now filled with weed seeds)

A View of the Farm from the "Main Highway"
(the farm is the dark patch on the right)

The Slough

Reta and the old combine she helped to operate

Reta with brothers Ted and Bill in the grain elevator

# Chapter 7

US, LIKE EVERYONE ELSE

By the time all the farms were going concerns, with half-grown children, each family had a certain status. It was known who were the successful ones, who were lazy, and who had the biggest say in the district – or perhaps these were just the noisy ones!

One outstanding man who didn't actually live in our district was a lively, entertaining and darkly-handsome fellow, Mr. Hoover. He lived to the northeast and was the one who threshed everyone's wheat for miles around, including ours. His farm had the most, including an attractive layout of buildings with rows of trees planted around as windbreaks. The government gave trees to anyone who would plant them. His house, barn and outbuildings were painted and well kept. This was unusual. Most people's buildings were make-do and looked it. His wife was a hard worker too, growing a big garden and making butter to sell, besides raising big handsome sons. I met one of them once at a dance. He pulled my sash undone as he went by, and then came back and asked for a dance!

Mrs. Hoover stayed close to home, but her husband, he was a bit footloose. We'd catch the grown-ups whispering about him. He liked women.

Across the road, down a short lane from his place, was a poorly run farm with a couple who were literally colorless. Mrs. Moody was pale and helpless and had light blue, protruding eyes. She had a husband who was just like herself. Mr. Hoover seemed to fancy her; he took her to town with him and gave her things. We kids thought he was just a kind man, but older people talked. We did wonder what he saw in her. Maybe her helplessness appealed to him.

Then the Fitzpatricks came! They were newcomers from the East and moved into the Scott Douglas house, right in our yard. Things changed. Mr. Fitzpatrick, known as Fitzie, was to be Dad's hired man, when needed. His wife, Lottie, and four sons just our ages, came too. They were a lively, wonderful family.

Mr. Hoover promptly took a shine to Lottie and forgot Mrs. Moody, who very soon moved away. We could easily see that Lottie liked him too. Dad began to have trepidations about the whole setup, and rightly so. Those boys were quite worldly-wise. They added very much to our school life and to our teacher's problems. Mr. Hoover not only took Lottie to town but even took her to dances! Once she asked if I'd like to go with them. Of course I would! I didn't know any better. Then she talked of how growing girls should dress. A corset! Sounded awful.

When I went home to ask if I could go with them, I ran into a stone wall. I was restricted, as I had never been before. And just when I was getting more wide awake to everything!

Dad fired Fitzie, who was a good man. He moved his family into Benton and he and his wife both worked there. She became the Post-mistress and he found such jobs as he could, but always managed to keep busy. Many years after I left home, a sad thing happened. They went to a dance one blizzardy night. They decided to walk home, not so far away. In the morning they were found frozen to death by the side of the road. Everyone liked them and mourned the loss.

I think this was the stage in life when I found less to do and was often bored when it came to play and I hated work. There wasn't the same satisfaction as to who could outshout the other, when crossed, by calling them, "hog, pig, goat." It seemed childish. But it was still done! It bothered me more than ever when one of the kids threatened to get into my things because now I had collected a treasure or two.

As it was for most people, my family's life had become very routine and settled. Many families were at that expensive stage of growth.

They were eating more and needing more clothes, and clothes were still hard to get. The number of animals per family had become standard. Horses might be the exception. Dad, for instance, now bought two smaller gray and white horses to be kept in for winter. They traveled faster with the sleigh and were not to be used for heavy work.

Now we had plenty of big, dark gelding workhorses, around twenty. A farmer's success could be told by the number of horses owned. How we loved them, and mulled over the exact right name for each horse as it came along, like Barney, Dock, Ernie and Prince. Don't they sound just like big fellows?

There were certain names for cows too. Molly for the white one, Bessie always did for a brown, and Blackie, of course, for the black and white. Dad liked a variety of cows, and kept only those who gave the mixture of milk that he preferred. All of them were mongrels, but some of them had signs of their original breed. Molly gave the rich milk and Blackie, mostly Holstein, gave the quantity.

Life was telling on Mom, more than on Dad. She complained of bad pains, but no one paid any attention. Dad said she was a complainer, and he gave us the feeling he knew everything. Years later they found that she had a gallbladder problem. When it was corrected she became a new woman. What Doctor out there had ever heard of gallbladders?

Dad was becoming more domineering. He had to be, very often, so I suppose the habit formed and was carried into all areas of his life. He'd always been strict, but now he lost all his sense of fun. Much of his strong-mindedness was good and we all gained by it, but there were drawbacks too. As a regular thing, it created too much tension.

Dad had no patience with what he termed lazy people, whatever the reason. He worked his horses hard, just as he did himself. All summer they had terribly sore shoulders where their collars rubbed for the long days of work. He didn't take time to put salve on them, unless they were so bad he was afraid they'd be good and sick. Mom fussed at him about taking some care of the poor beasts, but the end result was always the same. She would shake her head and say, "He is a hard man."

Some of his impatience with details can be understood because he had such big brute force jobs to do. As far as I could judge, his favorite pastime was arguing. While in his work he concentrated on the big jobs, he loved to argue about the tiniest little thing. This was difficult because none of us was allowed to contradict. Mom lost every argument, no matter what!

No man can be that right! Even though she knew he had no respect for her opinion, which was often right, she would wipe her eyes, manage a cheery smile and staunchly say, "Well, anyway, he's a good provider!" To some extent this idea compensated for his harshness because she firmly held to the adage, "When poverty comes in the door, love flies out the window."

TOWNS

When the railway was finished, places were already marked for towns. They grew to look very much the same: little clusters of buildings with a tall grain elevator seen for miles. Some grew bigger than others, so had more elevators. The town's size and importance could be seen at once by the number of these. It had to do with the land being good or bad in the area, besides the success of its cultivation by more industrious citizens.

Benton was a very typical small town. The land to the east of town was poor. Besides the inevitable elevator, there was the post office and "canned" grocery store, plus dwellings for their inhabitants. Mr. Landon lived above his grocery store.

This was the sort of store pictured in Wild West movies. In the middle of the room stood a stove, its pipe held up with wires fastened to the ceiling. It was a delightful place to gather round and listen. Men sat on chairs, leaning back precariously, or with shoes off and feet up to warm at the piping hot fire. They boisterously swapped tales and talked of the future. There were other times when the storekeeper became disquieted as to where an argument might lead. When the women came in, they clustered by the counter to talk to each other or to the storekeeper's wife, as well as to look over the shelves.

One passenger train went west through town at 2:00 a.m. and

another went east at 3:00 a.m. Needless to say, few people traveled on them or even saw them.

Benton was our town. Most of our business was done there. Oyen, to the west and south, was farther away from home. It was a town that went on growing. It was the one we usually considered for a Saturday night outing. Oyen boasted a wooden sidewalk, along with a row of stores, all with tall, square false fronts. There was the small dark drugstore with kindly Mr. Morrison. There was the hardware store, and the Picture House with its silent movies. By listening to the tempo of the piano music, we could tell whether there was excitement or romance in the movie.

The general store was the biggest building and was the most likely place to meet people. If there was nothing else to do, we could watch Mr. Miller tying up packages in brown paper. Paper bags were a rarity. On the end of the counter was a heavy roll of brown paper, supported by black iron legs. Always handy beside it stood a large white cone of string. The string went from the cone clear up to the high board ceiling, through a couple of loops, and then down within arm's reach of the counter. There it hung, handy to catch hold of for tying. After Mr. Miller finished tying a package, he wrapped the string around his fingers a couple of times and snapped it off with a flourish.

Once in a long while, a Canadian North-West Mounted Policeman stopped in Oyen. His horse was beautiful and so was he, all the way from the pinched crown of his tan felt hat to his shining black boots. With his gold buttoned scarlet coat and the yellow stripe down his navy trousers, he was a sight to behold. He stood very straight and rode tall in his saddle. Their reputations were the highest and it was said they "always got their man." It made one proud to be a Canadian.

They'd do for anyone's hero.

The only other thing of note about Oyen was a fascinating mound south of town. Some said it was an Indian burial ground. We begged Dad to see it because it looked so much taller than the ground around it. Climbing to the top would be great sport. And what if we found an arrowhead?

But Dad had a most prosaic outlook. To quote him directly, "I'm not interested one iota." He liked the word "iota," and used it when he got mad!

When snow time came people picked up a section of barbed wire fence and laid the posts on the ground. When the snow was deep, this made a short cut to town. Instead of following roads, we cut across fields and pastures. The drifted snow in the ravines was deep and must be firm enough to hold the horses. There were hazards involved if we tried this too soon. The fence or the ravine could cause accidents. There could be a job of shoveling out the team if there was a crust on the snow and the horses had sunk in it.

Dad went to town as little as possible in winter, mostly for staples such as tea, sugar, and matches and oil for the lamps. Perhaps a couple of us went along; he rarely went alone. He'd watch for the best possible day but, if supplies ran too low, there'd be no choice. He stood in the front of the sled to drive, but we could snuggle down in the straw. His face would get so red and cold he might crouch down momentarily. Then he went through a session of stomping his feet to keep warm. On them he wore heavy rubber boots with a pair or two of felt inner soles, depending on the size of the boots. He didn't bother much with sizes. It was the same with shirts. All men's shirts came with long sleeves. Men with shorter arms wore steel bands, reminiscent of expandable watch bands, above the elbows to keep the sleeve at the desired length at the wrists. Besides the felt soles in the boots, he might wear three pairs of heavy wool socks.

With his back to the wind, he whistled little singsongy bits. As short as our winter days were, it might be after dark when we arrived home. On the way he'd point out the Big Dipper or ask us to find it. His favorite stars were the Pleiades because he could see and count them all.

Everyone's breath looked like a spout of steam, which I didn't like. But I did like how Dad looked and how we felt. He was so big in his furry coat, standing all alone, whistling away so softly, and we'd listen quietly. It was not the ordinary sort of whistling but through his teeth and very pleasant sounding. It was cheery, and we felt happy and protected while snuggled down cozy and warm.

A storm might come up on the way home, so blinding we couldn't see. Dad then loosely wrapped the reins around the little post on the front of the sleigh box and let the horses find their own way home. They might have to be whipped going to town but never coming back home. They never got lost, but we thought they might. Dad enjoyed half-teasingly saying, "I wonder where we are?" which got us worried.

As soon as Mabel and I were old enough, we were left home to watch the little ones when Mom went to town on Saturday night. On these occasions, we were always scared to death. It was grim to see the parents drive off and to be left alone. Young ones, against orders, stayed up as long as we could keep them awake, for company. Then we'd mix some sugar in a cup with a bit of cocoa, if there was some, and add enough milk to moisten this. The stolen concoction was then savored in tiny spoonfuls.

After this, there was nothing to do but put coal on the fire and begin to hear noises. Once I did something startling and was sorry and ashamed afterward. On these occasions, Mabel was even more scared than I, if that were possible. She asked several times what we'd do if a burglar came. Then we hunted up a stick as protection and talked of how to "get him." She insisted I show her how to use it. I swung, not at a chair, but down on top of her head. Thank goodness it wasn't much of a stick!

The lamp was carried upstairs to check the covers on the little ones, and then brought back down to the kitchen table where it belonged. We got so tired and longed for bed. But who wanted to go upstairs in the awful dark and wait? We sat out the time in front of the kitchen stove, still gnawed by fear!

SEEDING TIME

As early as possible in the spring, usually in May, it was seeding time. The growing season is barely long enough, so no time was wasted after the fields dried out.

Dad coaxed for help to clean the seed drill. Our hands were small enough to reach down the individual pipes and clean out the sprouted remnants left from the last year's use. Dad next shoveled a wagon partly full of wheat. Buckets of water with formaldehyde mixed in them were poured over the wheat. This prevented smut, one of wheat's worst diseases.

The wagon was driven to the edge of the field as a source of supply for the seed drill. It took careful shoveling to fill the high, narrow drill. In these large fields, the drill looked very small. Today big dump trucks drive to the edge of the field and pour directly into low, wide sets of drills pulled by a tractor, cutting seeding time down to a fraction of what it was.

Spring calls to mind begging to go barefoot. Mom said, "Never before the 24th of May," which was Queen Victoria's birthday. This in turn reminds me of a rhyme we used to say at school:

It's the 24th of May
The Queen's birthday
If you don't give us a holiday
We'll all run away.

Sister Irene's birthday fell on that day and her middle name was Victoria, both of which she liked.

Hearing the frogs peeping at the edges of the slough started such ideas about wanting to go barefoot. We wanted to go looking for them and "We don't want to get our feet wet, Mom." When permission was granted we hobbled about the first days watching the terrain, until winter-shod feet toughened up and we could forget them.

There were barefoot feels to be enjoyed. One of them was following behind Dad when the first plow furrows were made for planting potatoes. The bottoms of the furrows had a soft dampness and it was cool on bare feet after running around. It was fun, too, to walk carefully on the smoothly cut, iridescent sod as it turned over. We would see how far we could go before sinking halfway up to our knees.

Potatoes almost came under the heading of gardening. They had to be planted by hand. Outside of the large potato patch there was very little gardening done. That was women's work and Mom wasn't cut out for it. Dad had the only wife around who didn't have a garden, but I never heard him scold about it.

Those horrid potatoes! First we had to cut them up with at least one eye per piece. Carrying a bucketful, we'd follow behind the plow, trying to plant them evenly, eye up, with Dad's, "Hurry up, hurry up."

A new furrow covered the row just planted. That patch seemed huge. The same rows and rows needed weeding all summer. Does anybody in this world like to weed? Dad usually ran a cultivator down the middle and gave up on kids pulling the weeds next to the plants. He was somewhat stricter when it came to picking off the potato bugs, though we started off willingly enough on that job. At least the first tin was a race to see who could get a tin full first.

When I come to think about it, Dad let us off on some jobs we could have finished, but not until we'd done enough to have a good taste of it. This gave some feeling of the unpredictable. Always being consistent is dreary.

Potatoes were a staple we depended on for eating every day, all day, breakfast, dinner and supper. Even the water they were boiled in was saved for baking bread and making gravy. We went from liking them, to putting up with them, all the way to hating them, and then back again to liking.

They were dug up with the plow in the fall, picked up in a bucket, poured into a sack at the end of the row and taken to the house. Those cut to pieces in the process were fed to the pigs and the cows. The rest were carried down to be stored in the cellar. The cellar was only a big dirt hole under the house.

The potatoes were dumped in a pile against a wall. That was gone over and piled into another pile several times a winter. This was because they grew sprouts that had to be broken off and any spoiled ones removed.

By spring no one liked potatoes, but we just had to eat them anyway. Sprouting them was a horrid job. They were pretty rubbery by this time and the number of spoiled ones had increased. At the end, Dad picked out the best ones for seed for the next year.

THE BOX CAR

Wheat was hauled to town and stored in the tall grain elevators. Freight cars were filled with grain from the elevators, then moved east. We were told that much of the wheat went to Port Arthur on the Great Lakes, and from there on to Russia by boat.

Sometimes Dad would order one of the big freight cars to fill himself. This saved the extra handling through the grain elevator, and meant a bit more profit. The box car was shunted onto a railway siding. Two large sliding doors on the side of the car pushed open, one on either side of the middle. As the car was filled with wheat, the opening was boarded up.

On one memorable occasion, Dad had ordered one, and took wagonload after wagonload of wheat to fill it. Perhaps he'd do some other work between trips. These cars were left on the siding for only a certain length of time. Never quite organized, Dad didn't keep track of his time limit.

One day he had an urgent telephone call. He said afterward he was taking a last big load of wheat to town. I must come to help. Help meant climbing into the box car, and, on hands and knees, pushing the wheat to the far corners as he shoveled it in. It was quite dark in there, and the car was almost full when we started to load the last little bit. I couldn't stand up, even in the corner.

Dad did everything fast, so he was shoveling away and I was hurrying to keep up with him, when there was a loud bump and a shudder. The car seemed to move in jerks ahead and then back. I crawled across the top of the wheat to see what was the matter and stuck my head out, shouting for Dad. He wasn't in sight and we were moving down the tracks!! In a minute I saw a man below me, running alongside.

He motioned with his hands and yelled, "Get back!" I'm sure because I was so frightened and blank-minded, I obeyed at once and fell back on the wheat.

What a sharp lesson I learned in obedience! The next minute the whole noise came to a sudden halt. The car stopped fast! Its big doors, on rollers, came crashing together, then bounced open again. I sat still on the wheat and thought how glad I was that I obeyed the man so promptly. My head would have been chopped clean off!

My ordinary reaction could have been to keep calling Dad and, in a panic, to try crawling out of the car. Dad didn't pay any attention to other people, and we weren't apt to either.

The train started up again and the doors slid quietly shut. I was plunged into darkness. We were moving again, smoothly and fast. Doomed, that's what I was! We were on the way to those Great Lakes! No one would look in a box car where there was only wheat. I'd end up being dumped down the chute into one of those big ships. I'd be smothered before getting to Russia. Russia, of all countries!

But, wonder of wonders, in a short time the doors slid open enough to see Dad's head from above, and he said everything would be all right. He had climbed the ladder attached to the end of the car as it started to move. Then he crept along the top on all fours. When the chance came to slide the door open, he was there to be reassuring, even though we were still traveling down the tracks. Eventually the car stopped and Dad helped me out. Then we went back to Benton.

What had happened was fairly common. Dad had been warned his time on the siding was up. Because he couldn't bear to have anything wasted, not even space, he'd hurried to town and tried to get a last load in. While he was loading, the freight engine, as scheduled, had coupled up the car to take it away.

It was worth a nightmare any old time!

LIGHT

Lighting was done with kerosene lamps. Such smelly, nasty things they were, and such trouble to keep in order. Our one lamp was never in order, unless it happened to be a new one. Dad fussed about it and Mom fussed back.

In the short winter days the lamp was lit by 4 o'clock. Perhaps the oil would last until bedtime, which varied. Homework was done within a three-foot radius of the lamp. Can't you hear the squabbling of several kids studying all at once on a rectangular table? "I can't see. She's got all the light on her side," and Mom's rejoinder, "Leave that lamp alone or we'll all be in the dark." If the oil ran out, someone groped in the cold dark shed to find the can of oil. If we were short on matches, a small piece of paper was rolled tight and lit from the coal stove.

After an undetermined length of use the wick had to be hand

pinched to remove the charred portion. The less thrifty cut them often and started fresh. We had no good sharp scissors, so more times than not, there'd be a horn off to one side of the wick. This smoked and then blackened the lamp chimney. Out went the lamp for trimming. If we burned the wick short, it was a calamity. We had no lamp until Dad could go to town for a replacement. The barn lantern, even poorer on the light, was brought in and used to see everyone to bed.

Whenever the lamp chimney wasn't clean, Dad had something to say. They became greasy and finger-marked as well as smoky. We kids were in fear of breaking the thing and never did please Dad with our best efforts at washing it. Nothing else in the house was so delicate to handle. We preferred staying away from it. Sudsy water and a soft cloth were needed, neither of which was available. Our only water was from the well, and it was very hard. Soap only made small curds, no suds.

The barn lantern's chimney was made of thicker glass and was more bulbous. It was easier to clean, but the dickens to get out of its wire frame. If we could see at all, no one fussed if it was a little dirty. Hung on the harness rack at the end of the stable, it was adequate for milking. It was also good enough in the pigpen to feed the squealing pigs. They made more noise than any other animal at feeding time. We were glad they'd be off to market or a neighbor's table by coldest winter time.

The lantern was also carried up to the haymow, where we held it high for Dad, who was pushing straw down to the mangers. It was firmly gripped; more than one barn burned when a lantern fell over in the straw. The barn floor now had at least two feet of straw on it.

Coming in out of the snow and wind, the barn was a cozy place with its weathered boards, dim light and soft, clean-smelling straw. Cows would be bedded down with feet tucked up close, munching away on their cuds. Horses seemed to stand all the time. I never saw one lie down, unless close to death. Cows must be more relaxed creatures. In the heat of the summer they did a lot of resting too.

How they all disliked leaving the barn's warm shelter! The horses ran back in, if they suspected a trip. The cows objected, even when they were driven out to the pump for a drink of water. With the trough covered with ice, we pumped slowly so's they'd drink all that was needed. Otherwise, it filled too soon with ice, and Dad was needed to chop it out with the ax.

It was cold all winter. We could tell when it was extra cold because, even in the well-banked barn, the animals blew out great jets of steam as they breathed. A word was exchanged then, between my sister and me, reiterating Mom's concern for the horses that were turned loose in the fall. We wondered if our faithful old work horses had found food and shelter out of the blizzard. Dad never mentioned them.

Years went by before the time came when an extravagant Coleman gas lamp, with its many problems, was brought home. Now we could see all the way across the kitchen as never before. It was forever posing riddles, especially for my mother. Halfway through preparing supper, she'd complain of not being able to see. The light had grown dim and needed something. Was it more air? "Where's the pump?" When it was located then, "How much air was enough?" The poor-quality mantles might be broken in the process, and only Dad could manage to make new ones. Or they clogged with carbon because the gas wasn't clean. Maybe a fly had landed on the mantle, breaking it. Anyone bumping the lamp, when unlit, broke them. They were very accident-prone. "Where's the old lamp?" Off went the new one for Dad to fuss with.

We spent all kinds of time watching him repair it one way or another. He was a little nervous of it too and would say, "Now everybody out of the way" or "everybody keep still..." There might be only one precious pair of mantles in the house, and he hoped they'd balloon out successfully when the handle was suddenly turned on with gas. We'd all heave a sigh of relief when it settled down to a steady burn with the flame contained in the mantles. Half the time this didn't happen. Perhaps the generator was at fault and the lamp had to be cooled again. Then more mantles were broken getting it out to run a wire through for unclogging. Maybe there was no more money for mantles.

The lamp was hardest to light after being refilled with gas. Some seeped out around the generator, and when that caught fire, the flames shot out alarmingly. More than once, when Dad wasn't there, Mom was convinced it had caught on fire. Worse still, it might explode. She snatched it up and threw it out the kitchen door onto a snow bank. Out came the old kerosene lamp and she relaxed.

In summer's long twilight, no lamp was needed.

CHURNING

When the cows were milked, some milk was set aside for family use, whole. Most was put through a hulking black separator and the cream saved for butter. It was poured into a large cream can, which held buckets full. Each day more was added and it became very thick and sour before the can was all the way full.

Everyone seemed to enjoy their butter strong so if it filled too fast they set it aside to age with even whiskers of mold on top. After the cows freshened in springtime there might be extra milk and a can of cream was sold in town, for cash, to be shipped for creamery butter.

The churn sat in the back shed. It was awkward and heavy and barely came in through the kitchen door. It consisted of a wooden barrel with a lid on top, and a cork near the bottom. This was suspended on an iron framework with another arc over it, used as a handle. On the floor, attached to its side, was a foot pedal.

After the cream was poured in and the lid fastened tight, Dad started it. By pulling the handle back and forth, and using his foot on the pedal, the barrel tumbled over and over. It was impossibly heavy for us to start. Dad had to push the barrel the first few tumbles, with his free hand, to help it on its way. When its momentum took over and it ran smoothly, he handed the job to us.

I don't know how long it took, but I do know that our arms got tired and our feet too, before Dad took over again. When it began to sound heavy we took a look or two before removing the cork to let the buttermilk run into a bucket. This was smooth and creamy-looking, not anything like what one buys in the stores. It tasted strong and pure and is very good, if you like buttermilk. None of us did, except Dad, who said, "You don't know a good thing when you have it."

Next came a fresh cold bucket of water from the well, to be poured into the churn. *handle* Back on went the lid for a few more turns. This washed the butter and lumped it together and was then run off. There'd be 20 pounds or so of butter. With a good-sized wooden paddle, Mom ladled the butter out into the dishpan to be worked. She pressed the paddle down with *mold* both hands, then scooped up a paddle full to put on top and press down again. This removed all air bubbles and compressed it, but most important was squeezing out all excess fluids. If bits of buttermilk were not completely removed they could spoil and ruin the flavor. Toward *butter* the end of working the butter, salt was added. Last of all it was ladled into a large earthenware crock and stored on the cellar floor. Mom really wasn't big enough to do this kind of work.

Mom had too much to do, but a few times she fixed some butter to sell. This brought a much better price than cream. Filling the mold and packing it in carefully took an amount of fussy work. The mold was an oblong wooden box and the handle was put inside with the stock through the top. It was held by this handle, upside down, to fill. When the mold was full it was turned right side up and carefully placed on store-bought paper, like parchment. The handle was then pushed and pushed until the butter slid out. It must have carefully squared corners, no finger marks, and it must land on the paper just so for neat corners. Next it was packed and stored, ready for town, to bring in some hard-earned money for necessities.

Now Mom had to make the buttermilk pancakes Dad had been waiting for!

CLOTHES

The most important clothes were the men's best suits. Anyone who was anybody had one – the one they got married in. Some were pretty ancient looking. When they became dusty from wear, they were hung on the clothesline and whisk-broomed. With no such things as cleaners, clothes were sponged off when necessary. There was no problem of growing out of them. The men worked hard and stayed thin. Suits were worn so seldom that when they were, it was a gala occasion.

I've never yet met a man who liked to shave! With all the time and bother of the long-handled straight razor, to be endlessly sharpened and carefully handled, hard water to be heated and a dubious cake of soap, it's small wonder the men didn't shave often at home. When neighbors were dusted off, shaved and all dressed up, it took a while to recognize them! A special dance or Christmas concert found the majority rigged up for the affair. Dressing up for a funeral was a must. We never went to one; there were very few at that time.

Dad owned a suit. His was navy blue. I think they all were. With it he kept his two good shirts, one a light blue and the other white. On top of the tall bookcase desk sat the two celluloid collars, to be worn with the suit.

Men's long leather pouches snapped shut at the top. When turned upside down, the change rolled out easily. It took much pinching and pushing to get a hold on the paper money. There were small, scarce 25-cent paper bills known as Shinplasters. Pennies were large, few in number and a novelty. No one used them. They were likely to be sent from the East to settle minor accounts.

Men wore caps or hats. Farmers never went out the door without something on their heads. In summer they wore a wide-brimmed straw hat to keep off the dust and the sun. Between seasons, they might wear a cap of the sort worn with sports cars today. Winter saw them in the caps with extras for warmth. The tops of their foreheads were white and smooth, but their faces were red and rough.

Work clothes were heavy blue denim overalls with bib and suspenders. Shirts were dark, impossible cloth. In the cold, they wore as many as three pairs of overalls all at once. The oldest pair was worn on the outside and perhaps a sweater was tucked between them. This saved the nuisance of a coat if they could possibly get by without one.

Inside their heavy rubber boots were lots and lots of socks. Boots were left on the porch, and only socks were worn in the house, whatever the season. Men's shoes were strictly for dress up. Shoes for both men and women were lace-up affairs, with hooks instead of holes for lacing.

How can I write about the clothes women wore then, when I see what they wear today? We now have one thing in common with way back then: nothing ever fit properly! Their clothes were that way by default, whereas ours are planned to be that way!

House dresses were worn both winter and summer. The newest was reserved for going to town. When it became worn it was used for everyday, and another ordered. Most of these dresses had all-over prints so's not to show spots. The fabric was a struggle to iron.

Women's hair was long and the ends were twisted tight and rolled into a bun at the back of their heads. Heavy wire hairpins kept it in place. These were good for a lifetime if they didn't get lost.

In the late 20's a few daring women bobbed their hair to the tips of their ears, and marcelling came into fashion. The curling irons were heated over a lamp chimney. Few of the older ladies bothered. Creating a swirl of waves around the head was well-nigh impossible to do by one's self.

Only loose women wore makeup!

Coats were dark, long and warm, that's all that could be said of them. But I will say something about children's clothes. They were always big enough. Anything new started out with sleeves turned back and legs rolled up, this being especially abominable when it was long winter underwear. Perhaps things would fit by the time they wore out. It was planned that way. No one could afford to grow out of his clothes.

WASH DAY

Wash days were horrid, tiring affairs for any farm woman. It wasn't so bad in warm weather, except for all the steaming untidiness in the kitchen. After all, the kitchen was where we lived!

Way back, I recall, Mom did wash in the same round galvanized tub we took baths in. She put it up on two or three chairs, facing each other, so's she'd not have to kneel at the washboard. This was a rickety situation! If she came down too hard on the washboard, a chair might slip and there went the tub! When she was feeling extra perky the tub stayed on the floor.

The oblong copper boiler was put on the stove and filled with soft water. It was so big that it covered the top of the stove. When it was full it was much too heavy to budge. A small tank on the end of the stove, called a reservoir, was supposed to be kept filled and handy for dishes and faces. It didn't hold much water, and didn't warm it much.

This warm water was scooped into the copper boiler to speed things up. When the water boiled, in went a white batch of underwear to spend some time. Mom found a stick for hauling out one boiling piece at a time, and dropping it into a bucket. The bucket of clothes was dumped into the tub, where everything was scrubbed on the metal washboard with Fels-Naptha.

In winter the tub was right next to the stove, but in summer it might be across the room, or even out in the shed, away from the heat. After a tub of white clothes was done, Dad's greasy clothes went in. When they were done, fresh water was needed for another round. All clothes were wrung out by hand. Dad helped with heavy things like flannelette sheets.

Barrels that had been used for gasoline sat under the rain spouts on the house. Dad felt they shouldn't be too scrubbed or they'd get rusty sooner. When they got rusty, water was scooped out carefully so as not to stir it up. Sometimes there was no rainwater in the barrels. If it wasn't a busy time, Dad rolled two of them up into the wagon and drove to the nearest slough. There was a sloshy ride home, but with a couple of boards floating on top (to help the splashing) enough water was left to be worth the trip. Wash day was always a wet affair, with water all over the kitchen floor.

There might be polliwogs and algae in the water. The muddiness would settle down. Mom strained it for most necessary wash and waited for another day. She wondered if Dad had gone to the best part of the slough. I went with him often to help, and he did take a fair amount of precautions. He had to back the wagon into the safest place or there'd be a problem getting out of the mud. It never was easy anyway. Where the slough was deep enough, he tied a rope on a bucket to scoop up the water. Being in his usual hurry, the rope was sometimes let down too far. Sometimes Mom wondered why he bothered to bring water home when the slough was in such bad shape. "You know men," she'd say.

When there was no rain and the sloughs dried up, it was unfortunate. Water from the well was so hard it was almost useless. If it had to be used, it was! Women had experimented over the years, trying to make well water usable. They tried homemade soap, lye, and anything else that came to mind, but no one ever found a good answer.

Our first washing machine was a thin-walled round one, with a copper coating on the outside. It was rather flimsy. A wobbly hand wringer clamped on the side. Underneath was a small, questionable gasoline engine. With its four cup-like dashers thumping up and down on the wash, and the engine running, the noise was fierce.

Later we got a heavy aluminum Maytag that was most durable. We had to be careful of the treacherous wringer on this machine! When one was absorbed with the problem of feeding in a tangled, wet piece of washing, a finger or the sleeve of a sweater could get caught. An arm could go in almost to the elbow before the top could be banged to release it. However, the advantages of this wonderful machine far outdid the hazards.

The Maytag was placed in the shed. Fastened down outside was a gasoline engine with a hole in the wall for the belt, very much like the pump setup, but with one decided advantage: there was a foot peddle to start it. This arrangement worked well, particularly during good weather.

Clothes in summer dried in a wink. They were hung outside even after frost and became frozen boards. After removing the clothespins, they were hard to get off the line and tore easily when pulled. We enjoyed dancing with the funny shapes when sent to bring them in.

Ironing was a game of chance. Clothes lasted longer without it, or at least were safer. The job was put off and off for one reason or another. There were no ironing boards. An old flannelette sheet was spread on the end of the kitchen table. A couple of sadirons (some people call them flat irons) sat on the back of the stove most of the time, handy. Where else was there to put them? The warming oven above was used every other day for loaves of bread to rise.

A spot on the stove with just the right temperature was needed to heat the irons. Maybe the stove wasn't hot enough and it would have to be stoked up. If the irons got too hot they had to be pushed aside to cool. Maybe a pot had boiled over and dirtied the irons, so they must be worked on.

A wooden handle with a catch was used to pick one up. Next came the guessing part. We wouldn't dare try Mom's method of testing, for fear of burnt fingers. She licked hers, and quickly touched the underside of the iron. By the sound of the sizzle, she knew when it was too hot. She could pretty well guess when the temperature was right. We used the irons as hot as possible, when starting out, because they cooled so fast. The first piece attempted was less important in case of errors. The perfect time between too hot and too cool came and went very fast. Back to the stove went the iron, and another was picked up while that one reheated. With such a lot of bother, not much ironing was done at our house. An attempt was made to press Dad's suit and our serge school dresses were ironed, after they were sponged.

DAD'S ORGAN PLAYING

The sitting room, where we never sat, was the only other room downstairs besides the kitchen. The door was kept shut, but we opened it to scoot 'round the corner and down the cellar stairs. There were three things in the room: a fold-a-bed couch by an outside door, a heater stove on the east wall, and a red-colored upright organ. That organ was really red! We were told it was cherry wood, probably the nearest it came to being so was its color. Anything that touched it came away red, like wine. This happened to the dust rag even after years of rubbing. I don't know where the organ came from, or when we got it. No one in the family knew how to play it, and we never had a visitor who could, either.

The heater stove was lit only on the very coldest nights. It was needed to help heat rooms upstairs. The chimney ran through the second-floor bedroom and out the roof. This was the parents' room. The kitchen stovepipes ran through the children's room. These pipes were made in two-foot lengths that tucked into one another and, if bumped, fell in a heap on the floor.

There was a damper to stop the heat from all going up the flue. When shut all the way, the pipes could get red hot in minutes. When the stove was burning full tilt, they were a fire hazard! Dad watched the spots where they came through the floor and where they went out to the roof. We warmed our hands on the pipes, when they were not too hot. They weren't enough to heat the drafty bedrooms but they took the chill off.

When Dad went in to the sitting room to light the fire or to add coal, he carried the lamp in and put it on top of the organ. With a little coaxing, he might be inspired to play. We gathered round to watch and tried to sing. Using his pointer finger, he haltingly played a one note version of a hymn or two. "Lead Kindly Light" or "Abide with Me" were his favorites and most often played. He sang them also. I didn't like them; when slowly played, they sounded forlorn.

Dad knew where middle C was and showed us how he found one note above or below, or down or up. A flat was a black one below and a sharp the black one above. That was the extent of the family's musical education. No one, not anyone in the family, had a musical ear. None had any singing voice, could carry a tune or stay on pitch, but we liked music with melody and rhythm.

P.S. When I was much older, I had access to a piano. I remembered Dad's instructions and learned to play "The Battle Hymn of the Republic," "Home Sweet Home," and a few such. Flats came easier than sharps but the timing left something to be desired! I'd still like to know how to play the piano!

Once during early high school, down East, a kindly teacher decided to help my education along by taking me to town – Philadelphia, no less – to see the sights. The crowning treat was to hear the Philadelphia Orchestra with the famous Stokowski conducting.

The building, which was the Academy of Music, was interesting, with lots and lots of people, but after twenty minutes I was bored stiff. A whole hour went by and the music had gotten nowhere. It seemed awfully noisy in spots and there were no nice rolling melodies, though once in a while it sounded hopeful. Could it be that the music was no good because there were too many players? The biggest orchestra at the very best barn dances at home had only three pieces!

After all the exciting sights of Philadelphia, such as seeing the Liberty Bell, the orchestra was a letdown. I had a bad time staying awake and looking happy about this treat. Another time a friend asked me to go to a concert, which was a family affair, held in a special studio. It was the same kind of thing!!

Besides, I'd not seen people be so polite nor sit so still for such a long spell in my life or I'd not have gone so willingly. Concerts at home were the Christmas concerts where they did all kinds of interesting things.

Classical music is an acquired, educated taste!

FOOD

We ate porridge for breakfast. We ate bread, meat and boiled potatoes three times a day and all year round. Once in a long while there might be something different. Life being simple, eating was the thing we looked forward to most. It wasn't any pleasure if today's food was the same as yesterday's and the day before that. There were long spells of this.

Children were told, "You eat what is put before you." Mom added, "Children should be seen and not heard," at the table or anywhere else with grown-ups present.

Some farmers grew big gardens and canned. Not so our family. Mom was too busy with washing, cooking and babies. She cooked meals and served them, but rarely sat down to eat with the family.

When all had finished, she cleared a corner of the table for her big pot of tea, with bread and butter. Being English, she loved her cup of "te'." She practically lived on this fare, which she also ate between meals. It was a treat to join her then. Ours would be Cambric tea, mostly milk. Tea stunted children's growth.

Breakfast began with homegrown wheat porridge and ended there, most often, for us. Once in a year Dad might buy a bag of cornmeal for a change. When it was gone, we'd be glad to go back to the wheat porridge we'd been sick of.

Dad ate heartily. His favorite breakfast was leftover boiled potatoes from supper. These were put into a frying pan with fat, chopped up with an upside-down baking powder tin and browned.

We had no chops or steaks, as they exist down East. Large square chunks of meat were boiled, and all tasted the same. Bread and butter stayed on the table all day. Maybe plum jam was added for supper. The jam in the pail got thicker with age. By the time the bottom was reached, it was dry and unappetizing.

A can of tomatoes or package of Jell-O made a rare, good dessert.

In summer, meat was scarce. There might be a cornstarch pudding made with eggs. Unless eggs were needed for a birthday treat or something special, chickens were kept for laying until the end of summer.

Once Dad and I were stranded in Benton until late. The store-keeper's wife, rather unhappily, invited us upstairs for supper. She served canned purple plums, and to this day I think them delicious. Boy, were the other kids jealous when I described them!

Vegetables were scarce and fruit more so. For winter we stored either turnips, parsnips or carrots in the cellar. Never did we have all three at once. During the Dust Bowl era these same vegetables were shipped in freight car loads to the starving people. Most of the roots had reached the rubbery stage and those who lived on them never cared for them again.

Mom baked all the bread, loaves upon loaves. The only thing we liked was the first outside slice of crust when fresh from the oven. Butter melted into it so deliciously.

Dad ordered one box of apples from British Columbia. He watched over them carefully. Each day he'd undo them and look for any with spots, then rewrap them in their paper. He'd eat one, brown spot and all. He carefully peeled it with his penknife in one long peel, round and round and round. He ate that. Then he ate one little thin wedge of apple at a time. Only the stem was left, not another piece was wasted. We oldest were allowed one apple a day, so we took it to school while they lasted. We watched him eat his after supper but we'd had our share. There was no chance of snitching. He counted them.

Often we found oranges in the toes of our stockings on Christmas morning. One year, when Dad was too poor to buy oranges, we found very small wooden balls dyed orange, instead.

We had very few chickens. Dad hated them. He considered them smelly, messy creatures. They got underfoot in the barn. Even with the door shut, they squeezed under it. He put up with having some only because he felt a few were necessary. We had a very big chicken house but nothing in it. The chickens stayed where they pleased. In the big chicken house there were only a perch and a couple of boxes for laying, which were rarely used. Hens like a cozy place.

Eating the eggs was chancy. No one gathered them regularly. Mom would remark, "No one has gone to look for eggs in days." In thinking about it, she'd decide some eggs were needed. Then it was, "Run out and get a couple, like a good girl." When Dad sent us out, it was to look for all the eggs. A still warm one was found in a horse's feed box. Another might be found under a granary, and maybe even one in the chicken house. Untrained hens! The problem was no one knew who had looked where or when the last time. What was found might be old, too old to use. If the egg was very light when picked up, it was bad. The questionable ones were those in between.

In spring, after the hens had been laying for a week or two, a cluck-ing hen would be discovered in some unlikely spot, setting on a nest of eggs. If she was in a safe place she'd be left alone. If not, we'd try moving her to the chicken house. They never liked it. They were cross and temperamental, feathers all puffed out, clucking and pecking. If she didn't settle down and stay on the nest, a box was put over her. A short time did for some, others not at all. It probably depended on how long they'd been setting. One hen was forgotten and the poor thing died. The chicken house was never a good thing. If too many nests were found, they were done away with in hopes the hens would go back to laying.

When they grew up, the roosters were eaten first. We'd be asked to, "Go get one for supper." Catching a rooster was a chore, but usually fun. There was only one way: we had to outrun him. Perhaps he'd be about wore out, then he'd disappear under a granary and we'd have to start on a fresh one. When caught and held by the legs, we'd swing him round and round over our heads until he was very dizzy. It was a cinch then to lay him over the old railroad tie at the wood pile and chop off his head.

Though we were young, we had no qualms about killing him. It was in the order of things.

Next, we grabbed him fast to pluck the feathers while he was still warm. If not done right away, the task was much more difficult. Sometimes they jumped up and ran around headless. We'd worry about them being really dead. Looking back on this now, it all seems absolutely appalling!

The chickens never laid eggs in winter. If left in the chicken house they'd freeze on their perch. So we kept none. If there were any eggs laid late in summer they were put down. A large earthenware crock was half-filled with a preparation called "water glass." The eggs to be preserved were put into this. This too was stored on the cellar floor. It was a murky, slimy substance that didn't improve with age. As the crock emptied we found it very distasteful, having to put an arm down in it and feel around for an egg. By this time, they were strong tasting and good only for Dad's buttermilk pancakes.

When it came to killing the larger creatures 'twas a different story. The calves had all been named and were our pets. We cried. We never saw Dad butcher a cow, thank goodness. After getting home from school some fall day, there'd be a carcass strung to the rafters inside the barn. The biggest job was skinning it. We saw none of the work in connection with it. The way we knew that the job was done was when Dad arrived in the house with fresh liver, or maybe a heart, for supper. Heart, stuffed, was the one meat sure to be roasted.

In the winter Dad cut up the meat with a saw and a big knife. The pieces were stored in the big galvanized barrel around the corner of the house, outside. There it stayed frozen all winter.

A tasty morsel was had after school by slipping outside with a butcher knife and slivering off a few frozen slices. These were cut as thin as thin could be, and they were eaten on the spot.

CALVES

One year, when the calves were half-grown, we had the greatest fun riding them, or at least trying to. We didn't have any riding horses. The calves objected strenuously, but we had fun seeing how long we could stay on. Most of them took off in a straight line, as fast as they could go. They all ended up throwing us off, one way or another.

One smart fellow managed to get rid of us in a hurry. He headed for the nearest barbed wire fence. If we'd been able to stay on that long he'd then run right alongside it. The barbs scratched our legs so we'd have to jump off promptly. Once I decided I'd not give in, but would teach him a lesson. As he came alongside the fence, I put my hand out to push against it. As luck would have it, a barb landed at the base of a finger. It hurt but wasn't a deep prick and was soon forgotten.

A few days later, though, it was red and sore around the small scab and some miserable times set in. The sore became red, swollen and discolored. The hand became so fat and painful, it was comfortable only with the arm up over my head, especially when sitting down. After noisily complaining, Mom looked at it one morning and, noticing red streaks up the arm, thought a doctor should see it. Dad even admitted that seeing a doctor wouldn't be mollycoddling.

The doctor now had a new office in town. As soon as he saw the hand he asked me to lie on the couch. Next thing I knew, I was sitting up with a big white bandaged paw. "Come back in a few days," he said.

When I went back to see him, he unwound the bandage, going faster and faster, and ending with a quick, painful pull. The finger bones I saw were a reddish brown. This was very surprising as all the bones I'd ever seen on the trails in the pasture were snowy white!

Calves are apt to be pleasant creatures, but a few are mean right from the start. Our gentle Molly had a roan calf that was almost the death of me.

Walking down to the pump one late afternoon, I didn't know what hit me or even that I'd been hit. I woke up in bed and asked, "How come?" Mom happened to see the calf run up behind me and knock me flat with the first impact. She'd called the hired man, who luckily was at home. The calf, not satisfied, had been busily butting me about in the meantime. The hired man had driven him off and carried me into the house.

Another time a couple of us were following Dad around doing the evening chores. We had to cross a fenced lane where the cows happened to be. That awful calf was there, and we were afraid. Dad, in his usual speedy way, with us trotting to keep up with him, had swung his leg over the fence and was on his way to the other side. He paid no attention to our, "Wait for us."

I had quickly crawled under the barbed fence and was standing, holding the lowest strand up for the youngest to crawl under, when bang, down I went again.

Mom began fussing at Dad to get rid of the beast.

Not long after this, teacher had a telephone call one afternoon. The phone never rang at school unless it was a thing of importance. She said it was Mom asking if she could send someone for Dad. He was working at a field in sight of school. It must be something bad for Mom to call. Teacher offered no more information and we waited to collect enough courage to ask. Her reply was that Dad was needed for young sister Lillian.

The minute school was over, four of us were strung out on the pasture racing for home. Mom was found at the top of the stairs bending over a cot bed. Sister lay unrecognizable, except for her dark hair and eyebrows. Her purple bruised and swollen face was full of cuts and scratches. That awful calf had gone after her. He was butchered young, and we kids all talked about how much he deserved to be chewed!

PIGS

In order of importance came horses, cows, chickens and then pigs. Some people thought pigs were not necessary at all, so they were a sometimes animal. That was the way it was for us. Dad didn't like keeping them, but they were handy for eating up the swill, which was the extra milk, weed seeds and potato peelings. He stood up for them as the one animal which always kept its bed clean. Other animals were not as fussy.

Pigs were not allowed in his barn but in a pen built next to it. When there was rain, they rooted their way out under it. They liked to root up anything – potatoes, for example – and wallow in any overflow by the trough. They are almost impossible to chase back into a pen, but will follow food at any time.

One big sow favored the chicken house. She was a mean one and we'd have to keep an eye out for her, if sent to look for eggs. The usual pig is a vegetarian, but this one ate the chickens, if she could catch them. She nearly bit off brother Leslie's finger when he rescued a friendly cat. We carried a stick when around her and used it with pleasure – I should say, with a feeling of justice being done. She even ate some of her own cute pink and white babies and was a most careless mother. She took no care when she wished to lie down, but thumped down on top of them.

By accident, I saw Dad slit the throat of a pig. It was a dreadful, awful sight, but was the standard procedure. Dad took precautions to avoid our seeing anything too unpleasant. He could slaughter a cow by himself, but needed the help of a neighbor with a pig. The time I saw him, Dad didn't choose to wait for help. He tied a rope to the pig, long enough to go around the corner of the hen house, out of sight and sound. I was to hold it tight. After quite a wait, I heard him call and came running. Instead, he'd wanted to know if I was all right, if I could manage to hold it longer, or some such question. I didn't hear. It was then I'd come back, at the wrong moment, before he was through.

After a pig was killed, it, like the cows, was strung up to the rafters by means of a rope and pulley. The cows were skinned but under the pig was set a large barrel of scalding water. The pig was dropped into the water several times. Then the men quickly went to work with sharp butcher knives to scrape off the bristles and outside skin. When finished, the carcass was nice and clean looking and almost pure white.

The German people kept lots of pigs. They enjoyed eating pork the way we did beef. Besides, they made all sorts of things out of the innards that sounded no good to us. The one exception we tasted and liked was headcheese. This supposedly was made from the tender bits and pieces of flesh from the animal's head set in gelatin they'd made from the animal.

Dad most often sold his pigs live. Neighbors offered to share half a pig after butchering and the favor was returned when we did one. Dad sold most of this meat but kept some for a change of diet. When he killed a pig he saved the bladder, washed and scraped it carefully, then blew it up as a balloon for us to play with. It lasted a good while if oiled because this kept it from becoming dry and brittle.

The Germans rendered down every bit of fat for lard. Any outside skin became crisp and delicious as a tidbit, called cracklings. If we ever used or needed any lard, Mom bought a small pail, refined and pure white. Once she found the grocery was out of it and had only a very large pail, so she bought it. She found it difficult to use up. When empty she considered it a nice bucket, but the handle wasn't sturdy enough to be dependable so she stored it away in the shed.

When Mom's last baby, sister Bea, was about to arrive, Dad called me into the sitting room where she lay on the fold-a-couch looking miserable. It was late, all of 9 p.m. Dad said he was going after Mrs. Newman, who lived ten miles or more away. I didn't know who she was.

I was left alone with my mother and no instructions given. Of course there was nothing to do anyway, but Mom certainly sounded as though she needed help of some sort. Maybe she was dying? Why did it have to be dark nighttime, which makes everything seem worse? It took such a long time for Dad to get back. How wonderful when he did, for with him was a large, pleasant woman who went directly to Mom. I went right upstairs to bed, tired out, and slept.

In the bright sunshine of morning we awoke to bustling sounds downstairs and found a new baby in the crib. Also we noticed the big lard pail simmering on the back of the stove and smelling so good. When we asked the woman what it was, she said, "Soup." She'd found no large kettle because we had none, so had hunted up the lard pail in the shed. We considered her soup delicious. That was the first and last time we ever had it, as Mom wasn't ingenious.

There was a doctor in the area, but who knew where? Everyone had their babies at home and thought the midwife as good as any doctor. The women preferred them and, in addition to their primary duties, they might help with other chores for a day or two. The doctor was making attempts to educate women to the hospital. The midwife and the doctor were not friends.

When I left home this youngest sister was 1 year and 1 month old.

Chapter 8

TREASURES

I don't know how it started, but it went back past remembering.
Whenever we quarreled amongst ourselves, and name calling wasn't
making any difference, we'd threaten to "get into your things." That
was the living end! We'd jump up and run into the house and up the
stairs to our room. There might not be a single treasure hidden at the
moment, but we took no chances in case something had been forgotten. If there was a tidbit, the hiding spot was changed from this corner
to that one, or under Mom's bed, or who knows where.

Our treasures were only bits and pieces of special paper or maybe
a magazine picture. Only a naive child would notice such things today.
One treasure I kept a long while, with much difficulty,
was a paper chair pasted together at school, like a child
makes in kindergarten. Actually, I can't remember anyone having their things ruined, as they meant too much.
To "get into your things" was only a dire threat; it was
never carried out.

We didn't have birthday celebrations with gifts. Someone would
remember when the day came, and ask, "How many lickings do you
get this year?" Dad usually was the one who kiddingly, but not too
lightly, turned us over his knee and swatted the right number of times,
with an extra one to grow on. This was no pleasure.

My first big treasure was given to me by Mom. Brother Leslie was a baby and got the croup, so a small vaporizer was bought. The lamp was so cute, we all wanted to be vaporized! The box it came in was bright orange, covered with very black printing. I begged for it, even though I knew that the lamp should go back in it when the croup was gone. Mom gave me the box.

Early one morning, soon after this, I was awakened by Dad standing over the bed with a lighted lamp in his hand. He asked for the box. I wasn't about to part with that new treasure! He sat down on the edge of the bed and quietly told me that a little baby had come to our house and that it had died. He needed the pretty box! When spring came, Mom planted a small circle of flowers in the corner of the yard.

Another time someone gave me a magazine with a Dolly Dingle on the last page (she was a paper doll with two dresses). This started two pastimes. One was to use the magazine itself as a scrapbook. Flour and water was used as paste to put pictures where there were none. The other pastime was inspired by this paper doll. Mom gave us the old Eaton's catalog. From this we cut out pictures of all the men, women and children. Hours were spent grouping them into families and writing their names on the back of each one. How many children should Mr. & Mrs. Brown have? etc. After everything was settled and labeled, they were jumbled up and we tried to sort them out again, without looking at the backs. We played with them until their arms, legs and heads wore out from all the handling.

The last treasure to horde was best of all. It was so special I couldn't find anything good enough to put in it for a long while. The gift was from Granny McDonald. Dad and I went out of our way to visit her on the way to town. As we left, she handed me a small tin box, richly covered with a red and blue paisley design. She said it came from Persia! More likely it came from England with tea biscuits. She added, "It would make a good treasure chest."

I was thrilled almost out of my wits, as Dad said, and didn't know how to thank her. I never saw her again. When I won a prize for making a doll dress, the dress was folded and put in the chest, which was then tucked away in Mom's trunk.

I went away to school and, four years later, I went back home and looked for my treasure chest. The younger ones had "gotten in my things," and it was gone.

GOODIES

One year Dad started an addition on the house. The wheat profits were too little to allow finishing it. Our house was fairly bulging with children.

There had been only two bedrooms, with a small hall between them. One room was strictly for the parents. The other room had been partitioned down the middle, with enough room only for a double bed on each side, and little else. It was cozy and warm sleeping in double beds, but we older ones each wanted a room of our own, which we never got. Soon a bed was put in the hall, making it almost impassable. Dad then decided the time had come for an addition, out back, with a bedroom upstairs and one downstairs.

The framework was completed the first year and the next year it was roughly boarded up. Then the bottom floor could be used for much needed storage, but there was no top floor yet. As it turned out, it stayed this way for many years and I never saw it finished. There was no door between the house and the addition. One went outside, around the house, to a small door which had a latch on it. 'Twas frigid in winter!

From somewhere, Dad was sent a food catalog that promised the lowest prices, to save money. This was an unusual happening. Mailboxes were not stuffed with pamphlets, magazines and all the sell we have now. Mail consisted of personal letters, packages ordered, and bills. Even very few bills were sent. The grocer told you when he saw you, "Better pay up, your bill is getting big." So when anything came by post, some attention was given it. Dad studied the small catalog and decided a few goodies could be ordered as a winter treat, but they had to last and not be eaten up too quickly. All I remember getting were some dates and figs in small packages, which were very good, but by far the best treat was a big, heavy paper bag of brown sugar. Dad put it in the new back-bedroom-to-be. He thought it was hidden! But we found it! For half the winter, we slipped out of the house, around the corner, to quietly open the latched door for just a pinch. Gradually, the sugar became hard and we could no longer manage to get even a taste. One day I remembered that the big butcher knife had been good for slivering the frozen beef, so why not try it on the sugar? I sneaked it out of the house, but instead of a sliver, I was after a chunk. I got the chunk, but with it came a good piece of my finger! No more brown sugar! Dad put a hook on the door too high to reach.

This reminds me of another snitching episode. In the corner of the kitchen was a narrow breakfront cupboard, painted gray. It was made of narrow car boards and reached to the ceiling. This was just about the only storage place in the house. It contained a variety of items, but was only partially filled. The upper shelves were impossible to reach, so Dad's bottle of whiskey (for medicine) was hidden away up there. There was also an old, cumbersome butter dish with room in it for ice. Handy shelves at the bottom held the jam and salt. All items came in bulk amounts. The salt, for instance, came in a 5lb. bag. Anything special was hidden on upper shelves.

One time it happened that Mom came home with a small tin of peanut butter. Etched on its side was a bushy-tailed squirrel. "Why was that animal picture there?" We learned then that squirrels ate peanuts. She pried open the lid, but there was nothing to be seen but oil. This floated on top until she stirred the peanut butter. It had to be stirred each time it was served. It didn't look all that good. We gave up and put it, untouched, high in the cupboard to be saved for some time.

When we came home from school, food was the first thing we thought about, and we looked around for something to eat besides just plain bread. One run was on bread, butter and a piece of onion, till the onion ran out. Another time a row of radishes from the garden was raided, sliced and eaten between the bread and butter. When we were old enough to climb on the cupboard and reach the upper shelves, we looked there. Thus, much later, we found that tin of peanut butter.

"No," said Mom, "it's for special occasions," which were mythical. We never had them. So it sat for a while longer, but I didn't forget it! I waited until I thought, perhaps, she had forgotten about it. When the chance came, with no one in sight, I swung up on the ledge, opened the lid, and whipped in a finger. The taste was pretty good, but my conscience wasn't! Another quick swipe, and Mom appeared. I suddenly got busy, just swinging about holding the main beam of the cupboard. "What are you doing? Get down."

My taste for the forbidden peanut butter grew! Then one day, getting tired of the old bread, butter and radishes, I had an opportunity to take several good big licks. The tin was getting alarmingly empty!

Soon I felt sick, awfully sick. For years afterward I couldn't stand the smell of peanut butter or of radishes!

TRAVEL

I suppose Dad always had a team of horses and wagon to get around in. I never saw him ride a horse, and we didn't own a saddle. He did tell me that he rode in the early days.

Wagons offered the world's noisiest and bumpiest rides. All farmers had the same sort of wagon, a buckboard, whether that is its official name or not. This included a set of wheels, a chassis, and a long tongue to which the horses were hitched. The wheels were large and steel rimmed, the rims always shining from use. When they were new, the wheels were painted red and the wagon boxes green – so we were told. I never saw anyone with a new wagon! Once bought, they seemed to last forever and were always the same gray, aged wood.

The usual wagon box was about two and a half feet high. It could be used for shopping or for taking a plowshare to the blacksmith shop. There the shares were heated and beaten out sharp again. Dad used his own small forge infrequently for mending chains and harnesses, but liked his shares done professionally.

Another section could be added to make the wagon twice this height. The back end was handled separately and added only when hauling wheat. Dad kept his wagon tall because he liked best to stand while driving, and this gave him something to lean against. With the back open, planks could be laid up for rolling oil barrels up or down. We climbed in the back far easier than clambering up over the wheels.

When the same box was used as a sleigh, it was much lower and easy to jump into.

A seat came with each wagon, resembling a bench on wide steel springs. It fastened on the top edges. I never did feel safe way up there! Dad sat on a full load of wheat, with his legs dangling over the front, so the seat was never used. It was set aside, by the tool shed, and we tried our strength by jumping on it occasionally.

Tank

When Dad's acreage became greater, he bought a large grain tank for hauling wheat. He carefully nailed the little post in front to wrap the reins around. The back had a small door that slid up and let the wheat pour out. It was like a long waterfall, cascading down into the elevator.

crack

door

He now owned two regular wagons also. One morning, he decided to hook up all three, loaded with wheat. They were connected one behind the other for a single trip to the elevator. Just thinking about those treacherous hills on the way to Benton worried Mom sick. Afterwards, when he told about his experience, she pleaded with him not to be so reckless. Of course he had to do it again! He was that way. We children knew that he himself was anxious about the trip. He whistled fast, fussed around, and didn't leave at once when everything was ready. He was the kind of man who would not be told, but who took every opportunity to tell others!

He never did it again.

Each farmer also had a set of sleigh runners as wide and as thick as wagon wheels. They were used for exactly the same chores in winter. Transferring the box from the wheels to the sleigh runners was a monumental job for one man. Dad maneuvered it up on the wheels with a two-by-four while we steadied it and what else I don't know. Getting it back up was even worse as sleigh runners are much lower. The sleigh was a pleasure to ride in, quiet and smooth going. No wonder they have never put jingle bells on wagons!

The buggies and cutters were for other people, mostly to get children to school. One reason Dad didn't like them was because he liked to go where he pleased.

A whip was needed for the horses. Dad kept two, basically the same, but one was longer. They were both long-handled, with a single strip of narrow rawhide knotted on the end. The longer one was taken to the fields where a larger number of horses were used. This way he could reach the furthest horse. When tired horses were stopped, he often had to use the whip to get them going again.

Some men used a cat o' nine tails, which is several whips in one, to whip their horses. Dad considered that unnecessary. His horses were trained to be obedient, and he used the whip only as a reminder. Sometimes there were lazy horses, which he wouldn't keep, except for big, spoiled Tom.

In a span of a very few years, the industrial world swept across the prairie and took away our farmyard way of life, leaving behind nothing living. First tractors, better roads, and then trucks. The one group that did come back were the wild ducks, to nest on the sloughs.

A Model T Ford stood in the yard as far back as I can remember. It was used rarely, perhaps because it was considered to be a luxury. It was used chiefly for pleasure, although that term was never mentioned. People called them Flivvers and Tin Lizzies. There were cloth tops to be pulled up and cloth sides to be snapped in. Along the sides were rows of tiny isinglass windows. These let in some light, but not a thing could be seen through them. Eventually they cracked into bits and pieces and fell out. Dad repaired one window by the driver's seat again and again. He wanted to keep out the dust, wind and rain. When it all wore out, there was nothing but the sky above, and that's the way I remember it best.

Late on a Saturday afternoon, Dad might pile the whole family in for a trip to town, always Oyen, and shut the doors, all but his. He'd be in and out of his, goodness knew how often, before the thing started, if it did. Stepping up on the bumpy tin dashboard, he'd sit in place to set the gas flow on the steering wheel. This handle was of shining, bright metal and stood out among every other dark and dusty part. Reaching for the dashboard, he gave a couple of pulls on the wire primer,

 then jumped out of the car in a hurry to crank it before the engine flooded. With his left hand on top of the radiator, the whole car bounced up and down as he cranked with the right one.

It wheezed, coughed and sputtered, making a terrible racket. A hush fell over everyone. Would it start? It never did right off, and perhaps not at all. When it didn't, after all the hurried preparations of getting dressed up, we'd have to climb out and be very disappointed. Dad didn't give up easily, but went on cranking until he was red in the face. Amid much backfiring, Mom would call, "Do be careful, Will." His arm was often hurt by the backfiring but never broken, as happened to some. Sometimes the engine started with a roar. Dad quickly ran back and jumped in his seat to push the lever up or down, back and forth, to keep the motor running. Leaving great puffs of dust, we headed up the lane to the highway.

Something was bound to go wrong on the way and we might have to turn back. The car had no trunk, so in the back seat, along with the young ones, were all kinds of paraphernalia used to keep it going. At a minimum there were wrenches, a tin of gas, and a bucket for scooping up water. Dad did not enjoy fussing with motors and objected to anything that needed as much pampering as did this car. At times it sent up great clouds of steam like a chimney. Then Dad stopped the car for us to race with the bucket to the nearest slough. Back in, we jogged along the road merrily singing and Dad whistling, perhaps one of his favorite tunes, "Pretty Red Wing" or "Clementine." It was great fun. Mom always sat up front with the youngest in her arms. The rest of us "squose" into the back, most of us standing up.

A special feature of this car was its horn. This consisted of about five brass pipes welded into a clump, which made pleasing musical sounds. It became quite a fad for each family to have its own individual-sounding horn. Mr. Hoover, for instance, made himself a very elaborate one. When anyone reached town, he honked and everyone else knew who had arrived, even before the dust settled down and he could be seen.

In 1928 the crops were good.

On a certain fall day, a man drove up to the yard in a most beautiful car. It was tall and green and square with real glass windows, and we gathered round to admire it. He opened the doors to show off the blue plush lining. Even the ceiling was covered in blue and the whole inside looked so cozy.

He was a salesman. After talking hard and Dad looking very serious, we chorused, "Buy it, buy it," a couple of times. And he did!! We were most proud of the shiny, new thing.

Everyone wanted to play in it. "Stay away and stay out of it," said Dad, but in the next weeks there were many tattlings. All of us were extra tidy and proper for the first trip to town. We sat waiting for Dad to get in and when he did, he started it mysteriously.

The riding was unbelievably smooth and so quiet. We climbed in happily, very sure that there would be no problems getting to town. How wrong we were! Our pleasure was short-lived. We weren't used to closed vehicles. What a sad lot arrived on Main Street! First one child was sick and then another. Dad always tried to stop the car in time. I stood up to get out and crashed my head in the doorway. No one sang. "The old car was much more fun," we children all agreed, but it had "had it."

THE LOAD OF WHEAT

Grown-ups were most busy at harvest time. Wheat piled up in granaries and not all of it could be stored. People counted on selling some at once, to pay debts left over from last year. Then they bought much needed things that had been postponed. It was hard to find time to haul wheat in the thick of things.

The neighbor boys drove loads of wheat to town. They were no older than I was, so, logically, Dad decided I could do this. The fact that I had gone with him on many such trips didn't cheer me up! I doubted that I could do it all alone. Reluctant feelings cropped up, but Dad mustn't know as he needed help. The things that bothered me were remembering his driving up and down those awful hills, and how many times he looked anxious and talked of risks.

Brakes on wagons were crude wooden blocks, often with gunny-sacks tied over them. They soon wore out and were almost useless with their poor leverage. We didn't use brakes. The dirt highways were graded round and high for the rain to run off. Ruts gradually formed in them. It was an unspoken rule that no one went to town after a rain unless it was absolutely necessary. If he did there were bound to be unkind words spoken. It was then that the troublesome deep ruts were started. These were formed chiefly in the low places. Everyone had to live with them until a road gang came along with scrapers to smooth them out.

There was that nasty little hill by the mailbox. Nearer to Benton there was another group of the nastiest up and down hills in the area. Going to Oyen was far easier. Even on regular hills, the reins were pulled hard to hold the horses back as they started down. As the bottom neared, they were let go and the whip was used to keep them running. This way the momentum helped the load up the next rise and saved the horses. The most awesome grade was the last one before Benton, long and gradually sloping, but out of the side of the hill. Dad surprised me. Instead of the small wagon and two horses I'd expected, he hitched up four horses to the big grain tank, and it was full of wheat! That meant I had to handle two pairs of reins instead of one. Oh dear! Mom argued with Dad (to no avail) about my taking on such a big job. Man, did I agree with her, but I said not a word!

The horses were waiting and there was nothing else to do but climb up, with my heart in my mouth. I dangled my legs down, just the way Dad did. All around me was a broad expanse of wheat. It looked as wide as the road and I didn't feel safe. I liked looking directly down at the road. From way up there I couldn't judge where I was on the highway.

With a slap of the reins and a "giddyup" we took off on that lonely trip, leaving my parents standing watching. Out to the mailbox was fairly level – so far all was well! Then I came to a sharp turn onto the road, and at once a hill to go down. It wasn't very big, but it was steep. Dad even had trouble there. I had seen him jump off the

sleigh and walk close beside it to get down. Thinking he'd done it to save the horses his extra weight, I now wondered if it was because he had felt unsafe! I was very afraid the wagon would roll too fast and bump into the horses. If they slowed down too quickly, after pulling hard, the tongue shot up in the air and could snap the tugs on the harness. Goodness knew what all could happen. Thumping and bumping, we managed and the bottom was reached safely, I don't know how. After a peaceful, level stretch, there were three or four more hills ahead. By the time the last long hill with the cut was reached, I felt the world on my shoulders.

The minute that last hill came into view, I saw a road gang at work and felt rather glad, thinking that maybe they would help me get down. Local people often worked on these gangs, but this time there was no one I knew.

The right-hand side of the road was cut into the hill, leaving a high bank. This was a big advantage – at least that side was safe! To the left the ground dropped almost straight down, and then rolled away into the valley. I could picture the horses, the wheat and me all rolling down there too! I had never thought that I had much imagination. That time I did, and it worked overtime!

The road workers stopped working to watch me. One of them yelled something fresh. Clutching the reins, busy worrying, I suddenly realized that this fellow was right beside the wagon, hollering! The long grade was about to begin. I noticed out the corner of my eye that he was trying to jump onto the wagon.

I yelled, "Get down."

The next instant he was hanging on and grinning over the top of the wheat. The horses had begun to move faster and needed watching. I quickly yelled, "Get down" again, but didn't allow him any time. He showed no signs of leaving, so I promptly let him have it with the whip. The end wrapped around him, and he dropped to the ground in a hurry, hanging onto the whip. My only thought was that Dad would be very cross to lose the whip!

The horses were frightened, but, after pulling unevenly, they settled into unison and began galloping down the hill. Pulling on the reins did no good. Rumbling and bumping, with wheat splashing over the sides, we raced downward. The horses had taken over completely. There was nothing I could do! At least it would all be over soon!

When we reached the bottom, everyone and everything was safe and sound. The wild-looking animals slowed to a walk, noisily snuffing and blowing, and the railroad tracks were crossed. A sharp turn to the left, and there was town. The elevator man was standing at the door. He kindly offered to drive the load in for weighing, and I gratefully climbed down. Whew!

It took a while to get over trembling and he questioned me. Was I sure the man wasn't trying to be helpful? Maybe he was. Maybe it was someone else who had made the fresh remarks. My only thought had been a recollection of Mom's warnings about men being awful, and I didn't trust them. Besides, under the circumstances, I'd been too rattled (in Dad's terms) to be sensible.

The elevator man was, after all, a stranger, so I told him as little as possible. He went inside to phone Dad. When the wagon was unloaded, someone was sent for me to follow, past the workmen, after which he waved me on and turned back. I guessed the elevator man could be thanked for that.

The mere thought of going again made me afraid. I knew Dad wished it, but he didn't make me. How disappointing for him and also for me! I'd set out so proud of the fact of being helpful, in spite of being a girl.

It was the first big job he'd handed me to do all alone, and I'd not been capable of meeting the challenge!

EIGHTH GRADE

From that harvest to the next, time went faster. I was an eighth grader now and almost grown up! Richard and I were conscious of this, and of each other. Jim was the same as ever, only taller, and still absorbed in learning things. He'd start to tell us about something, only to find he had no audience.

School had grown to a record number of children: twenty-six. Twenty of them were boys and six were girls, and all of these girls were much younger than I.

When school started again in spring, we felt that we were on the home stretch. We wondered what came next. No one had any plans, and there was no talk of high school. There wasn't one. The inevitable fate was to stay home and help out. The only kids older than us had come to that. All of this left us without enthusiasm, so we stayed away from the subject, lived from day to day and enjoyed what came.

The neighbor lady who had told me I was old enough to wear a corset showed me hers. What a nuisance! She also said to think about acting like a lady instead of a tomboy. No one had spoken of tomboys before and I wondered what they were.

I loved baseball. Being one of the oldest in school, I could smack nice home runs for the younger kids to chase. Jim didn't like to play and Richard was half-hearted, but he'd play if I would. The boys in seventh grade were good competition. We also played a form of tackle football, and I'd always been in the middle of it.

Then I got a pretty, white, printed voile dress with green collar and cuffs, and I had a problem. Torn between having fun and looking pretty, I was almost mad at Mom for letting me choose that one from the catalog. Each night it was carefully washed and ironed for school next day.

I'd begun to like Arthur best, even though he was redheaded and only in the seventh grade. He always looked nice and tidy and was so polite to girls. I wanted to look nice too. Before that spring, I hadn't noticed boys. Playing football would be ruinous to the dress, which did make me feel more like a lady, but I couldn't see giving up baseball. I tried to do away with hair ribbons because Florence (Richard's older sister, who was out of school) had shown me the latest things, which were bobby pins. I was hard-pressed to get and keep one in with such thick, straight hair. I took it out when I got home from school. I bent it into shape, and set it aside. This could go on only so long. After a while it gave out entirely and I had to beg a new one from somewhere.

What I wanted was bobbed, marcelled hair like Florence: "Then Mom, I wouldn't even have to have a bobby pin. Couldn't I please have a curling iron like hers?" "No," Mom said.

I had to have some kind of curl, so I tried wetting my hair every night and braiding it. Each time I unwound it in the morning there were only uneven bumps, hopeless looking, so I gave that up. I felt very plain. Believe it or not, I even tried eating dry bread crusts, on the sly, because someone said they made your hair curl.

I was a trifle naive! For example, another time I was told that a young wild duck could be caught if salt were sprinkled on its tail. I carefully walked to the slough with a handful of stolen salt. Somehow I couldn't seem to get close enough to throw the salt on its tail. It seemed to me that that was a pretty chancy way to catch ducks!

Richard and I talked about the awesome graduation exams to be taken, and wondered if we knew enough. The Provincial Government mailed them from Edmonton, our capital, in fat, brown envelopes. A scary occasion!

When the June day came, teacher brought them to school. She sat the three of us across the back of the room with at least one desk separating us. Everyone watched as she handed an envelope to each of us. We opened them, wrote down our names and addresses and went to work. Teacher timed us, since only so much time was allowed. There was no noise in the schoolroom or talking. The teacher was as anxious as we were. When we finished, the envelopes were sealed, handed back and sent to Edmonton.

Each subject was handled in a separate envelope, and it took a couple of days to do them all. When completed, I felt I'd known too little by far and hated to think what would happen if this meant failure. When we were finished we did not go back to school, but waited at home to hear the results. It was lonely and odd seeing the other kids off to school. Only babies were left at home.

One day I saw Richard on horseback, galloping in from the mail-box. It was fun to see someone coming. I'd recognized his horse and knew he was coming to see me. The occasion made me feel awkward, yet pleased. He'd been to Benton to find out if our exam marks had come. They were to be mailed directly to us, not to the teacher. His hadn't arrived and he was anxious to know if mine had.

I walked, not ran, to meet him, and he got down from his saddle and stood by the horse a short time while we talked. He found it as awkward a spell as I did. As he went off home up the lane, I began to think about him. It had been nice to have him come because he was in the same lost world. I'd even begun to be kidded a little in town about him being my boyfriend. I didn't like this, but I figured maybe he was, or should be. I couldn't see why a friend like him had to be labeled at all!

Before long, he came again, and I could see he had news. He was carrying mail, and he handed me a long, thin, gray envelope. Jumping off his horse he came to stand beside me, to watch while I opened it. I was half sorry and half glad he'd come. If all was well, it would be more of an occasion to have him share it. On the other hand, what if...? Standing undecided, I asked what his luck had been. He wouldn't tell his marks or even whether he had passed, so we teased around a bit.

Finally, fumbling it open carefully so he couldn't see any of it until I did, I pulled out a folded gray certificate. Horrors, marks for each subject were printed in a little box right on the certificate, instead of in a separate letter. Richard coaxed to see them. So subject by subject we talked them over. His marks were very much the same as mine. I was surprised to find that my highest grade was in Arithmetic. I wasn't fond of the subject, but it was good in that it was exacting. What had to be known was clearly put before you, whereas subjects like history and geography were beset with wonderings in many directions.

Richard and I stood to talk a bit longer by the edge of the pasture, both of us feeling very glad it was over. Then we reluctantly went home. That was graduation day!

MR. IUNGERICH

Within the next month, an unexpected visitor showed up. He was the Rev. E. E. Iungerich from down East in the U.S.A. He was a minister from our Church. One of these men had come once before from Denver, but that was years ago and I scarcely remembered. Mom must have known he was coming. She told Mrs. Pooke, who invited all of us to have the church service at her house that Sunday. We sat around on chairs in her nice living room, with Uncle Nelson and Cousin Norman. Mrs. Pooke was very polite but told us afterward she didn't take to Mr. Iungerich, so we heard no more from her about church matters. She thought he looked like a fat little monk. He was bald all over the top of his head and he did lisp!

I didn't like him much either. He watched everything we did, and asked why or how. No one had any answers; usually it was, "I don't know." Dad didn't let a minister interfere with his farm work, so Mom was left to entertain him. She wasn't at all comfortable doing so, and seemed to find more things for me to do in the kitchen while talking with him. I was sure some of it was for company.

He went out of his way to talk with us children. We were fascinated less with his talk than with his bald head! We had never seen one of these close up before! Within the first hour, he brought out large photographs of a beautiful wedding. The pictures were of a Brazilian couple in Rio de Janeiro and he told of their being married three times, or in three languages. He had married them in Spanish. We'd never seen anyone married.

We thought he was interesting when he talked, so we didn't, feeling we had nothing to say. Very soon he found out how old we were, our names, and where we were in school. He asked us to sing some songs we'd learned there. It took some pressure from Mom to get started but we launched into "De Camptown Races." He didn't think that was a very nice song and said so. "Do you know any others?" he asked. A bit of time elapsed before we regained the needed courage to go on. We decided to sing "Mr. Frog Took a Notion One Day" and he didn't ask us to sing any more. We whispered to each other that either it was too long or he didn't like that one either.

On the kitchen table was a shiny, flower-printed oilcloth. Dad felt that print ones cut down the glare from the lamp. Much of the color had worn off, but until it was full of holes, it was not replaced. Dad sat on a chair with an end to himself and we kids on benches, to either side, for many things besides eating. When suppertime arrived, Mom unrolled a new, pure white cloth, more suitable, she felt, for a minister. Because it was so plain she'd also bought a yard of bright blue crepe paper. The Fair had brought that to mind for decoration.

After the tablecloth was smoothed out, she handed me the crepe paper and asked me to cut out a doily for a centerpiece. I folded it in half, and half again, until it was pie-shaped, as we'd done in school. Then I used a pair of scissors to scallop it into a circle, with a leaf or two in the center.

Probably the reason why I remember this was due to Mr. Iungerich. With his usual curiosity, he came over to watch and ask more questions. This gave me a bad time, and the precious paper was almost ruined.

He stayed three whole days!

One afternoon he asked what I was going to do next year and, of course, I had no answer. "Why don't you go to Bryn Athyn?" he said. Where was that? He told of a school a person should go to in Pennsylvania. I was not at all keen about studies, and unsure of being up to such a risky undertaking. He did make it sound interesting. Mom said nothing, and Dad listened too, so they must feel Bryn Athyn was an alright place. I hadn't been told that it was a religious institution. Next Mr. Iungerich carefully wrote "Mr. C. E. Doering" on a piece of paper and said to write to him and tell him I wanted to go to school. He would be sure to answer.

It was no more complicated than that! If he'd only just talked about it and not been so exact I'm sure nothing would have come of it. Dad offered no help but he didn't stop me either. He mailed the letter. I didn't really think anything would come of it. Sure enough a letter came back promptly, saying I could have a working scholarship and to get a passport. So the summer was busily taken up with writing or waiting for letters.

We received a list saying what clothes I would need. This impressed me greatly, and seemed to me to be the biggest hurdle. There were fees to be paid, like $5.00 for breakage. What in the world was breakage? Having no money, I wondered how in the world any of this could be possible. If it hadn't happened in a year when the crops were good, it wouldn't have been possible! Providence does play a hand in things!

There was so much needed at home, but I couldn't worry about that. The first thing to get was the passport. The doctor gave me a vaccination, which didn't do a thing, not even leaving a scar. He gave me the slip of paper anyway. The hard part was getting to the city of Calgary, over 250 miles away, in order to see the immigration people. Dad hadn't been there himself since the very early days and still had said not a word about my leaving home. It troubled me; I couldn't picture him going to all the bother.

THE HAMMS

Within weeks of the minister's visit, and after my first flurries of activity, Dad decided to go visit the Hamms in Eastern Saskatchewan, about 260 miles to the east. The wheat was still growing and chores were put aside, I don't know how.

We'd heard the parents discuss this family. Old papa Hamm had two families. He'd almost raised the first one when his wife died and he'd remarried. Now he was raising a second family, and the parents hadn't met them. It was delightful to have Dad decide we'd go on a trip, and to pick up and leave. I and one or two sisters went with him. Mom was left at home. She'd never milked a cow, so I don't know who did the barn work. We kids didn't know why this came about.

The Hamms belonged to the same church and the minister had visited them before he'd come to see us. They must have been surprised to have us show up without notice and stay for a couple of days. Formalities were little thought about out West and never by Dad. It certainly saved the bustle and chores of preparation and perhaps added enjoyment because of the spontaneity. Mr. Hamm seemed overjoyed when greeting Dad at the door. His wife wasn't enthusiastic, shall we say, the whole time we were there, but her husband was clearly head of his household.

In general, they were a plump, jolly lot. Father Hamm had a white goatee, a big booming voice, and spoke to his family in German. Only his second family was at home.

Adelaide was the oldest. She had short, light, curly hair and she was awkward, slow and eighteen.

Justina was large, but at sixteen she was a dark and sparkly girl, full of vitality. We enjoyed each other at once. Emmanuel, with light, curly hair, was very quiet, but not unpleasant. He was fourteen, like me. Harold was small, dark and twelve.

We arrived after supper. The first thing they gave us was a bite to eat before going to bed: pork cracklings from a pan rendering pork rind on the back of the stove. It was there during our whole visit, with new pieces of rind added from time to time. It was delicious! Mom always said that the reason the Germans were so big was the amount of pork they ate.

 We had a most wonderfully noisy time during our whole visit. While Dad talked downstairs with Mr. Hamm, we big kids surprisingly played games such as Tag in the dark upstairs. We had a hilarious time. When the noise was too much, father Hamm bellowed up the stairs in German, which slowed everything down for a spell.

I found out that Justina was going to Bryn Athyn too, and she talked of her plans. Looking back on that occasion, I can see that this fact must have been the reason for our visit to the Hamms' home. Dad never said so! Mr. Iungerich had also interested Justina and told Dad about it. When the men had finished with their visiting, to their mutual satisfaction, we left. Mr. Hamm said that Justina and I should travel east together. This idea was never mentioned again, and, of course, we didn't.

A couple of weeks later Mr. Hamm phoned to say Emmanuel had run away from home and couldn't be found. In talking over our visit his father learned that the boy had taken a liking to me, which I hadn't known. They suspected that he had gone to our house. But he hadn't.

At a wedding in Pittsburgh thirty-five years later, I encountered, by chance, a handsome, well-informed young man. "I'll bet you don't know who I am." he stated. Then he proceeded to tell all he knew about me, which was considerable.

Completely mystified, I made a number of wrong guesses. Then he laughed and said he was Emmanuel!

MRS. POOKE

A most fortunate thing happened that summer. An ad was printed in the paper offering a package of remnants for $3.00. There would be a minimum of 10 yards, depending on the fabric. Mom considered this reasonable, and the order was mailed. A lovely, fat package came, with yards and yards of different pieces and colors. All looked most pretty and were to be made into dresses. The pink organdy was for best. I drew a picture for each piece.

Word got about that I was leaving home, and everyone asked many questions. Mrs. Pooke showed up, oh lucky day, and I can't imagine what would have happened without her. She looked at our ideas for my dresses and said that this was an enormous undertaking. No word was said about hiring her, as we couldn't afford to. Instead, she invited me to go home with her for a couple of days. She'd help me with the dresses, not do them.

Doesn't it always happen that, when one good thing comes along, others follow? Driving home in her horse and buggy I tried hard to think of what to say. The idea of staying at her house was even more absorbing than the prospect of having several dresses all at once. We had been there only once, for the church service. Her living room was bigger than any other I'd seen and as full of nice things as Aunt Kate's!

Jumping down out of the buggy upon arrival, I watched as she stepped casually down, then followed her inside, while her husband took the horse to be unhitched. It was suppertime, and she asked my help in setting the table. There were pretty things for this. Water glasses came from a china closet in the living room. When we sat down, the pretty sights and the quiet were alien. Everything was! Mrs. Pooke took the opportunity to teach me some of the niceties. A person asked for a piece of bread instead of reaching for it. A person waited to be asked, "Do you care for more meat?" rather than picking up his plate and saying so. Red Jell-O was served in tall, stemmed glasses, and I wasn't at all sure it even tasted like Jell-O. In spite of the lovely surroundings, I was already a bit homesick by bedtime. After two days of this, I was very happy to go home again where everything was easy!

While I was there we did sew, until our fingers and backs ached. I was miserably slow, having done little sewing before that time. I wanted to be sure that she didn't feel we had taken advantage of her wonderful impulse, which, of course, we had! I'm sure she'd hoped to be hired.

We used a few articles from her small collection of buttons, thread and ribbon. Mom and I had not considered this problem. She did charge for these. Not a dress did she question, but took the pictures I'd drawn and used patterns of sorts to cut out three of them. To think I never wrote to her afterward to thank her! She went to so much trouble, but then I'd no idea people did such things. Besides, after leaving home, I grew out of those dresses very quickly, and Mrs. Pooke was completely forgotten for years.

This was 1929, still the Flapper era. Dresses had no shape and tops were long. Hip lines had short, gathered skirts to knee level. These were just as shocking to the older generation then as 1968 skirts are to me!

The first dress we tackled was of sleazy rayon with white and blue stripes. Around the collar and cuffs was gathered, narrow ribbon as a ruffle, and it was black, the only color Mrs. Pooke had. It took me forever.

Next was another of the same fabric, all pink. It was copied after a style of Miss Kilberg's with a long collar to the skirt line. At its base was a black bow. Upon wearing it the first time, the remark was made, "If you must have a bow, make it a pink one." I had no money to buy a pink one but took off the black one. The dress looked too bare then so I put it away.

The best material, the pink organdy, was saved till last. The school list had said an evening dress. After discussing what that might mean, we decided it must be a party dress. Here at last was a chance for ruffles and lace, very special, nothing else would do. Lace must be ordered. Being such a rank beginner, Mrs.

Pooke set out to do all the machine sewing while I struggled with hems, etc., often becoming exasperated and exhausted. Best efforts didn't look very even and I wished she'd let me do the "easy" machine sewing in spite of the seams not being all that straight when done. But I could still dream of how pretty the results would be.

The pink organdy was taken home to finish, and to await the lace for the collar, puffed sleeves and ruffles. Then I tried it on. My sakes, what a disappointment! I felt all bumpy, lumpy and stuffy. A glance at Mom told the same story; she wasn't enthusiastic either. The fabric was very scratchy. I thought I looked like one of our clucking hens with its feathers all stuck out! I put the dress away. Surely it wouldn't look that bad when the time came for wearing it!

The clothes list was far from complete when what should happen but Mom decided to go to Calgary! She was going to travel two hundred miles, just to shop for me! I didn't know she had it in her. I was left battling seven other children – one a baby – and the cooking. I found out about work and what I didn't know about cooking. Mom came back beaming, with a brown coat, hat, purse and more. The purse caught my fancy with its cream-colored, shiny cloth lining and a leather handle.

lace sewed on flat

The most beautiful thing she bought was a peach georgette dress with ecru lace, for evening. Outshining everything else, it also made our sewing efforts look very feeble. That dress was almost worn out from folding and unfolding to look at again and again before it was put away! There was a feature about it that bothered me. From the waistline hung two little, wire half circles, one on each side, to make the skirt stand out. And that it did! When I walked, it felt funny and jiggled up and down like Grandma Even's crocheted hats had done.

I didn't complain to my mother, who maintained it was the latest thing. After I left home those bouncy things were carefully removed. After that the dress felt much better!

A trunk, which had to be brought home from Benton in a wagon, arrived shortly. It was small, covered with thin metal, painted shiny green, with wooden slats on the bottom. Packed on top was a brush, comb and mirror, all navy colored, and an umbrella. Schoolmates came to see and everything was taken out, marveled at and carefully repacked. The umbrella was the greatest novelty; nobody had seen one before. The little kids in my own family had to be watched. "Show me again how it opens and shuts." It had to be hidden to be kept safe.

There was nothing more to do at this time but wait and see as the days went by. Harvest was upon us and there was much work to do.

COMBINING

The past year Dad had had a bumper crop. His new disc plow turned over wider strips of earth each time around the fields and he was very pleased. Three furrows was the best the old one would do, but this one did eight or nine. Its large, round, hollowed saucers were no trouble at all to maintain, compared with the old plowshares which had to be sharpened so frequently. Farm machinery was bursting forth on the market with many new improvements. One important part of a seed drill, which had been made of wood, was now replaced with metal. Big tractors were mentioned. We children couldn't believe that they could replace horses. The very thought was unreal.

This summer's crop looked very good again. Implement agents were in readiness, primed for action with easy credit. They were very happy to talk with any likely fellow who came to town. What farmer isn't interested in better tools? Agents had a soft life compared with other residents and many times did a landslide of business. They had little compunction in pushing a sale without regard to the customer's real need, or ability to pay. With machinery costs in the thousands of dollars, I can hardly forgive them.

Buyers and seller knew one another personally. The farmers were honest folk and believed what they were told, seeming to have no shrewdness. These same men were rugged individual thinkers on issues concerning politics and other matters. When it came to farm machinery, they were just plain gullible! Their sons, left on the farm today, are the same. The greater part of their money was spent on implements and what an array was needed! Sheds for protection from the weather cost too much, so these expensive things sat outside year round. All their metal parts were exposed to the elements. Naturally they rusted, and soon had to be replaced. This was bad enough. But as Dad said, "What man wouldn't try something new in hopes of cutting down on the back-breaking labor? The only way to find out for yourself was to buy one," said he. At least they thought progressively if not with judgment.

This year waiting for sale was a revolutionary new implement costing more than Dad had ever dreamed of spending before. Supposedly it did away with stooking, binding and the whole threshing crew. It was called a combine, and it ended an era! Dad decided to buy a combine. He was the very first in the whole neighborhood. What a noise came from that monstrous thing! Tall and sprawling in all directions, how could anything of the sort be dragged around the fields? One side resembled a binder, but instead of cutting the usual six-foot swath, it cut fourteen feet! Attached at right angles and towering above was the bulk of its workings. In the back was a flat, rounded hood. The straw was blown from this as the combine circled the field. On the far side was a long, iron arm which pulled a wagon. Into this poured a steady stream of wheat, from a spout on its side. A gunnysack was tied to another smaller spout to catch the weed seeds and shrunken grain, which the pigs enjoyed later.

Where the cutting platform joined the main part of the machine there were many kinds and sizes of cogs, gears and pulleys, completely exposed. Beyond these, and two or three feet higher, was a small, wooden platform. To its front was attached a riding seat from which to drive the horses. I don't know how many. Sitting thus, the main engine was directly behind with the width of the platform between. Dad felt the seat wasn't tall enough. With 2x4s he fashioned a crude chair on stilts to be high enough so he could see over everything. He almost looked like some sort of king, way up on his expensive throne!

This wonderful machine posed a few new problems. At the top of the list was the fact that the wheat had to be dead ripe and still standing before it could be combined. No field ripened evenly. This fact gave Dad the most anxiety. Heavy winds and rain could easily flatten the wheat when it was so ripe. When this happened it would be difficult, if not impossible, to run the cutter blade low enough to pick it up.

Even an ordinary wind flattened some of the early ripened spots. Harvesting would take much longer because the machine was pulled round and round the field. Being so heavy and cumbersome was hard on the horses, very hard on some occasions. Then the worry. What if too much wheat ripened at once and was endangered?

As it threshed, the straw was left in a small trail behind the machine. There were no more strawstacks to play on. For Dad, there was no easily available source of bedding for the animals. This was a feature Dad did not like. Collecting enough straw was a new after-harvest job. The old, rusty rake was oiled up and used again. He drove round the field and collected straw into little piles, to be pitched high into the hayrick. He'd been able to drive up close to a big strawstack and in no time roll down fat amounts to fill a load. Oh well, work had slackened by then, there was the time, but what a nuisance it was! The only way to get rid of the straw that was left in the fields by the combine was to burn it off. This was more trouble, work and worry than firing the big strawstacks. No cultivating or seeding could be done until then. The soil would not absorb it as mulch if it was "turned under." Plowed rows of turned over sod, as fire guards around the fields, were now a must.

The day for burning was carefully chosen. There was no firefighting apparatus anywhere. If a strong wind came up during burning, a prairie fire might get under way and rage for miles. These fires had been common in the earlier days when the grass was longer from less grazing. Any sign of smoke was carefully watched by people and word spread quickly when a fire started; others were notified far and wide.

Men raced to the scene with buckets and barrels in their wagons, hoping for a slough near the fire. Plenty of gunnysacks were all important. Wet down from dipping in the barrels, they were used to beat the creeping flames and were the best method of combat. Shovels and brooms were taken also. Local men could get out to plow furrows ahead of the fire.

The women weren't to be left behind and miss all the excitement. They were best with the brooms. Hadn't they had much practice wielding these at cats, children, mice, floors and ceilings? Anyway, any excuse to visit was a good one! Hurriedly into wagons went coffee pots and sandwiches, whatever they had, as they climbed aboard.

The salesman's best pitch was that, with this new combine, one man alone could harvest his own crop. Above all things, Dad loved being independent, besides saving all the money a threshing crew cost. After the first day's trial, he at once found himself in the position of a one-armed paper hanger with too many jobs to do at once. Still determined to do it without outside help, he talked of it at supper and decided that I was all the help he needed! I was completely astonished by the idea, but I listened carefully and the job didn't sound too hard. Being asked made me feel very grown up. Faced with the actual machine next morning, it looked like a man-sized job and was really quite frightening. Not only must I judge the situation accurately, but I must be alert at all times, as I was to find out. Once during an easy spell, when complacency set in, the results brought me up short and everything came to a crashing halt.

Behind the cutting platform were two long, narrow V-shaped rods which supported it. I had to stand on these rods with my feet uncomfortably far apart. My toes were tucked under the platform for balance, as it rode along. The ride wasn't the smoothest going. In front was a three-foot wall of metal against which I leaned, watching the wheat fall onto the fast-revolving canvas belt. In my hands was a perfectly ordinary kitchen broom.

When the machine hit a patch of tumbleweed or Russian thistle, the canvas couldn't move these along. Instead, the stuff piled up and bubbled over the back, falling helter-skelter to the ground and the wheat along with it. Dad figured that I could ride on the platform to beat these weeds down. This would save time and wheat. He was right, it worked fine! But what a chore it was, keeping up with those nasty weeds.

There was another way I could be useful. At the bottom of inclines or slight valleys, the wheat grew heavier. With horses pulling such a heavy machine they could scarce be slowed down enough. As a result, wheat fell too thick and fast to be carried along to the feeder. It piled up layer upon layer with the canvas gaily slipping by underneath. The minute this happened, I pushed down hard with the broom, picking it up, and pressing down again. This often worked to keep the wheat moving. If this didn't work at first, the broom was quickly turned upside down so the handle could catch one of the little slats on the canvas belt. Thus the broom would ride along with the belt until out of reach, then I would pick it up and plunge it in to catch again. This would keep the wheat moving. There were slats every six to eight inches on the canvas, to keep it flat and rigid.

Usually the wheat fell neat and smooth and was carried along to the feeder. This was an open maw with a half dozen chopping cutter blades. These always appeared to be in a hurry. They moved up and down at different times, looking like a monster chomping its teeth. I spent a lot of time just keeping a close watch, ready for trouble. I learned to watch ahead, but could not always tell when a spot of weeds would be upon us. The mustard grew as tall as the wheat and was lost in the same golden color. Or the heavy patch of grain might be hard to judge. When these things did happen, they required instant action.

One time, we were on a comfortable, level stretch and I had become complacent. I hadn't been watching the terrain directly ahead, and the wheat began piling up. In hurrying to turn the broom upside down, it got away. There was too much noise for Dad to hear my calls. On rushed the broom into the jaws of the machinery. The noise that followed sounded like a dog chewing bones must sound to a dog! How Dad got the horses and engine stopped so fast I don't know – at least it seemed fast. You can imagine how he looked and felt. He set to work and worried, out loud, about getting all the bits and pieces of wire and wood removed from his precious machine. The broom could not possibly go through the whole machine. It would have broken or jammed the innards somewhere. What a repair job then! Luckily it hadn't gone that far. With the admonition, "Don't let that happen again," we went back to work.

This occurrence was tame compared to chances taken with life and limb at other times. Dad had a problem with the horses going too fast, particularly when we were going up a slope, like the hillside near the coulee. Then I worried about him sitting away up there. Maybe he could see everything better, but how could he possibly get out alive if anything happened? He was completely surrounded with hazards. I could jump safely off behind, providing I avoided one very wide flat wheel. Or I could make a long jump to the right to terra firma, if I was on the cutting platform to begin with. Naturally, with Dad riding it out, I never felt free to leave.

When there was a heavy stand of wheat on a down slope, I had my own problems. I had to leave my usual spot and jump over the awesome mass of gears and chains to reach the small, wooden platform above and beyond. The engine knob was accessible there. By pulling it out, the engine speeded up to handle the heavier volume of wheat, due to our speed down the hill. Then back down again quick to broom it through, while Dad seesawed hard on the reins, pulling back for all he was worth. Getting back down again was far more terrifying than going up. Such tense moments! After some particularly bad times, I remember Dad stopping the horses at the bottom and climbing down himself to stand a few minutes, now that the crisis was over. I wonder if it ever occurred to him those coulees did not have to be done? The loss would be minor compared with the chances he took on everything else.

Something should be said about the noises. I had never before heard anything like it! There was such a combination of sounds! Horses and harness, the long paddle wheel boards whirring around knocking the wheat onto the canvas, whose chains made a rattle, the cutter blades there in front and the big chopping ones to the left. The blower for the straw and the main central engine, which was noisiest of all. Even the creaking of the wagon could be heard from where Dad sat.

Dad knew by all the sounds whether or not everything was all right. Riding off to the side, as I did, wasn't so bad, but when jumping over the exposed gear I got the full impact. There the noise was deafening. It helped to add a feeling of cautiousness, which was badly needed. After being in the East a few years, I went back and took a look at that combine. I knew that never in this world would I be able to do all that again!

After the first day of harvesting I was wholly tired, and my face and eyes were windburned, scratched and sore from the chaff. Besides, I was completely covered with black dust. This fact was a surprise when my mother mentioned it. After becoming accustomed to the long day, I got immense satisfaction out of the job. Dad never savored more his first moments after he'd climbed on the wagon to inspect the year's wheat. He'd chosen the time correctly; the grain was dry, fat and ripe. He too felt satisfied. Best of all it did turn out to be a bumper crop year.

I recall the family going to town for supplies during harvest and being embarrassed by all the attention. Everyone wanted to know how Dad felt about the new combine and were surprised too when they learned I was his help. Dad enjoyed it.

That was the end of threshing machines. Neighbors all bought combines in the next year or two, but I was gone. Much better ones came along. Then the big step: buying tractors to pull them instead of horses, an enormous help in time, effort and safety.

Now the combines are self-propelled!

OUR FAMILY

In the late summer of 1928, Mom went to Oyen, to the hospital, for two weeks. It was harvest time and a hired man had come to help Dad with the stooking. The latest baby was very new, and I was anxious to do a good job of caring for it in Mom's place. I was 13 years old.

Dad encouraged everyone to help. He cleaned house and enjoyed it at first, but as time went on the going got rough. Getting the parts of the meal all cooked at the same time was the hardest thing to do. One day at noon, when we all sat down to dinner, Dad asked where the gravy was. I bawled! I didn't know how to make gravy and was too tired to even care.

All of us were mighty glad when Mom came back home. Dad gave each of us a big present to celebrate.

Bea was that latest baby. She was a year old when I left for Bryn Athyn.

Ted was a year or two older. He was a blond and not a very strong little boy. Mom pampered him and he had a hard time adjusting to difficulties as he grew up. A very pleasant fellow, he never married and was not really cut out to be a farmer.

Margaret was strong-minded, or at least she always knew what she wanted. She was called Lillian in school because there were two other Margarets. I think she was the handsomest member of the family.

Bill was nervous and skinny as a boy, but always full of fun.

Leslie was the oldest boy. He was responsible and thoughtful. He and Bill were inseparable.

Irene was bright-eyed, quick, and always naughty. She had no respect for clothes, wouldn't do the milking, and was Pop's favorite.

Mabel didn't learn as fast as the others. She didn't go to school because she couldn't keep up. She was particularly good at caring for the babies, whom she loved.

Mom was an orphan, and we really didn't know much about her past history. I don't think she remembered it very clearly, or at least we found it hard to decide from her stories what was fact and what was fiction!

This is her story as we understood it. Her maiden name was Rose Pearce, or perhaps Rosella. She grew up in Hull, England. Mom said she was driven in a horse and carriage and had a nice home. She was only a couple of years old when her mother died. Her father remarried and her stepmother was horrid. When she was eight the stepmother sent her to a Dr. Barnardo's orphanage. Her father had "died"?

The orphans once danced for Queen Victoria. Any mention of the royal family was a delight to Mom. She couldn't have loved them more if they'd been members of her own family! My sisters tell me that the best gift I ever sent Mom after I left was a beautiful book showing many English castles, the royal relatives, the palace guards, etc. She pored over it, and it was kept spotless!

She went to school until she had finished the third grade. She could write and add. However, she never did learn sentence structure and where to put her dots and capitals. I think she must have had educated people somewhere in her background because she had such good taste in many things, always had good manners, and wanted to be considered a lady.

In 1900, at the age of 11, she was included in a shipment of orphans that England sent to Canada to help colonize the country. From there, she went out to work in people's homes and had a very bad time of it.

Eventually she went to work for William Evens Senior, Dad's father. It was there that she met Dad. We understood that both Dad and Uncle Nelson were reticent about her. It was Grandma Evens who thought one of them might as well marry her. It didn't sound as if love was very important in Grandma's eyes! So Dad asked Mom if she'd be willing to have lots of children! She said, "Yes!" and they were married.

I was told that Grandma was supposed to make the wedding dress. She didn't finish it, so Mom wore it half pinned together for the ceremony. This dress was kept at home in a small trunk and Mom gave it to me when I went home. It was almost nothing but three pieces of wide, white lace. Under this she wore blue silk. I took it apart to make a beautiful bassinet for our first baby, our son Kurt. Sad to say this precious thing was lost when our house burned down.

Dad's grandfather was an innkeeper in Devon, England. He was hard and rough and ruled the family in tyrannical style. His father thought there was more opportunity in the "New World," and he sailed for Canada. I never saw him. Dad didn't seem to have much love for him.

Dad's father looked for a religion that would satisfy him. He came upon a volume of Swedenborg and became an ardent follower. It was through the church he met and married Dad's mother, whose maiden name was Scott. It sounded like she was prim, proper and strict. I guess that's where Dad's "no foolishness" came from!

They had twelve children and a farm in Penetanguishene, Ontario. Dad said that they had wonderful fruit trees and often talked about how good everything was there.

At one time, Grandpa tried his luck farming in Tennessee. I think Uncle Nelson was born there. It was a poor time, and they moved back to Canada. There the old man acquired a good-sized farm outside of Berlin, Ontario, which was renamed Kitchener during the First World War.

He studied the Writings of Emanuel Swedenborg diligently. Dad inherited most of the volumes. The margins are full of tiny written notes. For a while Grandpa was lay reader in the small society. Many stories are told about him. The story I like best was told by K.R. Alden. He said that old Mr. Evens decided to learn the Lord's prayer in Greek to surprise his family. He recited the whole thing at Christmas dinner, and his family thought he had gone crazy!

K.R. Alden also told a story about my grandmother. He was the visiting minister and went out to their farm. His train arrived at 10 o'clock in the morning. She was scheduled to serve him breakfast on arrival. When he arrived, there sat his oatmeal – stone cold! Breakfast in her house was served at 8! This happened every time he visited.

Grandpa beat religion into his kids, and it's interesting to note how they turned out. None of the other children followed their father's religion except Dad. I wonder if he would have been quite so ardent about it if he had not been isolated. Dad always said that his mother was particularly good to him. He had Bright's disease when young, and she stood between him and his father.

Dad said his father believed only in the theory that sparing the rod spoiled the child. They all worked very hard. Dad was one of the youngest in the family. The oldest was John. As a youngster Dad lived in fear of John. He was as mean as his father was hard. He'd do such things as pressing a floorboard down, having Dad put his fingers in the crack, then run off, leaving his little brother stranded. Uncle John was not well organized. His family looked bedraggled and were always late. When they visited they stayed too long. When John grew older he came back to the church. In the end, he left his farm to be used as the site for the Carmel New Church settlement in Caryndale, outside of Kitchener. Dad visited him at least once and they found that they could talk. None of his children stayed in the church.

Viola, Dad's sister, went down to the New Church school in Bryn Athyn for one year. She married a big, fat, unpredictable man, Uncle Marshal. She used to say she bought the biggest shirt she could find for him, then added half a yard of material to make his shirttail!

Viola is notable because Dad liked her, and, after he went west, she followed him a couple of years later. They had a farm halfway to Oyen. I can't remember them at all, but I do remember one thing in connection with them.

It seems Uncle Marshal had stolen someone's car chains, or at least he was blamed for the theft. The Mountie made several suspects bring their chains to town so the victim could show which were his.

Apparently, Uncle Marshal implicated Dad, and as a result they had a major fistfight. Dad came out the loser. I remember Mom being upset, and seeing Dad walking home all dusty, with a horrible hole in his head. Dad never believed in physical violence. Might didn't make right.

Uncle Marshal was booted out of town. The last we heard of him he was working as an ice man in Peace River. Karl Alden also visited him there. K.R. was sure he was a good man at heart, and thought he could bring him around. He and Uncle got along very well up until the time Uncle took the minister for a ride in his dump truck. K.R. rode in back and, as a joke, Uncle dumped him! After that their relationship went downhill and K.R. considered him a lost cause.

More about Dad. Dad's strongest language was "Land Sakes" and he wouldn't even let us say "Darn It." I received a liberal education one day in a far corner of the pasture when I heard a neighbor swearing at his horses. He was a bachelor who lived near the school on a small farm. His barn was never cleaned and the floor was so raised that the horses had to duck to get in. He was swearing because they hesitated. Our Dad kept his big barn in good shape!

Dad used to sit us all down often and read religion to us. It seemed

to us to be all theory and we didn't understand it. It was awful when he'd ask questions about what he had read and no one could answer. There wasn't a simple Sunday School aspect to these occasions. He did have one little book he read from called *Children in Heaven*. The part I remember tells how prettily the gardens grew when you were good, and the weeds if you were bad.

Dad did inspire us to want to be good and to be useful. In spite of his strict discipline, he wanted us to like him. We surely all grew up to be conscientious, maybe a little too much so.

The awful thing in the family was Dad's fighting and arguing with Mom all the time. They'd get to yelling, and Mom would end up in tears. Once he threw a big pitcher of milk at her. The milk stains stayed on the ceiling for ages as a grim reminder! He finally painted over them.

Here are the lyrics to some of Dad's favorite songs.

RED WING
(Dad's favorite whistling song)

> There once live an Indian maid
> A shy little prairie maid
> She loved a warrior bold
> This shy little maid of old
> But bright and gay he rode one day
> To the battle far away

> CHORUS:
> Oh the moon shines tonight on pretty Red Wing
> The breezes sighing, the night bird's crying
> And far far beneath the skies her brave is sleeping
> While Red Wing's weeping her heart away

> She watched for him day and night
> She kept the camp fires bright
> But far far away her warrior gay
> Fell bravely in the gray

Sketch from Reta's Art Notes book, made in eighth grade

GOOD MORNING MERRY SUNSHINE
(Sung in school first thing, with actions)

Good morning merry sunshine. How did you wake so soon?
(right hand over brow like a salute)
You scare away the little stars (point straight up)
And shine away the moon (hands form a circle)
I saw you go to sleep last night
(hands held prayer fashion to the left side of face with head tilted)
Before I said my prayers (hands in front prayer fashion)
How in the west (point west)
You sank to rest (bow head)
How did you get up there? (point to sun)
I never go to sleep dear child (shake head)
I just go round to see (circle hand down to right)
The little children of the east (end up with hand pointing east)
Who rise and wake for me.

Sketch from Reta's Art Notes book, made in eighth grade

MR. FROG TOOK A NOTION ONE DAY

Oh, Mr. Frog took a notion one day, mmhh,mmhh

Oh, Mr. Frog took a notion one day that he would ride a mile away mmhh, mmhh

He rode right up to Miss Mousie's home mmhh, mmhh

He rode right up to Miss Mousie's home and said Miss Mousie "are you all alone" mmhh, mmhh.

He took Miss Mousie upon his knee mmhh, mmhh

He took Miss Mousie upon his knee and he said "Miss Mousie will you marry me?" mmhh, mmhh.

Oh Mr. Frog I can't do that mmhh, mmhh

Oh Mr. Frog I can't do that you'll have to ask my Uncle Rat mmhh, mmhh

So Uncle Rat gave his consent mmhh, mmhh

So Uncle Rat gave his consent that they should marry and live content mmhh, mmhh

Oh where shall the wedding supper be? mmhh, mmhh

Oh where shall the wedding supper be away out under the hollow tree mmhh, mmhh

And what shall the wedding supper be? mmhh, mmhh

And what shall the wedding supper be, a slice of cake and a cup of tea mmhh, mmhh

The first to come was a little brown bear mmhh, mmhh

The first to come was a little brown bear who sat himself in the rocking chair mmhh, mmhh.

The next to come was a little yellow chick mmhh, mmhh

The next to come was a little yellow chick who ate so much he made himself sick mmhh, mmhh.

The last to come was a little black snake mmhh, mmhh

The last to come was a little black snake who curled himself on the wedding cake mmhh, mmhh.

The wedding cake lies on the shelf mmhh, mmhh

Very Slow:

The wedding cake lies on the shelf if you want any more just help yourself mmhh, mmhh

Chapter 9

A farmer won't give up harvest time for anything!

Winter came soon in the Northwest, and the season wasn't long for planting, growing and ripening. Some years might have had a very early snow before harvest was finished. If the temperature stayed low, and the snow was light and dry, harvesting was still possible but difficult. Rain or thaw meant a halt until the grain dried out. Dampness damages wheat, lowers its grade. This was more likely to happen with the new combine. Wheat stalks took longer to dry because they were fully ripened. There was also a longer handling time at this crucial stage. The farmer with a combine might be waiting for the wheat to ripen at a time when the old-fashioned man had wheat pouring safely into a granary. So every bit of daylight had to be used, once combining started. With shorter twilights this time of year, the days went all too fast.

I pondered the chances of ever leaving home. Dad still didn't talk about it. I got the feeling that perhaps my plans were all in vain. As harvest progressed and time ran out, the feeling grew stronger. I became anxious. We didn't push Dad. If he'd made up his mind, he wasn't likely to change it, but fussing could change it for the worse. I clung to the hope he'd take me sometime very soon, unsure myself as to what the right time was exactly. He had done what was needed up until now.

From the time plans started, I'd wished and hoped for an early harvest, knowing that otherwise there could be a problem. Dad didn't worry about getting places or being on time, but I did. He might even decide, "Why bother about any of it?" His most likely thought was that the particular leaving day wasn't that important and who knew how long it would take to get to Pennsylvania anyway? He'd never think to ask. It didn't matter that much to him when the train ran!

In trying to understand Dad, I would say he was strictly the boss at home. Aside from that, he tried hard not to get involved with anyone. He was not a participator, but rather a limited onlooker of life. The wishes and feelings of others became less and less important to him as he grew older. He could not understand why he had no friends. Being strongly opinionated, when he wanted to do or say something, he did. You can be sure that, if the school I was hoping to attend had not been a religious one, he wouldn't have been the slightest bit interested. Educating girls was foolishness! But religion did mean everything to him. When he was told that attending this particular school would assure his girls would stay in the Church, he was in favor of it.

On the first of September, as harvest neared its end and nights were cold and frosty, I finally asked him if I was to go. A trip to the city of Calgary was still a must for fingerprints and a passport picture. Then I had to be taken south, down across the U.S. border. The law stated that no one under sixteen was allowed to cross unaccompanied by a parent or guardian. I was only fourteen, so I had to depend on Dad. Getting to the border was the part that worried me most. It seemed one thing too many; maybe he'd object and leave me stranded! When I asked him directly, he said, "Oh, if it rains sometime, I'll take you," and no more. Rain wasn't likely to happen at that time of year, when frost had already come, but I hoped. Most of harvest was over. I had a strong feeling that, if we didn't go about the time intended, I'd never be allowed to go at all. From experience, I didn't leave anything up to chance. We were accustomed to looking out for ourselves.

Luckily, one morning about two days later we woke to the sound of rain! It rained at harvest time and my life was changed forever! Inside me crept an exhilarated feeling, not to be voiced, but something of the sort that is had when hopping out of bed early to find a beautiful day awaiting. Everyone was aware of the portent when they heard the rain. Mom was especially quiet.

My sisters got up and dressed, ready for the day. Dad seemed just the same as on any other morning. He went about eating his breakfast. When he'd finished, he started putting everything in the car. Mom looked sad.

There were no lingering farewells. Dad stepped up on the running board and into the car. I got in on my side, and we drove off very matter-of-factly. Because we were headed west for Calgary, which still seemed like Canadian home territory, I didn't yet realize the finality of it all. The idea of seeing a city was new and absorbing at the moment.

We drove and drove across the prairie. Suddenly the city was before us – the first city I had ever seen! The houses were so close together. How could anyone build that near his neighbor with all the space about? There were no sprawling suburbs. The city sat on the landscape like a box. Once into it there was no mistaking the main street.

Soon we had arrived and Dad was intent on looking at everything. I asked, "Please, can I get my hair curled for the passport picture?" I was fully expecting to be refused. He didn't say a word. Did he feel that with this landslide of wants, needs and doings for me, what was one more? By this time he probably felt a little like the father of the bride!

He appeared to know nothing about the city. After parking the car, he went walking down the street, gazing at its wares as keenly as I did. He never asked directions, but would hunt until he found the place by himself. He was looking for some kind of building where they gave you passports. We passed a beauty shop. I hesitated and then walked in. Dad followed. "Yes, the lady could do my hair now," and Dad sat down to wait. And wait he did, far longer than I'd thought possible. She lifted my heavy hair to do one layer of waves, and then another and another, with a curling iron. My neck was stiff and tired by finishing time. When she'd finished with the last top layer and I looked in the mirror the awful result almost brought tears!

My hair seemed to stand out straight from the sides, not at all flat and pretty like Florence Moore's had been. The woman brushed and patted it, to no avail. She looked perfectly pleased with her accomplishment. I didn't utter a word, and what more could she do anyway? I'd have liked to wash it out then and there, and felt we'd wasted a lot of time. She sold us a heavy, string net cap with ribbons to tie under the chin. This was for sleeping to keep the waves from getting "spoiled"!

With the picture taken and a stamp on the passport, we were ready to leave. The wonders of the city were glimpsed in passing but lost in the hurry to get going. We headed straight south for the first Montana town to be found across the border. It seemed like an endless trip. Never had I been on such a long ride. The country became more barren, and there were no farms. We saw an interesting thing: a rattlesnake curled up by the side of the road. Dad stopped the car and got out to look at it. The tail raised in a dull rattling whir, and I acted as mother would have, saying, "Dad, come back in the car."

After more miles of desolation, the border went by almost unnoticed. I'd expected a wire barricade and big gates, flags and something very important, maybe guards with guns. Dad had been quiet the whole trip and when my line of chatter about everything seen had about run down, we came to two very little piles of stone and cement. There was one on each side of the road. I asked what they were. Dad slowed the car and on a visible patch of cement on the north side was printed CANADA, on the south, U.S.A. What a letdown! After all the fuss made about crossing the border there was no one to stop us and no one to even talk with. Would we be caught later?

Further on the road skirted the rim of The Badlands area. We stopped the car to gaze below into a colorless, small version of the Grand Canyon. Varying strata of earth ranged from almost white to black. Not a blade of grass, water or any living thing was seen. Interesting but not pretty.

Sixty miles beyond the border, a small town came into view. We reached the railroad tracks and a little station on its outskirts. HAVRE was printed under its eaves. The building was somewhat better painted than the one at Benton. Dad took the suitcase out of the car and we went inside. A man behind a grill-covered window sold him a long pink ticket, folded every so often on black dotted lines. The money he handed back to dad was given to me, thirteen fat silver dollars. Now not only did I have some money of my own, the new purse was heavy with it. Then dad gave me a hurried goodbye hug and stated something like, "Don't exaggerate too much." He believed that was a frightful American trait. Out the door he walked, into the green Chrysler car and he drove away.

I carried the suitcase to the long bench against the wall, sat down, and suddenly felt completely deserted. That was the first moment I stopped looking ahead in a dreamy sort of way, and realized what was happening right now. It produced a terrible, lonely and unsure feeling, and I got a great big lump in my throat.

I sat for a long time, in a heap, thinking of home. Then the stationmaster stepped out of his cubbyhole. This was a bit scary, and I wondered how "safe" he was. Mom's "Never trust any man" came to mind. Glancing at him, he looked kindly. He told me that the next train coming was not mine, and it only had a couple of cars. He went on to say that, because the tracks were not very straight and level, this small train rocked and rolled. So the local people had nicknamed it The Galloping Goose. He asked where I was going in Pennsylvania. Sakes, didn't he know? Hadn't he sold us a ticket all the way there? Thinking this, I answered, "Bryn Athyn." "There's a beautiful cathedral there," he remarked. It was news to me, but the fact sounded in keeping with Dad's religious talk and gave me a safe feeling about my destination. I'd never been near a church and still didn't know the school was to be a religious institution.

The little train came and went; no one got on.

When it was almost too dark to see, I got up to look out of the window. There was no sign of a town, and nowhere to get any supper. There was nothing to do but sit down again and wait some more. Soon it was very dark outside, and the stationmaster again came out into the big room. Now what? More worry! He said he was leaving now and that the next train to come along, at about 10:00 p.m., would be the right one. "Will you be all right?" "Oh yes," I said.

After he left, the place was most lonely and I'd gladly have gone back home. It was late to be up, and I was tired. Never having been alone in my life before, being lonely was the hardest part. Feelings of uncertainty and worry came over me, or perhaps it was anxiety. The man's little grilled room had no light in it now, and the clickety-clack of the telegraph, which had almost seemed like company, had stopped. All was very quiet. The waiting room's one light hung from a cord, with a small green glass shade over the bulb. The outside world became frosty white, but the waiting room contained a small coal stove, so I was not uncomfortable.

Finally, I heard the noise of a train. There was a lot of huffing and puffing, and I went outside to watch and to be ready. The lighted windows came sliding up to the platform. Some went by before the train stopped. I had no feeling left at all of starting on a wonderful, new adventure. The only feeling now was one of pure relief.

A man in a dark suit and a very official-looking cap, stepped down from the train and helped me up with the suitcase. Then the train started moving.

THE TRAIN RIDE

I had never before seen a passenger train, and now I was inside one! It wasn't as pretty as I'd pictured it. There was no one to say where to sit, and so I chose an empty seat in the corner. The conductor had left the suitcase and walked down the aisle and out of sight. A whistle blew. Soon he was back and asked for my ticket. He tore off a piece and handed the rest back to me, then disappeared again.

A person would feel less alone on a raft in the middle of the ocean than I felt on that train! The car was almost dark. By craning to look about I could see one or two people slumped down in their seats. Were they asleep? Bed was the only place to sleep! Besides, how could I watch my belongings if I were asleep? There was the suitcase to keep within touch and the pocketbook with all the jingling money.

Mom hadn't tried to give me advice about the future. She had said long ago, "Trust no one you don't know" and "Trust no man." In the time before leaving home she'd added, "If you are ever stuck, look up the Traveler's Aid." Now the unknown void held a note of security, with my knowing there was someone somewhere to be depended upon.

After staring out of the window into the darkness for what seemed like hours, I decided I should get some sleep. A large boil had just healed on my arm. Another boil was brewing almost on the end of my nose for everyone to see. Oh, horrible luck! I always felt ugly anyway. Then, too, my feet were cold. Wouldn't it feel good to take those uncomfortable new shoes off and tuck those cold feet under me on the seat? But, "people don't take off their shoes in public."

After much experimenting, the seating problem was solved. I found it quite comfortable to sit in the corner of the seat, with my feet stretched across the suitcase, which was standing on edge on the floor. This also guaranteed that no one would run off with the suitcase while I slept. Next, I found that I was warmer when I took the coat off and draped it kitty-corner to cover more of me. Has anyone ever taken a coach ride in winter and not had cold feet?

Now, what to do about the purse? There was so much money in it! It made such a noise when it moved! I was afraid of being robbed. I devised a way to take care of that. Putting an arm through its short-handled strap and pulling the purse up safe under my armpit, I could rest in peace. The next day another trick was discovered after watching someone else. By reversing the back of the seat ahead, two seats faced each other. This made a big, square, comfortable space. The suitcase was still on the floor to fill the gap between the seats, and the coat was over all. I rode this way for four nights and three days!

A man who looked like a conductor came down the aisle three times a day carrying a large, flat, steel basket. In it were sandwiches of bread and meat, or bread and cheese, with no butter. Most times he came by I bought a sandwich. I didn't do it every time because I didn't know how long the trip would last. I didn't want to run out of money. The sandwiches seemed very expensive. I bought the ham ones because they were meat. At home, we only ate very brown cooked meat. I'd not had cheese or ham before – such pink meat! There was drinking water at the end of the car.

I knew we were headed for Chicago, that dreadful gangster city, headquarters of the notorious Al Capone. Richard had talked about that. The idea gave me the shivers! Every so often I asked the conductor where we were, so as not to miss the right place. By the second night I hunted up the string granny cap to put on after the lights were turned down. This kept my hair-do from getting tangled. Gradual changes took place outside the window. The most wonderful change was seeing trees, lots and lots of them. There began to be fields with other crops besides wheat. Some gardens were mere patches. Dad's machines would scarcely be able to turn around in them. Nothing different had happened inside the train, except a few more people had been picked up. Then we arrived at Minneapolis-St. Paul, which the conductor called The Twin Cities.

The train stopped in the darkness, on what seemed to be a trestle over water. The passengers began to stir. I raised the blind to take a peek, and saw two men directly below me. One pointed his finger at my window and both went into gales of laughter. Embarrassed, I ducked from sight. Women weren't seen then in caps and curlers. Still, I couldn't see what was all that funny. Maybe they were laughing at my red, bulbous nose and wondering why such a one would bother with a cap for tidy hair. Oh dear, again? A new day dawned and the next time the train stopped we were in the city of Chicago. "You have to get off to change trains, this one doesn't go any further," explained the conductor.
To go back:

Before I left home, an older girl who lived in a place called Glenview, near Chicago, had written to me, saying that she was going to school in Philadelphia too. She described her looks and said she'd wear a red flower and meet me at the station in Chicago. I thought, "How nice," but didn't know what to write because I'd no idea of when I'd leave home or of how to make such arrangements.

Farmers, at least at home, were apt to wait and see what happened. Dad never planned ahead. He went to town when he needed something. Years later this trait was exasperating when we tried to pin him down on his proposed visits. He preferred to wake up some morning and feel like coming. The first we'd know about it would be his arrival on the doorstep, which often meant a rapid rearrangement of the household.

At the last minute, as it turned out, this girl wrote again to say that her sister had decided to get married in Bryn Athyn and that she was leaving ahead of schedule for the wedding. Another girl would take her place and meet me. Lois Nelson was the girl and Bea Synnestvedt the sister who got married. I gave up thinking about it after that.

So, the train rolled into Chicago. As we moved past the city, everything seemed speeded up. There were more houses flying by the window. Many passengers had been picked up at Minneapolis and now were fussing with their bags and standing up. Dozens of railroad tracks ran alongside and then we pulled in under the cover of a big shed.

I followed the conductor as he carried my suitcase down the aisle and put it outside at the bottom of the steps. People were everywhere, and everywhere there was confusion. A big black man in a red cap picked up my suitcase. I snatched it away from him! Imagine trying to steal my bag in broad daylight, and right from under my eyes! His color was startling too. With a firm grip on the suitcase, I walked quickly in the direction everyone else was going. This led to a cavernous room. Shoes clicked on the stone floor. It had a very high ceiling. There were a few desks, over by the walls. Stopping a few feet inside this room to gaze up at the tall ceiling, I noticed the stupendous variety of people. Some of them were strange colors!

Wondering where to go next, I carefully looked around the room. There, above a desk, was a huge sign. Across its face was printed "Traveler's Aid." While hesitating, I saw a tall girl with a red flower on her shoulder standing under it! I walked over, still uncertain, until she started asking questions. Sure enough, she was the replacement for the girl who was supposed to meet me. Our meeting like that was pure dumb luck.

She led the way up wide stone steps to a place called a Rest Room, where her mother was waiting. The mother was resting, lying down on a long bench with a shawl over her face and head. When we spoke to her, she sat up, with the shawl still over her head. She said she was "going to rest a bit longer." There was food in a paper bag, which the two of us sat down to eat.

This all had a strange air about it. I felt impatient, and couldn't eat much. I was anxious that I might miss the train that was to take me East. However, being on solid ground for a while felt good. The world didn't wobble when I got a drink of water, and there was a respite from the noise of the clacking wheels. The girl asked to look at my ticket and said, "It's too bad we're going on different railroads. We'll have to meet in Philadelphia." I had a ticket on the Baltimore and Ohio. The other girl, Luelle Starkey, was riding the Pennsylvania.

Again I was riding alone on a train, feeling as if I'd been going on forever this way. Such a long way to go. The scenery had become prettier all the time. So had the houses, with flowers and green bushes snuggled up against them. Nowhere at home were there green lawns, or flowers planted around buildings. Houses out there were stark and bare, and usually surrounded by bare earth.

Whole fields of corn could be seen from the train's windows. Whatever did they do with it all?

Then came the mountains and, best of all, the Horseshoe Curve around the sides of a river. These mountains weren't huge rugged rocks jutting into the sky, like the pictures of Alberta's Rockies. I wouldn't have called them mountains at all, but rather big hills with their rounded tops and soft coverings of trees. The river at their base was a disappointing muddy color, but with trees hanging over its very edge, it was a lovely sight. This was the best scenery of the trip, but I was too tired to appreciate it. My nose was a major problem. If only it could be bandaged to hide the boil! Also it hurt. At least this ride didn't turn out to be as long as the previous one. Next afternoon I arrived in Philadelphia.

When I walked down the train steps, there was that same girl, wonder of wonders! Again we were in a great big maze of a railroad station. I was very disappointed. I thought that this train would let me off right at the school! "No," said Luelle, "the school is twenty miles further and on another railway." This idea was most distressing. It's lucky she was there to cheer me up.

Having been a Senior at the school the year before, Luelle knew the ropes. When she looked at my ticket in Chicago, she'd known I had the longer route on the B&O whereas she'd ridden the "Pennsy." She had gone to a lot of trouble in Philadelphia to stay in town to meet me. I was too tired to care. I guess that, without her help, I would have sat in that railway station and waited for another day! I was so tired, so dirty, and my nose hurt. I hurt both inside and out. Inside I was full of anxiety and uncertainty, going further and further away from those familiar, simple things at home. So I dumbly followed the girl, who was wonderful because she seemed to know just what to do.

I REACH MY DESTINATION

After walking in eerie, underground, cement passages, upstairs and downstairs, we boarded a much smaller train. Sitting side by side we did some talking for about an hour and arrived on the five-o'clock mail train in Bryn Athyn.

Apparently the arrival of this train was the occasion for a social outing! Men arrived from work in the city and wives were there in the family car to meet them. Some walked. Only men drove cars at home. Many young people met, some as dates strolling down from the dormitories to collect mail from home. There seemed to be too many people about for such a small station. The tan and brown station building sat in a hollow, near a creek. Roads led out in several directions. One road went directly up a steep hill, one went over the creek on a bridge, and one went along on the level.

It was September 7, 1929. I had arrived on the last day students were expected to come for school. This was a happy accident; no one back home had planned it that way! Almost everyone left the station quickly. Luelle spied a young man she knew by name, Andy D. He'd been sent to look for me!! She took off. I looked up at that big blonde with his hands stuffed in his pockets. He wore light tweed knickers with buttons fastening them just below the knees. It sure looked funny to see a man with no pant legs on his trousers. He wore a short-sleeved shirt with bare arms. He picked up the suitcase and carried it for me. My, that was kind of him! He looked so nice! I promptly got a "case" on him that lasted a long while, about two whole years. He never paid the slightest attention to me. I suppose that first look had been enough. To explain where I was going to stay:

I found I wasn't going to live in a dorm like everyone else, and I was quite disappointed. The big Depression following the stock market crash had just started. A half-dozen homes in Bryn Athyn needed domestic help. These people had asked the school for girls to live in and earn their board. I had been chosen as one of these unfortunate girls.

Much later, when I asked the people who housed me how they picked me out, they said they'd chosen me from the list because they knew nothing of that section of the country nor of my family. They thought it would be interesting to have me. What I suspect is that they knew I came from a farm and thought I would be used to hard work! And work hard I did! Their time schedule for me was almost impossible. I was rather proud of myself, as I was the only one in this experiment to stick it out. I not only lasted through the first term, but stayed for three whole years. There wasn't even enough money to go home for vacation.

When I got off the train that day, I saw how fancy everyone was dressed and how pretty everything looked. I pictured going to work in some big place and being a servant, like Mom talked about in England. I didn't mind a bit. Mom, being English, felt people should know their place. But I did have a lonely feeling when I thought of not knowing a living soul in town. The only one I had met, Rev. Iungerich, had moved to Pittsburgh.

Walking up the hill, the young man had nothing to say. I was embarrassed and acutely aware of my appearance. I was also thinking how warm this country was for the time of year. Left behind at home were heavy frosts and cold. I wore a bulky, brown pleated wool skirt and long-sleeved sweater. They were warm enough at home. Here they were much too hot and scratchy. Besides they looked awful! With no permanent pleats, they were a rumpled mess.

Glancing up at this blonde giant again reminded me of how much smaller and skinnier the people at home were compared to what I'd seen in the USA. Going up the hill a ways, we took a footpath over the side as a short cut. There sat a little white house with a pink rambler rose over the door. Stepping into the living room, I saw a tall, dark-haired woman with no welcoming smile on her face. After one look at me, she half swooned onto a couch with arms outstretched, and said, "Ye Gods, another child to raise."

This sounded mighty like swearing, so I was rather leery of her.

I thought of my mother with her hugs; she would have said of this woman, "She was as cold as a cucumber."

Andy, who was her brother-in-law, left at once. There I was with this awesome woman! While still standing in the same spot inside the door, I took a good look around the living room. At least there were fabulous sights to see. On the floor was a soft green carpet, slightly the worse for wear, but, to me, elegant. There was a brick fireplace. What was that for? I could hardly wait to see a fire in it, although that must be dangerous. There were such soft places to sit down!

Almost her first words to me were, "I guess you know all the facts of life, coming from a farm." I asked what she meant and she said, "You've seen animals born." I was shocked. At that moment she didn't appeal to me at all! The question wouldn't have seemed so bad if she had asked it at some quiet later time. As an opening comment, it was shocking!

She saw me looking around the room and asked what was so interesting. When I mentioned the soft places to sit down, she told me that the couch was called a "davenport" and pointed to a big "easy" chair.

Then she led me down a tiny hall. There was a room where several pieces of furniture were painted gray, and an iron bed. The table was for study and the dresser had a mirror. This was to be my room, all to myself! I was thrilled! The next door to this was the family bathroom. A bathroom inside? The idea was somewhat hard to fathom all at once. And everything in the room was white. Boy!!

Then there was the pure wonder of running water. You turned on the tap and water came out! She stood watching me wash the baby's bottle a few hours later. After running the tap (the spigot to her) till the bottle was half full, I shook it, then carefully poured it over the nipple. Her watching made me uneasy until she said, "How wonderful to be so careful and not waste water." They had to pay for it!

In the kitchen was a small white stove. By merely lighting a match, a flame popped up for cooking. The flame could be regulated to any height you wanted with a little white handle. The brown wooden ice-box in the corner was full of many different foods. Lights went on all over the house by pushing little buttons.

It took me days to discover all the wonders of this place. This little home was one of the smallest and poorest in the town. Yet, to me, it seemed like living in the lap of luxury. The contrast with my home, as regards physical comforts, was extreme.

The people here were another story. They did not make me feel wanted, or at home. They kept me at arm's length. I felt they preferred it to be that way. Thus began a long period of living on my own, trying to understand how these strange people thought, talked and dressed. The woman's very standoffish manner made it hard for me to ask questions. Instead, I watched everything carefully to learn how. I could never guess what dress was right for what occasion. At home there had been only one dress for all occasions!

During the first few days I went to church, a tea party and later a football game. Each situation presented a problem. It was bad enough not knowing what to say, let alone not knowing how to look. Young people learn pretty fast what others are wearing. Besides, I had the problem of a very limited wardrobe, with many items missing. Take shoes, for instance. Those brown laced-up Oxfords didn't look very dainty for tea! I noticed that some girls wouldn't even wear them for school. In those days there was not the selection of style, color, and size that there is today, but there was some choice. Black was usual for winter, navy for spring and white in summer.

I cried into my pillow at night but didn't want to go back home. If you asked me, I couldn't have told you why I cried. Perhaps it was "growing pains," as Dad might say, or perhaps it was the sudden, drastic change in my way of life. Maybe it was being plumb worn out at night. Probably it was a little of all of those.

The bad part was that the Mr. of the house caught me crying. Their rooms were all upstairs on the other side of the house, but he crept around at night. Even though I was careful, he heard me crying. He asked me to come out to the living room, where I got the dickens. His long, boring lectures were the usual: "You don't appreciate all that's being done for you, etc., etc."

After the first few days of settling in and being allowed out some, there was no free time and much too much to do. They had three small children and she ran a beauty shop in the basement of the house. They allowed me only eight minutes to walk to the school, which was at least a mile away. There were many rules, and they were strict. It was rough after my relatively carefree life on the timeless prairie.

I literally did all the work in the house, and they were fussy people. She did not cook one meal while I lived there, nor make a bed, nor vacuum. Woe betide me if she ran her finger over a baseboard and discovered dust!

The job I disliked the most was the hand wash. There were mountainous amounts of this. There were the usual delicate clothes, her nighties, slips, etc. The whole family's nasty cotton socks were washed by hand so they'd last longer. Babywatching was perpetual. When I was there, I booked the appointments for the beauty shop and swept up the hair promptly after she cut it. I also washed the towels from that shop.

When the six o'clock train from the city arrived, I was to keep watch in the kitchen. When the top of the Mr.'s head appeared over the hill, supper was to be dished up. We must sit down to eat the moment he arrived.

Every job I did involved clock-watching. I lived in a perpetual state of anxiety. At home there had been no rules. Here everything was governed by rigid rules. After doing the supper dishes and hurrying the three children through their baths, there was little time left for studying. My light must be out by ten. With so much to learn in school, I had a terrible time keeping up. So I resented his lectures, and him.

Not a word did I ever say back. I think he went out of his way to catch me crying. The third time this happened and the usual lecture began, I cried louder so as not to have to listen! Next day, I overheard him say something to the effect that I was a psycho. That was the end of my crying, for good (to this day I can't cry). I'd just be feeling sorry for myself. I didn't understand why he crept silently about the house. Why did he do it? More than once he startled the wits out of me. Was he expecting to catch me doing something I shouldn't?

Another thing that was new to me was their sarcasm, such a nasty form of communication. However, it too was accepted, though rather uncomfortably, as another of the ways of these people. Very soon the words "subtle" and "hint" were added to my vocabulary. This further complicated a life that was already too complex.

Being subtle apparently meant beating around the bush. When this was done, one had to ask additional questions to find out what was intended. This was done gingerly by both parties. Even then, they never gave a direct answer. The educated rarely seemed to be patient with gaps in another's knowledge. Hinting was just as bad. It meant you were doing or wearing something wrong. You had better think of something else! But what? Why didn't these people come right out and say what they meant?

Things were much simpler out West. People were what they were. They looked pleased or displeased with their children. They came right out and said what they thought. These subtleties wasted so much time! One had to worry and puzzle out an answer to some obscure situation. Chances were it was an uncomfortable and unsure answer.

In spite of all this I was quite happy. In many ways I felt lucky to be there and looked forward to each new day. I learned much more than they guessed. They were hard-pressed financially, and busy folk themselves. Besides, they were just not outgoing people; they were too wrapped up in their own problems.

After supper on the first night I arrived in Bryn Athyn, two smiling girls, Joyce Cooper and Alice Fritz, appeared to take me to the dorm. It was a custom for all B.A. girls to collect there on opening night, to meet and greet old students and newcomers.

My hair had been brushed and my face scrubbed free of all the train soot and cinders. Something new called a Band-Aid was pasted on the sorest part of my nose.

Those girls looked so pretty dressed in summery cottons. I felt dowdy in the rumply, pale brown woolies I wore. Everyone was happy and friendly, but I sat in a corner. They all seemed to know each other and could talk of so many things I knew nothing about. I felt so strange in a new land. One woman, a teacher named Wertha Cole, came over to talk. She was soft-spoken and kindly in her manner. She looked so pretty in a white silk dress with lavender feather stitching on the collar and cuffs. She'd made it herself, she said. I thought only poor people sewed! I went home feeling that I had had a wonderful time.

For a long while, I enjoyed the dances. I felt lucky to be an onlooker. There was one unusual happening. While I was sitting on the sidelines, a handsome older fellow came across the room and asked me to dance. I felt sure he'd made a mistake, had gotten too close before realizing, and then was too polite to back off. Everyone here was so quiet in their ways and manners, I couldn't tell. I quickly replied, "Oh, I can't dance, thank you." The lively square dances at home were a far cry from these formal waltzes and foxtrots. He politely sat down and asked a few questions, in a friendly way, before leaving.

One of the two girls who'd taken me to the dorm saw this happening and afterward rushed up to ask, "Do you know who that is?" It must be someone important, judging by her excited voice! "That is the bishop's son," she said. I could forget that one! My general premise was that all handsome people were for each other. Better to try for friends in one's own category.

I soon found out that I was unpopular with the boys and considered a wallflower, whatever that was! Anyways, I went to every school dance and had a delightful time. When there was an extra of "all the men left" in a big circle with the whistle blowing every so often to change partners, I jumped up to join the circle. The rest of the time there were other wallflowers to sit beside and visit. They became nice new friends. As time went on, the one thing I yearned for was a chance to visit with other young people. School dances were the only opportunity for a break from constant work.

People talked about a "Depression." Dad used the word often, meaning little hollows on the surface of the land. What did these people mean? I came to know what was meant, in a vague sort of way, but could see no signs of it. How could these people talk about hard times? They didn't know how good they had it! But I kept very quiet about the poverty at home as a matter of family pride.

Everyone had so many different kinds of clothes and varieties of food, the likes of which I'd never seen before. Outside every window, lovely things were glimpsed. Bright green lawns, flowers and bushes, that everyone at home would have said were "awful pretty." All houses had paint on them. None were of bare, beat-up boards like our house. How wonderful the trees looked.

When I told Mrs. how I'd like to run and put my arms around one, to see and feel how big it really was, she thought I'd lost my mind. She was very prosaic and remembered my saying that all her life. I wrote home to tell Richard all I saw and did. He answered and said I exaggerated.

Down by the station was the prettiest tree-lined creek, the Pennypack, where water ran rushing over the stones. It seemed so big to me that I thought it must be a river! The day after I arrived, I went back to the station to take a peek and to see if my trunk had arrived. It had. I hurried home to tell the Mrs. and she gave me instructions as to how I might get it: "Go up the road a piece, to a certain gray house, and ask the man there if he will go and get it." She carefully said his impossible name, Doren Synnestvedt, which I repeated all the way over. When the door was opened by a woman, I could only stand there, having plumb forgotten that awful name! Collecting a few wits, I asked if her husband was home? "He is not," she said and closed the door.

Late the next afternoon, when the list of chores was done and the lady of the house not yet home from visiting, I again walked to the station. The weather was very warm and I needed the cooler things in that trunk very badly. There must be some way of getting it moved! I had worn that wooly sweater and skirt for a solid week, plus the four nights of sleeping in them on the trains.

The tall stationmaster, Mr. Clayton, was a pleasant man. Looking into the grilled window, I could see him busy tapping out code on his clicking telegraph machine. Soon he came to the window, and I asked to see the trunk. He went outside and unlocked the storeroom door. He looked very surprised when I asked him to get my trunk out.

He then hurried back to his noisy little room. I hoped that someone would come along to help with the trunk. Nobody did, so I started dragging it, which was slow and hard. Worst of all, the cinders were scraping the bottom and the green paint would be ruined. So I stood it on end to inspect the damage and to rest a moment.

Suddenly I looked up to see dozens of men, yes, dozens, pouring down the hill, walking two by two. They seemed to have appeared out of nowhere. When I resumed trying to push my trunk up the hill, not one of them offered to help. Every last one went right on past me. What helpful people! They must be fine fellows! Later I learned that these were the artisans and craftsmen who worked on Bryn Athyn's beautiful Cathedral. They were catching the 4:30 train into Philadelphia.

After standing the trunk on end, an idea popped into my head. Why not try rolling it instead of dragging it? So I pushed it up on end and pulled it clump, down, end over end, across the station yard, diagonally across the road, up the hill and across the field. I maneuvered it up the front steps and finally into the house, and into my room.

The effort had been worth it. When the lady of the house arrived home for supper, I'd had a bath and was wearing a thin green dress with short sleeves. She asked who brought the trunk and I told her. Again she swooned, in her make-believe fashion, onto the couch and said, "Ye gods," in an unpleasant voice. It seemed to me she was awfully fond of that expression!

At school the next day, a number of people knew about my adventure with the trunk. Some mentioned the fact. Even the redheaded principal of the Boy's School, Karl Alden, came through the dividing, swinging doors to shake my hand and say, "You'll never fail in life." I could not understand him. Instead, I cringed with embarrassment, thinking they'd feel I knew no better. What I had done seemed to me to be conspicuously unladylike! I had contemplated waiting until after dark, but I needed the clothes!

Thus, I left a sea of farms and tumbled into a new, fascinating world of doctors, lawyers and merchant chiefs.

ABOUT THE AUTHOR

Reta Evens, later Simons, grew up on the Western Canadian prairie nearly 100 years ago. In many ways the life she describes seems entirely different from what most of us experience today. In other ways, related to human nature and behavior, we are all too much the same. While conditions she describes were often difficult, Reta brings levity to the mix with her impromptu illustrations, sprinkled throughout the text. Originally, these sketches were rendered in ball point pen in the margins of her handwritten manuscript. Sketches from an art notes book she made for school are also included, art history class being one of the highlights of her early education. These were done with the pen shown below. Drawings and a few adventuresome sewing projects she undertook, with no training, give hints as to skills she developed later in life.

This book deals with her childhood years. At the end of the eighth grade, there were no high schools on the prairie and she faced the rest of her life working on the farm. A combination of events, along with the fact that it happened to rain one harvest day, changed her life forever.

And this was just the beginning.

ABOUT THE EDITOR

Dr. S. Leigh Matthews is a Lecturer in the Department of English and Modern Languages at Thompson Rivers University in Kamloops, British Columbia. She reads, researches and publishes mainly in the areas of Life Writing and Canadian Literature and has published a book titled *Looking Back: Canadian Women's Prairie Memoirs and Intersections of Culture, History, and Identity* (University of Calgary Press, 2010).

CPSIA information can be obtained
at www.ICGtesting.com
Printed in the USA
BVHW031243050819
555095BV00013B/1849/P